TEAMSTERS METROPOLIS

TEAMSTERS
METROPOLIS

RYAN PATRICK MURPHY

UNIVERSITY OF MICHIGAN PRESS *Ann Arbor*

For questions or permissions, please contact um.press.perms@umich.edu

Published in the United States of America by the
University of Michigan Press
First published July 2025

A CIP catalog record for this book is available from the British Library.

Library of Congress Cataloging-in-Publication data has been applied for.

ISBN: 978-0-472-07753-3 (hardcover : alk. paper)
ISBN: 978-0-472-05753-5 (paper : alk. paper)
ISBN: 978-0-482-22227-8 (ebook)

DOI: https://doi.org/10.3998/mpub.12398418

Cover image credit: Gottlieb, William P., photographer. *52nd Street,
New York, N.Y., ca, July, 1948.* Photograph courtesy of William P. Gottlieb/
Ira and Leonore S. Gershwin Fund Collection, Music Division, Library
of Congress.

Authorized Representative: Easy Access System Europe, Mustamäe tee 50,
10621 Tallinn, Estonia, gpsr.requests@easproject.com

For Peter Rachleff, who signs his every message
"love and solidarity." Thank you to my mentor
and comrade for teaching me to live my life according
to those two beautiful principles.

Contents

Digital materials related to this title can be found on
the Fulcrum platform via the following citable URL:
https://doi.org/10.3998/mpub.12398418

Acknowledgments

A core premise of this book is that people crave middle-class comfort while also seeking the meaning and the joy that comes with cultural dissent. Those who helped make *Teamsters Metropolis* possible inspire me because they, like me, struggle with the tension between conventional and unconventional ways of living. A tenured academic job gave me the money, the health insurance, the relatively low teaching load, the schedule flexibility, and the space to speak up that I needed to write my second book. But as I took full advantage of that privilege, I—and many of my personal and professional comrades—had the same debates as the historical figures in this book: how to conduct oneself in a society whose values and laws are often unfair, how to raise children in a country that provides no support to do so, what it means to be faithful to family, friends, and lovers, how—or whether—to align with heteronormativity, marriage, monogamy, domesticity, and other traditional institutions, and how to open a space for pleasure in a culture forged in Protestant asceticism. My friends and colleagues' efforts to answer these questions are the lens through which I interpreted all the sources that I collected for this book.

Teamsters Metropolis is a testament to the interdisciplinarity and intergenerational solidarity that flourish at liberal arts colleges. Administrative bloat and endless accreditation flow charts threaten to snuff out our intellectual lives. But with organizing—and preferably through unionization, which we seek at Earlham College where I teach—liberal arts schools are nevertheless remarkably rewarding places to work. Library Director Amy Bryant was immensely influential to this book. While coleading our summer research seminar at the Library of Congress four times, Amy's technical skills helped me find much of the primary source base for the project. Midnight Manuscripts, Earlham's research and writing group for junior faculty, generated useful feedback, and I am especially thankful to

Becky Jestice, Victor Kumar, Elana Passman, Joanna Swanger, Rebekah Trollinger, Michael Weinstein, and many other group members for their ideas about my work. Thank you to all my academic contingent worker colleagues at Earlham who, despite facing the labor exploitation that defines the culture of our industry, were some of the most ambitious, skilled intellectuals I know, especially Amanda Gray Rendón, Michael Schlie, Viet Trinh, and Michael Weinstein. I thank Chief Academic Officer Greg Mahler for his tireless advocacy for research time and money for junior faculty. His leadership helped keep me at Earlham. My conversations with students made me so excited about this book, and they inspired me to keep writing. My spring 2022 course "Teamsters Metropolis"—a discussion seminar based on the primary and secondary documents for this book—was among the most rewarding courses I have ever taught, and it sharpened all the arguments I make herein. Thank you to Isa Ajanee, Margaret Bartimole, Connor Del Carmen, Quinn Doden, Jacob Gurt, Skyler Hayes, Emi Hinosawa, Jack Johnson, Mehmet Ali Schubel, Amal Tamari, and J. T. Todd for making me so excited to come to class every night. My student research assistants' sharp eyes helped me find the information that makes this book compelling, and I thank Olivia Chabowski, Taylor Frisbee, Opal Harbour, Jasmine Lorenzana, Amalia Silverheart, and Amal Tamari for their dedication to that work. Thank you to Myrrh Grossman for so many illuminating conversations about the Old Left. Fearless student labor activists also inspired this book, especially Jace Grissom, Asa Kramer-Dickie, Gisselle Salgado, and Della Walters.

I thank all the scholars who helped foster my thinking, research, and writing skills. Thank you to Sara Cohen at University of Michigan Press. Sara's eye for a gripping story, her thorough, caring feedback, and her pragmatic problem solving allowed me to write a book that I am very proud of despite a pandemic, despite illness in my family, despite the intense time constraints that come with a liberal arts job, and despite the chaos of a union organizing drive that I have chosen to lead. This book would not have been possible without the generosity of David Witwer, whose encyclopedic knowledge of the Teamsters union I constantly referenced. David sat for interviews, planned conference panels with me, wrote letters of recommendation, and gave me a wealth of feedback on this project, all which have deepened its contribution to labor history. Thank you to Jack Goldsmith. Sylvia Pagano's story is central to this book because of Jack's generosity in sharing the story of his family with me, and of talking through all the ideas I have about Pagano and her kin. Thank you to Emily Filler, whose relentless attention to historical detail—few others enjoy discussing the history of salad dressing over drinks—and rigorous analysis of Jewish thought have made me a more original, more iconoclastic thinker. May we someday find a way to teach a course together. Thank you to Daniel LaChance, whose friendship and support have always given me the confidence to keep writing. Thank you to Hayden Kindrat, whose brilliant eye for mid-twentieth-century fiction made for so many fascinating, funny late-night conversations. Your ideas helped make this book more readable and more interesting. Many people commented on drafts of this manuscript and on the funding proposals that helped support it, and I am especially thankful to Julio Capó, Tracey Deutsche, Korey Garibaldi, Aaron Lecklider, and Kevin Murphy. Thank you to all of the conference panelists who helped shape my work, and especially to Alex Burnett, Margot Canaday, Janet Davis, Brooke Depenbusch, Lane Windham, Elissa Marek, Shay Olmstead, Amanda Gray Rendón, and Rahima Schwenkbeck. Thank you to the anonymous peer reviewers of the initial and final drafts of this book as well as of my National Endowment for the Humanities fellowship proposal. Your thorough, creative suggestions helped me see what was most original about this book, and to transform its argument around that originality.

I built this book like many of the people described herein built the International Brotherhood of Teamsters, through conversation with chosen and biological kin at all hours of the day as we walked the streets, relaxed in parks, swam in lakes, and ate and imbibed in bars, taverns, restaurants, and cafes. Thanks to James Andrew for always changing the way I see the world. Los Angeles is a long way from the Midwest, but our conversations about cities still bring so much joy to my life. Dan Luedtke has given me twenty years of friendship and solidarity. So many interesting conversations about the word lifestyle—and the art show Lifestyle Form Bundle that he helped create—gave me many of the original ideas for this book. Thank you to Adam Klaus and Ben Turner for being our West Coast chosen family, and for providing so many beautiful, sun-and-wine-filled writing breaks. I look forward to being old gays together. Thank you to Peter Crandall, Matt DuBois, Sam Robertson, and my whole Minneapolis friend group for always making me feel so happy in the place I call home amid a life otherwise lived in motion. Thanks especially to Sam Robertson for reminding me to see the pleasure and the joy in the world even when things are painful. I am so grateful for mutual care and support we have given each other through all of our ups and downs. Thank you to Soniya Munshi. Our trips to Lucienne on First Avenue in Manhattan, and conversations on the—slow—Queens Boulevard Express late at night are my favorite annual ritual. A queer history bike tour of Minneapolis brought Travis Eckman-Rocha into my life as I was writing this book. Thank you to Travis for reminding me that despite getting older and regardless of the responsibilities that come with ailing loved ones and busy jobs, there is still room for new, joyful forms of queer kinship in our lives. Thanks to my sister, Mary O'Connell Murphy, for being a rock of professional and familial support. Mary and I have navigated the academic industrial complex at a particularly dark moment in its history while supporting our mother on her journey through cancer. I could never have done either of those things alone. Thanks to my father, Mike Murphy, for talking to me like an adult from the time I was a child. I got to know about the Teamsters through his eyes because the union represented the truck drivers at our family business, Murphy Motor Freight Lines. But even though he was on the management side of the table, he is an immensely open-minded person, and that openness helped me see the Teamsters with the nuance and the complexity that I strove to write into this manuscript. Thank you for always treating me with the love and the care that have given me the confidence to be able to write, and thank you for all of the vivid anecdotes about the past that make me a successful historian. My mother, Mary Lynn (Nelson) Murphy, taught me to, as she would say when I was a child, "slow down and smell the roses," to let myself be shaken by the beauty that exists in the ordinary details of the everyday. That wisdom guided me as I looked through my mind's eye at the places that make up this book, from hotel lobbies with bejeweled chandeliers and tropical palms to dingy warehouse loading docks and hot, loud commercial laundries. I hope this book passes her gift for seeing an enchanting world along to my readers. I am so thankful that as she courageously weathered the storm of cancer's unwelcome arrival, we have still been able to do the thing I most cherish: go out and talk about the world over a long lunch. Finally, I thank Andy Hamp for fourteen years of love, camaraderie, and friendship. Andy has taught me so much about the intersection between autonomy and interdependency. I find Andy particularly compelling because he is a man of strong interests, one who knows more about culture—film, fashion, and especially music—than anyone I know. Those ideas, and the space that his passions give me to pursue my own arcane obsessions that became this book, make for a beautiful connection when we do our favorite thing: sitting down at our dining room table in Minneapolis and eating the dinner we make together. The International Brotherhood of Teamsters is a union forged in movement, and I thank you Andy for sharing a life on the road that always makes me feel at home.

Building a Metropolitan Union
Service Labor Activism
in the Age of Suburbanization

Sylvia Pagano drove in style and she drove fast. January 8, 1963. Pagano walked into a Detroit car dealership and purchased a brand-new, steel gray Pontiac Grand Prix. Along with a wide, split chrome grill, stacked headlights, and a low-slung silhouette, Pagano's car was equipped with a fiery four-barrel V8. When she got behind the wheel, Pagano used every one of the engine's 302 horsepower.[1] Soon after buying the car, she was caught in a speed trap near her downtown apartment not once, not twice, but three times in four days.[2] Despite angry calls to her lawyer and an indignant refusal to pay the tickets, Pagano would have had no problem coming up with the money. She bought the Grand Prix in cash, laying today's equivalent of $35,800 on the counter before signing the title.[3]

Pagano's liquidity came in part from her twenty-five-year career in the International Brotherhood of Teamsters, the largest, most aggressive labor union in the United States in the 1950s and 1960s. There is incontrovertible historical evidence that Sylvia Pagano worked as an adviser to Teamsters general president James Riddle Hoffa on investment deals between the union and the Jewish and Sicilian underworlds.[4] Pagano grew up in Kansas City as the daughter of Sicilian immigrants. Though her mother had been a seamstress and her father worked his way up to factory foreman, Pagano's family was also involved in the liquor trade during Prohibition.[5] Probably because of the specialized knowledge about the Sicilian syndicate that she gained from her family, friends, neighbors, and coworkers while coming of age, and after earning Hoffa's trust as a confident, gritty Teamster organizer in Depression-era Detroit, Pagano began to vouch for the legitimacy and the trustworthiness of underworld operatives. With Pagano's nod, Hoffa would loan the operatives money for their small businesses in exchange for protection for his unceasing effort to organize workers in the transportation, light manufacturing, and service industries.

In addition to lucrative commissions on the advice she gave to Hoffa, Pagano's work delivered physical mobility that was remarkable for a middle-class white woman in the mid-twentieth century. Although only a quarter of white women held paid jobs during the decade when Pagano was most active in the union, and while the average marriage age bottomed out at 20.8 years in 1956,[6] Pagano was a single woman who traveled globally to support the union and who owned multiple small businesses within and beyond metropolitan Detroit. January 2, 1963. Pagano arrived at Detroit Metropolitan Airport to catch Delta flight 815, a sleek silver, gold, and navy blue Douglas DC-8 jetliner that would carry her nonstop to Miami. While cruising southeastward at six hundred miles per hour, Pagano would be offered a hot lunch, cocktails, and complimentary cigarettes that she could smoke while playing cards in the first-class lounge. Earlier that morning, Jimmy Hoffa had boarded Delta flight 812, another DC-8 bound for Miami. The following day, Bill Bufalino, president of a large Teamster local in Detroit, would take the same route as Hoffa.[7] It is unclear why the three made this particular trip, or why they traveled on separate flights to the same destination in one twenty-four-hour period. It does appear, however, that Pagano was working to connect Bufalino to her friend George Rubin, a higher-up in the Jewish syndicate who owned the Atlantic Towers Hotel on Miami Beach's Collins Avenue oceanfront. The six-story art deco tower was built around an L-shaped, crystal blue pool and a two-level sundeck dotted with lemon-, lime-, and orange-colored umbrellas. Rubin hoped that with a loan from the Teamsters—one that likely came with a kickback for Pagano, Bufalino, and Hoffa—he could renovate the hotel, making it a desirable place for rank-and-file union members from the Midwest and the Northeast to rollick in the sun and the surf.[8]

While the geography of Pagano's affairs was particularly unusual for a woman, her male interlocutors also gained economic and social mobility from the Teamsters that would have been unimaginable to their immigrant parents or grandparents. Like Pagano, whose hands were permanently scarred from the burns she suffered on the job at a potato chip factory as a young woman,[9] Bill Bufalino had come of age in the hardscrabble world of Detroit's service economy. By the early 1940s, he owned a small business that installed, serviced, and resupplied the jukeboxes that played big band and swing jazz hits in the nightclubs of wartime Detroit. By mid-decade, Bufalino had gotten involved with the Teamsters union, recruiting other second- and third-generation eastern and southern European immigrants to join the union as part of a wider effort to bring operational stability, economic security, and a living wage to Detroit's service economy. He excelled at the work, and by the end of the 1940s, Jimmy Hoffa—a rising star in the union who was an architect of its rapid expansion—made Bufalino president of the Local 985, the Teamster affiliate that organized service workers.[10]

Bufalino's activism paid off, and by the middle of the 1950s, the Teamsters allowed him—and hundreds of thousands of rank-and-file union members across the United States—to build a comfortable, middle-class, metropolitan lifestyle. While the small, family-owned produce warehouses, car washes, barber shops, and taverns of central city Detroit remained the focus of Local 985's operations, Bufalino left the working-class neighborhood of his younger years for the leafy boulevards of the suburbs. He had started a family in the Ravendale neighborhood in the 1940s, having moved into a small bungalow built in the shadows of the hulking Mack Truck and Chrysler Kercheval assembly plants.[11] But as his salary rose with Local 985's breakneck growth, Bufalino left Detroit for the verdant enclave of Grosse Pointe Shores in 1961. He bought a brand-new, four-bedroom, four-and-a-half-bathroom, 4,300-square-foot brick colonial. The house was three times the size of the one he left behind in Ravendale and came with a flowering crabapple tree in the front yard. He and his wife made full use of the space, raising four children in their new home.[12]

Deeply contradictory meanings stem from Sylvia Pagano and Bill Bufalino's journeys through metropolitan Detroit. In one sense, their endeavors were the foundation of the dominant culture of the mid-twentieth-century United States. Pagano and Bufalino helped the Teamsters negotiate lucrative contracts that allowed second- and third-generation eastern and southern European immigrants relocate to affluent, racially restricted suburbs, where they would assume the full privilege of middle-class American whiteness. Key to that process was the performance of heterosexual domesticity, in which a breadwinner husband and a dependent wife raised obedient children, lived in the privacy of a single-family home, and confirmed their middle-class status through conspicuous consumption.[13] But in another sense, both Pagano and Bufalino's lives were far more complicated than the story that historians, sociologists, writers, and filmmakers often tell about the 1950s. Although Pagano had been married twice, her intellectual and social credibility—and the financial war chest that she displayed flamboyantly—came from paid work outside the home. While she and Bufalino drew paychecks from the Teamsters, both became power brokers in the union because of their connection to another, far more transgressive working-class institution: La Cosa Nostra, our thing, that which law enforcement and the middle-class press called "the Mafia." And while a roaring mid-twentieth-century economy could have allowed Pagano and Bufalino to sever their connection to the blocks of the central city and to settle into hermetically sealed suburban lives, both continued to build businesses, kinship networks, and intimate relationships[14] in the old, gritty blocks of downtown Detroit. These antipodal trajectories—and the role that both city lifeworlds and comfortable suburban landscapes played in the meteoric rise of the Teamsters union— are the subject of *Teamsters Metropolis*.

Jimmy Hoffa's Teamsters Metropolis

Sylvia Pagano and Bill Bufalino were building a union on the leading edge of the mid-twentieth-century labor movement. The International Brotherhood of Teamsters grew by at least one hundred thousand members in every year of the 1950s, and won watershed wage and benefit gains that made long-haul truck drivers—the largest group of workers in the union— better compensated than highly paid workers in coal mining, meatpacking, and manufacturing.[15] The Teamsters' rapid advances diverged from the flagging performance of the remainder of the labor movement. By the middle of the decade, the industrial unions in the steel, automotive, and meatpacking businesses had slowed down their organizing. Multiple factors drove the decline, from public backlash against the wave of strikes that rocked core industries in 1946, to the Taft-Hartley Act's restrictions on aggressive organizing tactics in 1947, to the merger of the once-militant Congress of Industrial Organizations with the less strident American Federation of Labor in 1955. As labor historian Nelson Lichtenstein has argued, the "union idea" that transformed American culture around the concerns of working people during the Great Depression was already evaporating in the 1940s. Ominous though the warning signs were for all union members, the Teamsters bucked the downward trend.[16]

Teamster dynamism stemmed from a vigorous, unceasing, and uncompromising commitment to union organizing in the service sector of the economy. Accounts of the early twentieth-century US economy often assume that the large corporation and the sprawling factory were the driving forces behind the era's unprecedented vitality. A labor historiography that has centered the manufacturing sector, as well as popular cultural texts from Fritz Lang's *Metropolis* to Upton Sinclair's *The Jungle*,[17] illustrate this trend. But as historian Andrew Wender Cohen demonstrates, small-scale craft production in services and light manufacturing also boomed in the new century. "If steel and oil were the sinews of the new national economy," Cohen argues, "bread and meat, coal delivery, garbage removal, as well as housing and plant construction underpinned (cities') commercial life. Stores, restaurants, bars, and barbershops did not provide essential goods, but they were the important neighborhood institutions and spaces that defined public life in the city."[18] Activists formed the International Brotherhood of Teamsters in 1903 as a craft union for workers who drove teams of horses. Every day, those drivers delivered goods to thousands of the small-scale shops Cohen describes: bakeries, grocery stores, bars, construction sites, and manufacturing lofts. By the early 1910s, President Dan Tobin began to expand the union by organizing both teamsters and the workers at the small businesses they visited along their routes. Two decades later, and after motorized trucks had replaced horse teams, West Coast Teamster leader Dave Beck intensified Tobin's commitment to the service sector. Beck funneled resources to the union's "trade divisions," umbrella organizations for workers at dairies, in the laundry and dry-cleaning business, in warehouses, and in other service and light manufacturing industries.[19]

Jimmy Hoffa amplified his predecessors' commitment to service-sector unionism after he was elected general president of the International Brotherhood of Teamsters in October 1957. Hoffa's interest in service-sector unionism stemmed from an iconoclastic view of metropolitan life in the 1950s. Most other union leaders held a sunny outlook, embracing the increasingly central role that scale played in an urban economy where large firms signed lucrative union contracts that lifted an ever-wider swath of the population into the middle class. Hoffa's take, however, was dark. Vast conglomerates wiped out family businesses, turning the city landscape into an archive of loss. "Unfortunately, and again I use those words unfortunately," Hoffa began as he described his own pessimism about the state of industries not long after he was elected president of the Teamsters. "Every time I see a large supermarket or large department store built into a shopping center area, I see the surrounding merchants who have been there from their fathers to their grandfathers to the present people gradually going out of business."[20]

It is this negative critique that inspired Hoffa's commitment to expanding the Teamsters as aggressively and rapidly as possible. Like the family companies whose vanishing troubled Hoffa, he insisted that many unions were too small and too parochial to meet the challenge of an economy that increasingly favored large corporations. For the labor movement to adapt to economic change, Hoffa insisted, the size of union bargaining units would have to grow, with standardized, industry-wide contracts replacing local agreements between workers and individual companies.[21] Rather than abandon the small family firms that had shaped the Detroit neighborhoods where he had lived and worked since he was a teenager, however, Jimmy Hoffa made those small businesses the core of his effort to build a bigger, stronger union. He intended to organize every worker at every small business on every corner in every neighborhood. All truck drivers, all bakers, all jukebox mechanics, all uniform cleaners, all bartenders, and all cabbies would have to become members of the Teamsters. Through this commitment to mass organizing among marginal workers on every block, Jimmy Hoffa aimed to turn every US city into a Teamsters metropolis.

Jimmy Hoffa had begun to put his mass organizing vision to work in the 1940s, when metropolitan areas were undergoing their greatest spatial transformation in US history. According to LaShawn Harris and other historians, the Great Depression had turned the central neighborhoods of industrial cities into heterogeneous, unsettled places. The surge in immigration immediately prior to the 1924 restriction had made Russian, Yiddish, Italian, and Chinese more widely spoken in some neighborhoods than English. Stigmatized eastern and southern Europeans—Jews from the Pale of Settlement in Russia, Polish peasants, landless Sicilians—competed for low-status jobs with a growing stream of Black people leaving the Jim Crow South under duress. Multiple generations of aunts, uncles, cousins, friends, and boarders packed into dilapidated nineteenth-century railroad apartments. Life in crowded private and public places transgressed the boundaries of race, religion, language, class, and gender.[22]

To stabilize the population after years of economic crisis and war, the Roosevelt, Truman, and Eisenhower administrations used the power of the federal government to encourage people to relocate from the old central city to a brand-new suburban landscape. Taking advantage of mortgages insured by the Veterans Administration and the Federal Housing Administration (FHA), and using the infrastructure financed by watershed laws such as the Interstate Highway Act, first- and second-generation eastern European Jews, Greeks, Italians, Hungarians, and Ukrainians joined better-heeled, old-stock American Protestants in an affluent new suburban world. Once they arrived in their subdivisions, they moved into single-family homes with lush lawns, trimmed shrubbery, fenced-in back yards for the dog, and an abundance of electronic gadgets and labor-saving devices to make life more pleasurable. These modest yet comfortable homes that historian Dianne Harris calls "little white houses" allowed people who were once poor eastern and southern European immigrants to pass as middle-class American white people.[23] Part of the way they passed was by following—or at least pretending to follow—the narrowly defined gender roles that emerged as markers of middle-class identity in the nineteenth-century US and western Europe. Men were breadwinners and wage workers. Women were mothers and caregivers. Sex was contained within the institution of marriage and in private space. Friendship took place in leisure time, either among married couples or in same-sex groups. Business was separate from kinship and occurred between men at the office. As more people moved to the suburbs and adopted suburban culture, American cities became metropolitan areas, regions defined by a central core designed for commerce and suburban enclaves designed for domesticity and mass consumption.[24]

A million workers joined Jimmy Hoffa's International Brotherhood of Teamsters in the 1950s because membership in the union helped deliver access to these new suburban landscapes of safety, comfort, and indulgence. Lila Corwin Berman and other historians have argued that metropolitan mobility came to define white middle-class US culture in the mid-twentieth century. Families drove back and forth between old ethnic enclaves in the central city and their new world in the suburbs, building lives on both sides of the urban-suburban boundary.[25] Even with the federal government's robust subsidy, however, multilocal metropolitan living was expensive. Joining the Teamsters helped people cover those costs. High hourly pay bought the patio furniture sets, the pontoon boats, and the station wagons that defined suburban culture. A husband's family wage allowed some Teamster wives to stay home, to go to the supermarket, and to drive the kids to school, to the movies, and to the shopping mall. Indeed, by the mid-1950s, and as Bill Bufalino's family history demonstrates, selling the old, humble house in the city, moving upward and outward to the suburbs, and living a mobile, metropolitan lifestyle defined what it meant to be a Teamster.

The problem for Jimmy Hoffa, however, was that painful antagonisms lay just below the varnished surface of Teamsters' metropolitan lives. Most importantly, the federal government had racially restricted the suburbs, which made segregation a defining feature of metropolitan geography in all regions of the United States. Since its founding in the 1930s, the Federal Housing Administration had used detailed, block-level maps to insure mortgages for buyers in white areas of the city and to withhold that insurance in racially integrated areas, a process that came to be known as redlining. To access the giant pool of buyers who qualified for federally insured mortgages, the FHA ordered developers to restrict newly built suburban enclaves to whites only. And as historian Richard Rothstein has shown, even after the Supreme Court banned many of these racist practices in the 1948 *Shelley v. Kraemer* decision, the FHA flagrantly violated the court's order by continuing to insure mortgages for segregated developments until the mid-1950s.[26] Because of racist collusion between the federal government, developers, builders, real estate agents, and white home buyers, Teamster collective bargaining gains delivered deeply inequitable outcomes for union members.

Such disparities were blatant within Bill Bufalino's union in Detroit. For example, Annie Mae Anderson was a member of Local 985 who worked ten-hour days at Duke's Five-Minute Auto Wash. Like tens of thousands of her Black neighbors, Anderson's family had fled to Detroit to escape the poverty and the white terrorism of the Jim Crow South. Anderson had begun washing cars in 1953 when she answered a classified advertisement in the *Detroit Free Press* that read "Car Washers—Colored."[27] Although she worked a low-wage service job, Anderson had a vision for a better future for herself and her kin. Each week, she placed a small portion of her paycheck into a fund that she hoped would allow her fifteen-year-old daughter to attend the college of her choice. Through her savings, Anderson sought to allow a younger generation of Black women to build the skills necessary to avoid the indignity of exhausting, dangerous, segregated service work.[28]

Detroit's metropolitan housing economy was a daunting barrier to Anderson's dream. In the late 1950s, Anderson and Bufalino lived four miles apart, a short ten-minute drive on the streets of central city Detroit. While Bufalino's Ravendale bungalow was north of the Chrysler Kercheval factory, Anderson lived in a similar bungalow due east of the plant.[29] Like Anderson, Bufalino wanted to spare his children the economic scarcity and chronic instability of the service work he had grown up doing, and thus he made plans for the move to Grosse Pointe Shores that came with safer streets, better schools, and more space. The problem for Bufalino, however, was that the new neighborhood was restricted. Real estate developers subjected prospective buyers to a screening system that assigned points for particular ethnic characteristics. The lower the score, the more desirable the buyer.[30] All Jews automatically received a handicap of 85 points, all Italians 75, all Greeks 65, and all Eastern European Christians 55. Additional points were assigned based on the answers to questions such as "how swarthy is the buyer?" and "is the buyer's way of life American?" Much to his chagrin, as a somewhat dark-skinned person who spoke the Sicilian dialect of Italian fluently, Bill Bufalino failed the test and was denied entry.[31] Annie May Anderson, meanwhile, would not have been allowed to take the test even if she had the money to build in Grosse Point Shores. Even though the Supreme Court had banned racially restrictive building covenants thirteen years earlier, developers, real estate agents, lenders, and hostile white neighbors continued to prevent Black people from buying homes in the development where Bufalino hoped to move in 1961.

The resolution of Bill Bufalino's dispute with Grosse Point Shores illustrates the economic consequences of the racial divergence in metropolitan mobility. Bufalino had added a law degree to his activist portfolio for the Teamsters, and he promptly sued the developer who rejected his application. Well aware that the legal foundation for explicit housing discrimination was collapsing in the early 1960s, the developer terminated the ethnic scoring program, and Bill Bufalino built his house. Today, that home is beautifully maintained, with handsome red bricks gleaming white trim, and a current market value of $770,000.[32] Meanwhile, his old bungalow in the central city fell into disrepair. As people and capital moved to the suburbs, demand for urban residential real estate declined sharply after 1960. Today, the house sits boarded up. It last sold for $19,000 in 2016, and currently has a tax-assessed value of $14,400.[33] Annie May Anderson's former house met an even more troubling fate. After its value depreciated to zero, and to prevent the fires that often result when people strip abandoned homes of precious metals, the house was demolished, and today the lot is one of thousands in Detroit that sits unkempt and overgrown.[34] If Bufalino or Anderson were alive today, Bufalino would have nearly a million dollars in home equity, while Anderson would have none.

The urban geography of Anderson and Bufalino's lives emphasize the tensions that defined suburbanization. The move across the urban-suburban boundary came with strict regulation of style, comportment, and desire for those who were allowed to make the move. And while people who complied with the regulation received the rewards of comfort, space, safety, and status, those who were unwilling or unable to perform middle-class American whiteness were categorically denied those privileges. As a consequence of these and other tensions, many union members—and a notable number of union leaders—were ambivalent about the journey from the city to the suburbs that Teamster membership delivered to some workers. Jimmy Hoffa, for example, never moved to the suburbs and never fully embraced the conventional domesticity that defined suburban culture. For most of his adult life, Hoffa lived in an unremarkable 1,500-square-foot home in the Belmont neighborhood on Detroit's northwest side. The house was similar to those where Bill Bufalino and Annie May Anderson lived during the 1950s, with four tiny bedrooms, a small but manicured lawn, and an eat-in kitchen.[35] Hoffa bought the house in 1940 and lived in it until he disappeared on July 30th, 1975. Although Hoffa married his wife Josephine in 1936, raised two children with her, and remained married until his vanishing, Hoffa's domestic arrangement regularly involved people outside his nuclear family. Josephine Hoffa's mother lived there for many years, as did Chuckie O'Brien—the son of Sylvia Pagano whom Hoffa referred to as his "foster son"—and O'Brien's small children. Hoffa, Pagano, and O'Brien were part of a social group where men and women pooled their ideas, their time, and their money to advance the positions of their businesses, of the Teamsters union, and of the Jewish and Sicilian underworlds.[36] There is also evidence that some people within Hoffa's kin network mixed friendship, romance, sex, and long-term intimacy outside of marriage.[37] Therefore, while Teamster contracts provided the economic resources for some union members to prove their compliance with the cultural values of heteropatriarchy and domesticity that suburbanization required, it appears that Jimmy Hoffa and his friends lived far beyond the boundary of those institutions.

Rather than an impediment to his leadership of the International Brotherhood of Teamsters, however, I argue that Jimmy Hoffa's hesitancy about suburbanization was the foundation of his success as an organizer. Hoffa was by no means alone in his sense of cultural discontent. In her work on the suburbanization of American Jews in the 1950s, for example, historian Rachel Kranson "challenges the notion that American Jews welcomed their post-war economic rise without reservation or hesitation," arguing instead that "Jewish anxieties about upward mobility emerged out of the dissonance between financial and social success and their deeply felt histories of exclusion and want."[38] In Kranson's account, the move to the suburbs was anxious and ambivalent, one in which newfound security was painfully discordant from the outsider status and cultural dissent that had long defined American Jewish identity. A central claim of this book is that the Teamsters succeeded in the 1950s because the union helped mitigate the ambivalence that many of its members—especially eastern and southern European Jewish and Catholic immigrants—experienced when making the journey from city to suburb. It did so by paying the wages that allowed entry into desirable new suburban neighborhoods, while solidifying economic and cultural ties to the small businesses, the bars and restaurants, and the working-class neighborhoods of the old central city. A million people joined the union in the 1950s because Teamster membership granted access to both the comfort of suburban affluence and the brash, unruly, defiant culture of immigrant life in the industrial city. As Annie May Anderson's family history demonstrates, life in the Teamsters metropolis was rife with inequity and unfairness. But the culture of the union nevertheless resonated with many working people across the United States, making the Teamsters the dominant labor organization in the United States by the end of the 1950s and delivering a livable wage to hundreds of thousands of workers on the margins of the economy.

Cultural Maximalism and an Unruly Union

The reticence about suburban middle-class culture that made the Teamsters attractive to many workers originated in its particular practice of trade unionism. That practice diverged sharply from the model that had become dominant during the Great Depression. In 1935, at the peak of his unprecedented popularity, President Franklin Delano Roosevelt signed the National Labor Relations Act, dubbed the Wagner Act after its primary sponsor, Sen. Robert F. Wagner of New York. The new law aimed to tamp down the unrest that union organizing often spawned, whether such violence came from the anarchist radicals of the 1910s or the right-wing private security forces who led the "open shop drive" against unions in the early 1920s. In the place of these contests of physical force, the Wagner Act outlines a system based on the liberal model of political representation that gave rise to the US republic in the eighteenth century. Workplace leaders identify a common set of interests, recruit their colleagues with reasoned arguments in favor of unionization, ratify the union through a secret ballot election supervised by a government agency, elect representatives who convey workers' needs to the employer, and leverage the power of the courts to enforce the contracts that result from measured negotiations. The new system was a resounding success for working people in the United States. On the eve of the Wagner Act's passage in 1935, 12 percent of private-sector employees were union members. Fifteen years later, that number had nearly tripled to 35 percent, and union representation brought robust increases in compensation in construction, manufacturing, transportation, and other core industries.[39]

Advantageous though the Wagner Act was for most workers, the International Brotherhood of Teamsters rarely followed it. Instead, as Teamster activists built the union block by block through the country's industrial cities in the 1930s, they used tactics that resonated with the first- and second-generation eastern and southern European Jewish and Catholic immigrants who did much of the most difficult, most dangerous work in those neighborhoods. Members of this cohort of immigrants often arrived in the United States unfamiliar with the idea of representation that inspired the Wagner Act, as they had come from the Russian Pale, the Romanian peasantry, the Sicilian countryside, and many other places where the state, public institutions, and private employers had never subscribed to such Enlightenment ideals. Therefore, when they came to North America, many of these immigrants organized using their own notion of the political, one steeped in a history of dispossession, racist pogroms, famine, and war, and one that would meet the needs of the small, unregulated, and sometimes extralegal businesses where they worked.[40] Unruliness defined this unionism that skirted the boundaries of the law; that blurred the line between workers, owners, activists, and entrepreneurs; and that challenged bourgeois standards for physical comportment.[41]

Unruly tactics were the core of Bill Bufalino's practice as president of Teamsters Local 985. Bufalino focused his organizing among people like him: second- and third-generation immigrants who faced ethnic and linguistic discrimination at large corporations and who mitigated that mistreatment by building their own small businesses within their ethnic communities. They started those businesses in the sectors of the economy where they could afford to, in the undercapitalized, highly competitive, tumultuous light manufacturing and service industries. During the same years that Bill Bufalino got into the jukebox business, for example, his brother tended bar in a hotel and started an open-air Christmas tree lot as a side hustle.[42] Frontline workers at businesses like the Bufalinos' were marginal, working long shifts for low pay at establishments with high turnover. Rather than make an appeal to workers who bounced between sectors and firms, Bufalino and other Teamster activists often approached the most stable worker at a given business: the proprietor. Instead of assuming that workers and owners constituted discrete groups with opposing interests, Bufalino framed union membership as a resource that would benefit both parties. Signing up with the Teamsters would raise wages for frontline workers and would help set an industry-wide wage floor that would protect small businesses from being undercut by new competitors who paid workers less. Therefore, the Teamsters operated as both an advocacy group to improve the plight of workers and as a cartel to protect immigrant-owned small businesses from unfettered competition.[43]

In many cases, all parties—the Teamster organizer, the rank-and-file worker, and the shop's proprietor—agreed to a mutually beneficial deal. But in the cases where companies or workers balked, the Teamsters would turn to more aggressive tactics. Most common among them was the organizational picket. Whereas the Wagner Act frames the picket line as tool for rank-and-file employees to gain leverage over managers after negotiations break down within the workplace, Teamster picketers often came from outside the firm where the dispute took place. In working-class neighborhoods steeped in the union idea that ascended during the Great Depression, crossing a picket line was a moral outrage. Therefore, if the owner of a beer distributor or a produce warehouse or a laundry refused to do business with the union, Teamster operatives would hire people off the street to surround the business holding picket sings alleging unfair treatment of workers. The pickets would stop Teamster truckers—who always honored picket lines—from dropping off supplies to the business, and would shame the establishment in front of neighbors who supported the cause of organized labor.

When moral pressure proved ineffective, Teamster operatives sometimes turned to physical force. In June 1954, for example, Bill Bufalino's Local 985 had been picketing Bright's Bar in Detroit's Woodbridge neighborhood for failing to use a unionized mechanic to maintain its jukebox. Bright's proprietor James Patterson refused to back down and continued to service the jukebox with a nonunion company that paid less than the Teamster wage. Amid Patterson's intransigence, and according to a report that Patterson filed with the Detroit police, Bufalino's associates backed up a truck to the bar, barged through the door, and stole the jukebox. They then held it for ransom, returning the machine only when Patterson finally agreed to transfer service to a union company.[44] Similarly, a few days before Christmas 1954, Hugo Guensche told police that Bufalino attacked him inside Local 985 headquarters. Guensche was the owner of a jukebox company called Brilliant Music, and Bufalino accused him of hiring mechanics without paying union dues. He entered Bufalino's office and an argument soon broke out, during which Bufalino lunged at Guensche. After he broke free of Bufalino's stranglehold and bolted out of the building, four of Bufalino's lieutenants took off after Guenche. They hurled rocks as he sprinted across the parking lot to his car. The operatives caught up to Guensche as he dove inside and locked the door, and they kicked dents into the car's side panels as Guensche gunned the engine and sped away.[45]

Teamster operatives also turned to property destruction, sometimes using sabotage, bombings, and arson to organize workers and build cartels in undercapitalized industries. In January 1957, for example, Bill Bufalino approached Gerald Duff, the owner of Bubble Bath Auto Wash, about having his workers join Local 985. Duff rebuffed Bufalino, and for the next sixteen months, despite the occasional presence of organizational pickets to shame customers and workers at Bubble Bath, Duff held out against the Teamsters. According to Duff, during the wee hours of a Sunday morning in April 1958, Bufalino's associates lobbed dynamite charges through the windows of the car wash. They detonated, blowing Bubble Bath to smithereens in a flying cloud of scorched foam wands and flaming bristle brushes. Given Duff's lack of business insurance, Bubble Bath permanently closed after the bombing. Duff alleged that Bufalino had dynamited no fewer than eleven other car washes that refused to agree to the union standard in the late 1950s. While no definitive historical proof of this string of attacks exists, the fact that Duff believed such accounts enough to testify to them under oath—which he did in April 1959—is evidence of widespread associations between the Teamsters union and illicit activity[46]

Conduct as reckless as Bill Bufalino's was ultimately rare in the pantheon of Teamster tactics. Nevertheless, these and other less dramatic confrontations between workers, union officials, and small business owners reveal that unrestrained bodily comportment defined Teamster organizing. Big, loud, unyielding, flamboyant, and bejeweled, the Teamster body was the opposite of the controlled body that the Wagner Act encouraged through the liberal model of political representation.[47] Whereas the voice and the facial expressions of the Wagner Act's prescribed body were measured to avoid provoking conflict, the Teamster often shouted, voice at full volume in the native language of the small business owner. Whereas the speech of the Wagner Act body was formal to meet the standards of personnel departments and federal mediators, Teamster speech was often colorful and crass. Whereas the clothing and accessories of the Wagner Act body were subdued to suit the formal environment of professional collective bargaining, the Teamster body was sometimes boldly adorned with hand-painted ties and fur coats and carrying roles of fifty-dollar bills.[48] And whereas escalating conflicts compelled the Wagner Act's adherents to seek assistance from attorneys and the courts, Teamster conflicts involved waving arms, flying fists, and, on rare occasions, hurling dynamite through smashed windows at three o'clock in the morning.

A discerning reader might ask why, when the terror of smashing fists, hurled rocks, and exploding car washes plagued the metropolitan landscape, did so many workers actively support the union that was the source of the terror? And why was Jimmy Hoffa—the architect of some of that unrest—among the most popular leaders with rank-and-file workers in the 1950s? The answer, I argue, lies in the regulation of working people's bodies. In her provocative essay "Sex + Freedom = Regulation: Why?" political theorist Janet Jakobsen argues that the discipline of the body has long been a constitutive foundation of American freedom.[49] Drawing on the German sociologist Max Weber's 1904 book *The Protestant Ethic and the Spirit of Capitalism*, Jakobsen argues that freedom depends on the regulated activity of the body that helps the free market operate efficiently, regulation that Weber famously called "worldly asceticism." For people to accrue the material resources necessary to live according to their own desires and not by the command of a monarch or the pope, work must be a calling, an end goal in life rather than a means to an end. When people answer the calling to hard work, they dedicate their bodies to the productivity, the endurance, and the efficiency that allow one to be an independent agent in the free market. This requires both self-discipline and what Weber calls the "regulated enactment of activity along particular lines" by the government and by employers.[50]

Just as Jimmy Hoffa launched his effort to organize the Teamsters metropolis in the 1940s, this "regulated enactment of activity" became more intense and more personal for working people in the United States. As Jakobsen argues, heterosexual marriage had replaced celibacy as the core Christian sexual ideal during the Reformation. Luther and Calvin pushed everyone to marry because celibacy—which bound one to the church hierarchy rather than to another free individual—was the foundation of the Catholic abuse of power and perversion of the gospel.[51] In the secular context of the mid-twentieth-century United States, while marriage remained a cultural ideal, marriage was articulated with a particular spatial formation: suburban domesticity. Domesticity solved two problems during the immediate postwar period. First, it provided a cultural mooring, one that would stabilize kinship, sex, love, procreation, and ethnicity that had all been knocked off kilter in the Depression-era central city. By containing sex and containing kinship in the single-family home, domesticity would shore up the whiteness and the Americanness of Italians, Greeks, and Jews who had previously lived in ethnically marked multigenerational households and who would now adopt the "traditional" American family form. Second, domesticity would buoy the economy, stimulating the macroeconomic consumer demand that would prevent the return of the Depression. The ranch house, the wood-paneled station wagon, and the suite of kitchen appliances that came with suburban domesticity would fund the economic growth, the corporate profits, and the union contractual gains that would make for a stable market society. Whereas we might think of family structure, sexual relationships, and procreation as private matters in US culture, these intimate concerns had become the centerpiece of public policy in the 1950s.[52]

The regulation that Janet Jakobsen describes explains why so many workers were drawn to the International Brotherhood of Teamsters. The culture of the union, I argue, became a way for workers to challenge the disciplining of their bodies and desires. It is not that the Teamsters union or rank-and-file members rejected suburbanization. Quite the opposite, many Teamsters saw the suburban single-family home and heterosexual nuclear family as the primary privileges that union membership enabled. Rather than wholesale condemnation of suburbia, many workers saw the Teamsters union as a place to forge an alternative to the bourgeois cultural values that workers were supposed to embrace as they became middle-class, values that included self-denial, deferred gratification, the avoidance of pleasure, and personal responsibility. In the place of that minimalism came what Jewish Studies scholar Emily Filler calls a "maximalist aesthetic." Filler argues that maximalist aesthetics involved an externalization of the newfound material wealth of eastern and southern European Jewish and Catholic immigrants in the 1950s. Rather than hiding their economic privilege, suburbanites were encouraged to display the cars, pools, patio furniture, and vacation photographs that defined their emerging prosperity. The culture of the Teamsters exacerbated that externalization, and encouraged members to indulge to the maximum in public space: to eat succulent foods, to adorn their bodies with flashy clothing, to lie on Miami Beach on a paid holiday, and to talk, laugh, argue, dance, and imbibe late into the night without restraint.[53]

As she sped across Detroit's wide avenues, pedal to the metal and the window down so she could smoke the Newports that she loved[54], Sylvia Pagano was particularly illustrative of the maximalist aesthetics of the Teamsters union. Lore has it that Pagano was a dramatic, indulgent person. She apparently carried a cigar box in her purse full of twenty-dollar bills that she would use to hold sway over vendors and union operatives.[55] Neighbors in the late 1950s spoke of a captivating woman with jet black hair who wore flashy, tight toreador pants and whose lilting Italian filled the hallway outside her apartment.[56] People gossiped about Pagano's sultry love life and described the strong, handsome men who frequently rode the elevator up to her apartment. They claimed that Pagano had been married many times, including to several men at the same time.[57] While there is zero historical evidence to support that claim, her maximalist lifestyle clearly made Pagano a subject of desire for many people in the Teamsters' orbit.

What made Sylvia Pagano alluring to so many people was the same cultural dynamic that attracted workers to the International Brotherhood of Teamsters more broadly: the ability to contest some of the foundations of mid-twentieth-century US middle-class culture while embracing the consumer pleasures, physical mobility, and economic benefits that came with it. Pagano's resistance was always inexplicit. She never endorsed notions of feminism, lesbianism, bisexuality, polyamory, or alternative lifestyle that would become the defining terms of the new social movements by the end of the 1960s. Instead, and as historian Lauren Jae Gutterman so compellingly demonstrates, mid-twentieth-century dissidents like Sylvia Pagano opened a space to live beyond the boundary of conventional bourgeois culture by being—or at least appearing to be—so normal. Gutterman argues that 1950s heterosexual marriage "maintained its dominance not just through its rigidity, but also through its flexibility as a lived relationship."[58] Marriage—and, I argue, other normative institutions such as domesticity, traditional femininity, and mass consumption—allowed some people to engage in unacceptable behavior while providing the social and legal cover for those transgressions. Part of the reason that Sylvia Pagano got away with being a woman who was single, who was an entrepreneur, and who was an underworld operative was that she also used her husband's last name long after he died, doted on her grandchildren, cooked opulent meals for the men she worked with, and aided and abetted powerful men without explicitly challenging their authority or claiming credit for her work. It is my premise here that the Teamsters union was popular with workers precisely because it gave Sylvia Pagano, Bill Bufalino, and a million rank-and-file members a space to push the boundaries of domesticity and heterosexuality while reaping the full privileges those categories endowed.

A Map of Teamsters Metropolis

Sylvia Pagano was an iconoclast who paved her own path in an era where sexism tightly constrained her options. But many readers will find her story—and the stories of Bill Bufalino and the many other operatives who appear in *Teamsters Metropolis*—as disturbing as those stories are interesting. Is it really okay, we might ask, to involve unions in sketchy underworld rackets that pilfered money from people who desperately needed it? Is it okay to terrorize people even if some of those strong-arm tactics benefited some workers? And more philosophically, shouldn't the labor movement appeal to people's belief in a greater good, in a principled commitment to workplace justice, and shouldn't unions' daily practices reflect those lofty goals? Most Teamster activists in the 1950s would have said of course union activism should be about big ideas, and it often was. Many local Teamster leaders were like Harold Gibbons in Saint Louis, who in tandem with local NAACP president Ernest Calloway built a cross-racial movement around what they called "total person unionism." For a time in the 1950s and 1960s, every member of Gibbons's local had a shop steward for work and a shop steward for home. The neighborhood stewards would fight for housing access, food security, and physical beauty on the blocks where rank-and-file Teamsters lived. Much like Bill Bufalino, Harold Gibbons sometimes used physical persuasion against his adversaries in the 1950s. But he often did so in the explicit ideological pursuit of workplace justice. When white cab drivers in Saint Louis walked out on a hate strike to stop Black workers from integrating their industry in 1956, for example, Gibbons deployed muscle—some of which he likely recruited from his underworld contacts—to force his own members to back down and to work with their new Black colleagues.[59]

What Teamster activists would also have said about organizing, however, is that there is no single way to mobilize. Heterogeneity defined the metropolitan world of the 1950s. Driving a truck, washing a car, fixing a jukebox, loading produce, and tending bar were all different work experiences. The nature of the tasks varied if a Jewish, Italian, Black, or Chinese person was performing the work. Jobs that took place in a hot creaky manufacturing loft in New York's garment district were different than work in a brand-new car dealership in Chicago's posh north suburbs. For union organizing to be successful, each one of these niches required its own approach to organizing. Although some activists broke the law and abused their power, a few of those same activists were experts in their niche. What defined the culture of the Teamsters in the Hoffa era is that the union encouraged those local experts to use whatever tactics they needed to get the job of organizing finished. Labor historian and Teamsters expert David Witwer argues that this decentralized, wide-open approach to organizing made the Teamsters a uniquely cosmopolitan union. Witwer invokes the concept of cosmopolitanism not in the sense of sophisticated urbanity, but rather as a wholehearted embrace of a heterodox, heterogeneous set of strategies, values, and ideas.[60] Teamster activists understood that there are a hundred different ways of being on every city block of every neighborhood and thus a hundred different ways to build a union. It was that cosmopolitan worldview that made the International Brotherhood of Teamsters the largest, boldest union of the mid-twentieth century.

And then there is the issue of Jimmy Hoffa himself. Hoffa undeniably betrayed his members, as irrefutable evidence presented in every chapter of this book shows that Hoffa became a millionaire by skimming money off the union's pension fund and that he used his commitment to centralized bargaining to suppress democracy in the union and to undermine rank-and-file participation. Although these nefarious practices are painfully real, the Hoffa genre[61] of popular writing muddles our understanding of these events. From the *Saturday Evening Post* to *Playboy*, men's lifestyle journalism[62] made Hoffa into a caricature, telling a teleological tale about mob ties, corrupt locals, and nefarious deeds that ended gruesomely on the red velvet back seat of an Oldsmobile outside the Machus Red Fox restaurant in suburban Detroit as the labor movement withered in the long hot summers of the 1970s.

Fifty years have passed since these events, and it is time to move past the paranoid readings of Hoffa the crook that emerged during that painful time. *Teamsters Metropolis* does so not with a reparative reading[63] of Hoffa the hero, but rather by using historical documents to place Hoffa's ideas and actions in the context of the era in which they took place. Despite his many flaws, Hoffa motivated rank-and-file workers because he was a countercultural person. As CBS radio journalist Eric Sevareid said so succinctly in 1958, "Hoffa was a man at war, in his heart, with orthodox society."[64] According the Harvard Law School professor Jack Goldsmith, rather than follow professional best practices for union leadership, Hoffa read Billy Graham's sermons and saw the ecstatic unrestraint of religious revival as an inspiration for union organizing.[65] He bought tens of thousands of copies of George Orwell's *1984* for front-line Teamsters to teach them about the perils of government overreach.[66] He campaigned fiercely for prison reform, launching a speaking tour that explained to workers and to the press how rape, emotional abuse, and isolation ruined people during lock-up, and he demanded a humane alternative to the US carceral state.[67] Perhaps because his countercultural outlook opened his eyes to people on the margins, Hoffa pushed the Teamsters union into some of the most exploitive sectors of the economy, recruiting workers in dangerous, high-turnover, sweatshop work. Organizing these workers is paramount in an era when US metropolitan areas run on undocumented work, temporary work, gig work, and sex work, and labor historians must ask how and why Hoffa's generation of leaders took on these tasks.

The unruly organizing practices of the International Brotherhood of Teamsters in the age of Jimmy Hoffa are the subject of every chapter of this book. Each chapter describes working people's yearning to trade the hardscrabble world of the central city for suburban landscapes of comfort. Each chapter illustrates these same people's ambivalence about restraining their bodies and tempering their emotions to comply with middle-class cultural regulation. And each chapter addresses the intensifying counter-mobilization among the poor people, the Black people, the Brown people, and the queer people who had been locked out of the suburbs categorically. Chapter 1 is written from the perspective of the operatives who built the Teamsters metropolis, focusing on workers who installed and fixed coin-operated vending machines, the pool tables, pinball machines, juke-boxes, and shuffleboard alleys that entertained patrons in neighborhood bars and taverns. Activists built the union by harnessing a cultural con-flict over the meaning of suburbanization, one in which Catholic and Jew-ish immigrant families from eastern and southern Europe struggled over how to fit into the city, how to be white, and whether or not they would embrace traditional middle-class domesticity.

Chapter 2 inverts the perspective of the first chapter, telling the story of the Teamsters metropolis according to its greatest antagonist, Chief Counsel Robert F. Kennedy of the Senate Select Committee on Improper Activities in the Labor Management Field. The "McClellan Committee" subpoenaed fifteen hundred witnesses over thirty-seven months and told lurid stories about malfeasance in the Teamsters and other unions. Ken-nedy probed the ways that Teamster operatives violated bourgeois stan-dards of comportment: the overly flamboyant clothes, the unnecessarily indulgent dinners, the preposterously inappropriate ethnic nicknames, the jarringly violent confrontations, and the constant use of aliases, dual identities, extorted money, and forged documents to flagrantly violate the law. Through chronicles of brash overconsumption, nefarious desires, and unrestrained, overadorned bodies, Kennedy and the other commit-tee members strove to bring union activists under control, to regulate the undisciplined bodies that constituted the Teamsters union.

Set in the resort hotels of Miami Beach, chapter 3 focuses on the role of pleasure in the Teamsters metropolis. Beginning when Jimmy Hoffa was elected president of the Teamsters in 1957, the union invested millions of dollars in the construction of flamboyant oceanfront properties where activists conducted union business, where workers took paid vacations, and where retirees enjoyed the benefits of their union pensions. In the sweet smell of suntan lotion, the joyful glow of pink neon, and the clicking of the ice in a Tom Collins sipped next to the pool, the chapter argues that Teamster Miami Beach rejected the prowork, antipleasure ideology of the Protestant work ethic. The irony, however, was that while Jimmy Hoffa build this landscape of desire for his members, he eschewed pleasure in his own life and renounced the mass consumption and bourgeois domesticity that defined suburban culture.

Chapter 4 tells the story of young Black and Brown dissident union activists who, like Annie May Anderson, had their own vision for the future of the Teamsters metropolis. Union membership provided unprecedented metropolitan mobility for eastern and southern European Jewish and Catholic immigrant families. But for young people coming to New York in the 1950s from the Caribbean, Central America, and the Jim Crow South, city life was tightly constrained, as they were locked out of the suburbs and forced into overcrowded housing, segregated schools, and an overtly racist two-tier labor market. This chapter presents a conflict over urban space, one where young workers challenged exploitive practices by business owners and Teamster operatives to secure their own access to middle-class consumer comforts.

Teamster kinship practices are the subject of chapter 5. At the center of the narrative is Sylvia Pagano. The chapter argues that Pagano's social group practiced what historian Nayan Shah calls "queer domesticity,"[68] a heterogeneous form of kinship that transgressed the boundaries of friendship, love, business, family, and the household. Challenging assumptions about the Teamsters union's cultural conservatism, the chapter demonstrates that the unconventional kinship practices—Pagano's peers' tendency to share productive and reproductive labor between men and women, to build evolving relationships that included love, sex, solidarity, and betrayal, and to mix intimate ties with professional and political ones—were the foundation of the union's organizing success.

The book concludes with an epilogue that explains why all these unruly events matter. In the fifteen years after World War II, the Teamsters recruited more than a million workers in the service sector and in other marginal industries, organizing that has remained elusive despite decades of unceasing efforts. The epilogue upends the common assumption that the labor movement was an agent of heteronormalization in the mid-twentieth century, an apparatus that handed access to mass consumption, suburban domesticity, and whiteness to European immigrant union members who willingly accepted it. It instead argues that unions grew in the 1950s when they were countercultural: when they challenged the work ethic and other bedrock American values, when they expanded the domain of the family, when they addressed the anxieties that came with economic and spatial mobility, or lack thereof. It is these countercultural practices that turned industrial cities into the Teamsters metropolis. To these contentious events—on the smoky dance floors of neighborhood bars where the neon glow of the jukebox was the only light—*Teamsters Metropolis* now turns.

CHAPTER ONE

Organizing the Teamsters Metropolis
Unruly Unionism in New York City's Service Industry

Salvatore Caruso's troubles began in the summer of 1958 with a brand-new Wurlitzer jukebox. A slick new package for the year's hit songs, from the Everly Brothers' "All I Have to Do Is Dream" to the Silhouettes' "Get a Job/ Sha-na-na" and the Coasters' "Yakety Yak," Caruso hoped the machine would encourage people to linger over martinis and Manhattans in the lounge of his Levittown, New York, restaurant. Caruso had been a successful small businessman before the arrival of the Wurlitzer. He chose an ideal location, nestled amid middle-class families' newly built Cape Cod homes, and with the intersection of bustling Wantagh Parkway and Hempstead Turnpike providing ample automobile traffic. To capture the attention of passing motorists, Caruso built a tall, bold marquee featuring an image of himself tossing a pizza crust in turquoise and tomato-colored neon.[1] The marquee became the center of the restaurant's branding, emblazoned on the glossy black matchbooks that Caruso bought from the Maryland Match Company in Baltimore.[2] Even his choice to name the restaurant after himself was shrewd, as Caruso's surname would remind a local population still adjusting to life in the suburbs of the cuisine they left behind in the old immigrant neighborhoods of Brooklyn and Queens: thin crust pizza, ragu with tagliatelle, and panino Napolitano stuffed with mozzarella.

The Wurlitzer, however, was a mistake. To make space for the jukebox and for a Smokeshop cigarette machine he also bought, Caruso broke the contract for his old jukebox with the Nu-Way Vending Company, which operated pinball machines, shuffleboard alleys, billiard tables, and other coin-operated equipment in twenty-five bars and restaurants around the Long Island suburbs. Nu-Way's owner Herbert Jacob did not take the news well, as he worried that Caruso's move would encourage other small businesses to follow suit, buying their own machines to avoid sharing the proceeds of customers' entertainment with service companies. On September 12, 1958, Jacob drove out from his home in Sheepshead Bay, Brooklyn, to pay Caruso a visit. He began by offering to purchase the Wurlitzer and the Smokeshop in cash. When Caruso refused, Jacob threatened him, saying that Caruso could "get hurt" if he failed to honor the service contract with Nu-Way. Jacob also threatened Hal Zimmerman, the man who sold Caruso the jukebox, calling him on the phone and telling him, "You can't sell your machines to Caruso. You have a nice wife and child; you had better get smart."

Unfazed by the intimidation, Caruso continued to entertain customers with his Wurlitzer. Jacob then further escalated the situation, calling Teamsters Local 266, a union that regularly did business with Nu-Way. Teamster leaders agreed to help and notified Sylvia Goldberg of the trouble in Levittown. Goldberg managed the logistics of mobilizing the union's most powerful tool: the picket line. Twelve days after Jacob's visit, a man appeared under the restaurant's marquee, holding a sign that warned customers that Salvatore Caruso was unfair to labor. In a neighborhood home to many eastern and southern European Catholic and Jewish residents, many of whom had been active during the labor struggles of 1930s New York in their youth, crossing a picket line was a shameful act. Caruso quickly recognized that absent a deal with Jacob and the Teamsters, his long-loyal customers would vanish.[3]

This chapter explores the small Catholic and Jewish family businesses like Salvatore Caruso's and Herbert Jacob's, those that were the economic foundation of the Teamsters metropolis. New York City's coin-operated vending machine business is the primary focus of the chapter, though I also point to similar dynamics in commercial laundering, uniform supply services, electrical and plumbing manufacturing, office equipment, car washes, beauty salons, taxicabs, and scores of other industries in the light manufacturing, service, and retail sectors of the economy. Prominent historians, from Nelson Lichtenstein to Robert Self to Kim Phillips-Fein, have framed mid-twentieth-century society as structured by bureaucratic institutions, those that defined a Walter Reuther–style corporatist capitalism: the agencies of the federal government, large corporations, and the industrial unions that grew out of the CIO movement of the 1930s.[4] In both scholarly accounts and in a spectrum of critiques from John Kenneth Galbraith's *The Affluent Society* to Lorraine Hansberry's *A Raisin in the Sun* to Herbert Marcuse's *One-Dimensional Man*, the suburban cul-de-sac, General Motors, and the United Automobile Workers signify the dominant, heteronormative, and often racially segregated mass culture of the Cold War era.[5]

Salvatore Caruso, Herbert Jacob, and Sylvia Goldberg rejected that homogenized world, refusing to embrace the restrained personal demeanor, the controlled bodily comportment, and the respect for authority that were defining features of the middle class of the 1950s. Rather than containing themselves on the cul-de-sac, Caruso, Jacob, and Goldberg lived metropolitan[6] lives, mixing home and work both in the new suburbs and in the older, central city neighborhoods of their parents and grandparents. Rather than rely on the large corporation for a wage, they worked for themselves and continued to foster the small service businesses their families had built decades earlier. And rather than join large, amalgamated locals of the steelworkers, the mineworkers, the autoworkers, or other CIO industrial unions, they built small, AFL craft unions, many of which would end up affiliating with the Teamsters by the end of the 1950s. I argue that these small businesses and Teamster locals were the primary venue for the cultural struggle over the meaning of suburbanization—and the attendant investment in whiteness and heterosexuality[7]—for the children and grandchildren of Jewish and Catholic "new immigrant"[8] families like Caruso's, Jacob's, and Goldberg's. Jimmy Hoffa understood this, which is why he made the service sector a crux of his rise to power in the Teamsters. I thus frame the International Brotherhood of Teamsters as a mechanism for eastern and southern European Catholics and Jews to struggle over where they would fit into the city, how they would be white, and if they would be normal sexual subjects.

While chapter 4 will analyze how Black and Latino activists built their own political structures in the Teamsters metropolis, this chapter examines cultural unrest among the particular cohort of Jews and Catholics whose whiteness, as Mae Ngai so sharply demonstrates in *Impossible Subjects*, had been stabilized by the immigration, housing, and labor policy reforms of the 1920s and 1930s.[9] The bars and restaurants such as Caruso's in Levittown where this cohort socialized were deeply contradictory spaces, those where Catholic and Jewish people could cavort, where libidos rose as jukeboxes played music from Black artists to white audiences, where people refused to cross picket lines when the Teamsters warned of trouble, and where people took full advantage of the segregated world that the Federal Housing Administration, labor policy, the police, and their own physical violence created. That unruliness, that which Jimmy Hoffa so shrewdly harnessed, is the subject of this chapter.

Acid Attacks on Pool Tables: The Search for Order in the Coin Machine Business

Coin-operated vending machines existed for the pleasures of people of modest means. While the proprietors of small-scale restaurants, bars, and taverns provided physical space, food, and alcohol, they often lacked the funds to hire bands, comics, or theater troupes to entertain guests. It was therefore the coin machines that directly encouraged people to talk, dance, and carry on. Most important among these devices was the jukebox, which played and amplified 45 rpm vinyl records. Jukeboxes were built to attract attention, with sleek modern lines, polished wood, chrome piping, and flashing lights meant to lure people to peruse the songs. Design features matched wider style trends. The 1958 Rock-Ola jukebox, for example, included a gleaming chrome chevron that made its speaker look like the grill of that model year's Chevrolet. The machines were named after the founder of the company who made them, an operative in the Prohibition-era Chicago crime syndicate who was fittingly named David Rockola.[10] Jukebox operators like Herbert Jacob would regularly restock the records inside the Rock-Ola, pulling out last year's hits—the Del Vikings' "Come and Go with Me" and Elvis Presley's "All Shook Up"—to make way for the music of 1958. A good jukebox would get bar patrons dancing, arousing the social, romantic, and sexual capacities of the body with fast songs that allowed people to show off for their friends, and with slow songs that enabled a more physical, erotically intense connection.

Other coin-operated machines facilitated social interactions in a less explicitly intimate context than dance. Shuffleboard alleys, for example, were narrow wooden tables where competitors would use their hands to slide discs toward a scoring zone, a game modeled after the more common patio sport where players stand and use long cues to accomplish the same task. In another case, "ball bowlers" or "bowling machines" worked similarly to coin-operated shuffleboard, but instead of sliding discs players would roll heavy balls down a long, thin table toward a set of pins, following similar rules and tabulation procedures to a full-size bowling alley. Shuffleboard and bowling machines featured modern electronic technology to dramatize the competition, broadcasting point totals on boldly lit, brightly colored scoreboards. Pinball machines were widely popular coin machines, as were billiard tables, which encouraged people to return to the tavern night after night to build their skills. Game machines promoted connections across social differences, as the structured nature of sport was less obviously transgressive than the openly sexual realm of dance, especially in the fraught context of same-sex, interethnic, or interracial interactions. Particularly crucial to facilitating such mixing was the cigarette machine, in which neatly displayed rows of colored packages encouraged people to pull the lever, light up, and let go of any social inhibition that remained as the cocktails went down.

While tavern owners installed coin-operated vending machines for the pleasure of their patrons, the economic rewards of doing so were lucrative. The more fun a guest had dancing, playing pool, and smoking cigarettes, the later into the evening they would stay, driving up revenue as they bought more drinks. Barkeeps, thus, sought a wide variety of the newest, most eye-catching machines. The problem for many owners, however, was that the machines were expensive. A state-of-the-art jukebox in the mid-1950s cost about $1,100, the equivalent of $10,000 today.[11] Many bar and restaurant owners had grown up in immigrant neighborhoods during the Great Depression. Capital was scarce, as large banks often refused to lend to poor, Italian-, Yiddish-, Polish-, or Russian-speaking families. Even amid a booming 1950s economy, and even as the significance of ethnic differences waned, the risk-averse, heavily regulated midcentury banking system often avoided small businesses with little collateral like Salvatore Caruso's.[12]

Other immigrant family businesses stepped in to make up for tavern owners' undercapitalization. Beginning in the 1930s, a new, mostly Jewish cohort of entrepreneurs became coin machine "operators," using what little money they had to purchase machines, installing the machines in bars and restaurants, and splitting the proceeds with barkeeps, who they called "location owners." Operators charged the location owners a monthly fee that, when combined with the take from the coin box, made for a sustainable business. With the operators assuming the risk of buying and maintaining the machines, the location owners were able to access an array of bowlers, pinball machines, jukeboxes, and other equipment for a modest monthly charge. Herbert Jacob ran just such a business, having started the Nu-Way Vending Company with his brother Eugene in 1950 and subsequently taking a financial stake in fellow operator Max Gulden's business that ran seventy machines in Pennsylvania, West Virginia, and Ohio.[13]

The problem for the Jacob brothers and other operators was that, like most businesses in the light manufacturing, retail, and service sectors, barriers to entry were low. While buying a jukebox or a commercial washing machine, starting a lampshade or cushion factory in a small industrial loft, or opening up a corner beauty parlor or barber shop was an expensive prospect for an ordinary person, many individuals and families found ways to pool enough resources to start such businesses. The consequence was a chronic instability among such firms, with proprietors facing a steady stream of new entrants vying for market share. In the coin machine business, the practice was called "jumping." Jukebox and game technology evolved quickly, which created an opportunity for new firms to displace older businesses by offering bars and restaurants the latest equipment. Why, for example, would a bar continue paying for a dated, early 1950s Wurlitzer jukebox with staid wooden columns when they could get a brand-new 1958 machine with chrome and flashing turquoise neon for a lower rate? The threat of jumping thus drove up operating costs, as established operators like the Jacob brothers had to continually buy expensive new equipment to remain competitive.

Operators took collective action to discourage jumping and to bring a sense of order to their business. Organizing dated to the 1930s, when small business owners began to band together to limit competition. The grassroots nature of their mobilization challenges dominant historical understandings of the response to the Great Depression that tend to center the federal government and large corporations. From the Glass-Steagall Act, which controlled banks' lending practices, to the National Labor Relations Act, which allowed workers greater control over the labor market, to the regulation of the transportation, utility, and communications industries that set prices and established barriers to entry, New Dealers used the power of the federal government to control the way businesses were financed, staffed, and structured.[14] The new regulations transformed the way that U.S. Steel, General Electric, and United Airlines did business. But for Salvatore Caruso, the Jacob brothers, and the proprietors of tens of thousands of small family firms in services and related industries, New Deal reforms did little to protect them from the volatility of an unregulated marketplace.

Small business people thus took matters into their own hands, building trade associations in an effort to regulate themselves. In New York, for example, jukebox operators formed the Music Operators of New York (MONY) in 1937. Members of the association would pay a flat initiation charge for every jukebox—which ran the equivalent of $700 in today's dollars—and then a monthly fee for each machine. Members of MONY promised not to jump each other's locations, and the organization hired a staff person to visit sites to ensure that the machines were well-maintained and to discourage bars, taverns, and restaurants from operating jumped equipment. Similar structures were adopted in other service industries and in other locations. Coin game operators in New York formed AAMONY, the Associated Amusement Machine Operators of New York during the same period, and in Miami, they started AMOA, the Amusement Machine Operators Association. Barkeeps in suburban Chicago created the Retail Liquor Dealers Protective Association, for example, and commercial laundries in Detroit joined the Detroit Laundry Institute. Membership rolls of the associations reveal the competitive and unstable nature of these industries, where scores of small firms struggled to win and retain market share. According to the jukebox association MONY, by the mid-1950s there were about eleven thousand machines in New York City and the surrounding area. While there were a few large operators such as the Suffolk-Nassau Music Company, which ran seven hundred jukeboxes in the Long Island suburbs, most of the 160 operators who had joined MONY ran very small businesses. The average member had between thirty and forty machines, and grossed about $20 a week from each one, meaning that total annual revenue for their business was about $330,000 in today's dollars. Many operators were so small that they chose to forgo joining MONY altogether, hoping to save the money that would have been spent on monthly fees and to leave the door open to the practice of jumping, which, despite the anger it provoked among competitors, was an effective way to build market share. MONY initiation fees had indeed been paid for only 72 percent of jukeboxes in New York City in 1957.[15]

Absent the regulatory apparatus, the political stature, or the economic capital to compel their peers to join the association system, operators turned to a valuable asset that generations of Jewish and Catholic family business owners had cultivated in unstable industries over decades: muscle. If a proprietor refused participate in the collective effort to bring order to the industry, association members often intervened to force the individual to comply, threatening family members, destroying property, and attacking or maiming the intransigent parties. On April 13th, 1955, for example, a group of men appeared at the warehouse of the Southern Music Company in Miami after its proprietor, Robert Norman, refused to follow the mandates of the local jukebox association. They launched stink bombs through the windows, which soaked Norman's equipment in nauseating fumes. According to Norman, a gagging odor still permeated the eight-thousand-square-foot warehouse four years later, making jukebox maintenance in the space virtually impossible.[16] In another case, three assailants entered Vilius Niemantus's corner tavern in the Bridgeport neighborhood on Chicago's near southwest side in January 1958. The bartender noticed the men's conversation in English, which stood out in a bar where nearly all patrons spoke Lithuanian. Before they left, one of the men doused the pool table in acid, which rendered it inoperable and which destroyed all of the bar towels that the staff had used to try to clean up the mess. Niemantus had recently changed vendors to a coin machine operator who was not a member of the local association, and he quickly understood that the pool table was a casualty of his decision to participate in jumping. Three weeks later there were more casualties. A man came in, sat at the bar drinking for three hours and then, when the bar had quieted down before close, took a hatchet out of his jacket and chopped up the bowler. Refusing to back down, Niemantus continued to operate the jumped machines, which soon brought physical reprisal. A customer pulled a revolver on Niemantus, threw him against the pool table, and broke three of his ribs. Niemantus knew that other local taverns that refused to follow association protocols were also experiencing reprisal. Late one evening, Leo Romaskiewicz, the owner of a nearby bar with a Polish clientele who had begun operating jumped machines, witnessed a man dousing two of his machines in acid, and cutting up another with a large pair of shears.[17]

The violence that Niemantus, Romaskiewicz, Caruso, and others faced raises the question of why they continued to run small family businesses in the 1950s. The famous "Treaty of Detroit" had just been signed between big labor and the automobile industry. Unions across the manufacturing sector were negotiating a breadwinner wage, free health insurance, ample vacation, and company paid pensions for the children and grandchildren of eastern and southern European immigrants.[18] Why would people continue to work in the service industry, undermining their physical safety, jeopardizing their investments, and exposing themselves to criminal prosecution for relatively meager remuneration when they could easily secure a job at a large corporation that came with higher pay, better hours, and far less risk?

The answer begins with the financial networks among two groups who arrived late in the "new immigrant" wave during the 1900s and 1910s: southern Italians and eastern European Jews. For both populations, the licit and the illicit were the intertwined foundations of public economic life. In the Italian case, illicit economic practices stemmed from a fraught relationship with the Catholic Church on both sides of the Atlantic. Sicilians were often deeply anticlerical, blaming a corrupt Church hierarchy for the political and economic paralysis that pushed them to cross the Atlantic.[19] Upon arrival, they struggled to find a place in an American church with an overwhelmingly Irish episcopacy. According to historian John T. McGreevy, localism and parochialism defined the Catholic culture of northern US cities, with pastors seldom visiting the parish next door and rarely building relationships across ethnic lines within parish boundaries. Newcomers from Naples and Palermo thus often met an unwelcoming Catholic institution. Italian priests, for example, were often forced to say Mass in church basements while Irish priests worshipped in English and spoken Latin from the altar upstairs.[20] In the dual contexts of Sicilian anticlericalism and episcopal defensive localism, the home and the family became the core of Italian Catholic popular theology in the United States, which made Italians the least churched among early twentieth-century Catholic immigrants.[21] Therefore, and unlike their highly observant eastern European counterparts who often used the church as a mechanism for integration into the wider industrial economy, family ties were the centerpiece of Italian Catholic economic networks. With the household rather than the large corporation providing the primary venue for Italian business dealings, immigrant families continued to rely on both the licit and illicit practices—the family-owned shop and the muscle of the organized crime syndicate—that had defined the economy of southern Italy. Small firms, a diffuse capital structure, and scant government oversight made the service industry well-suited to already existing southern Italian business infrastructure.

Eastern European Jews' presence in ancillary firms also had transnational roots. By 1920, Jews from eastern Europe outnumbered their wealthier western European counterparts in the United States nine to one.[22] In the shtetls of eastern Europe, Jews were outsiders, formally excluded from state protection in the Russian Pale, Romania, and Ukraine, among many other places. Out of necessity, and as Michael Alexander argues in *Jazz Age Jews*, business took place on the law's margin, and Jews of all social locations—including the establishment—embraced those marginal endeavors because they recognized the injustice of the law itself.[23] Once they arrived in the United States, eastern European Jews came to cities where "good government" reformers were cracking down on the corruption of Tammany Hall and other Irish Catholic machines. Immigrant Jews applied the business techniques they had honed in eastern Europe to the formerly Irish-controlled gambling, bookmaking, and liquor-dealing operations that the native-born middle class both scorned and adored, those disdained pastimes that Alexander calls "deliciously illegal."[24] Therefore, despite a significant Jewish presence in the upper management of above-board businesses in entertainment, dry goods, and finance, the illicit remained a visible component of Jewish American economic life. Arnold Rothstein, the infamous bookmaker who helped throw the 1919 World Series, ran his business from reserved window tables in Ruby's and Lindy's delicatessens, the social hubs of both working- and middle-class Jewish life in New York.[25]

Although the history of immigrant family businesses helps explain why Salvatore Caruso and Herbert Jacob opened up shops in the service sector, even stronger structural forces were pulling southern Italians, eastern European Jews, and other "new immigrants" in the opposite direction, away from the small, central city firms that their parents and grandparents had built. New Deal–era reforms—FHA-backed mortgage lending, GI Bill education, and Wagner Act–refereed collective bargaining, among others—disproportionately benefited eastern and southern European immigrant families, often allowing them to leapfrog native-born white Protestants into the middle class. Two-thirds of American Jews had moved to the suburbs by 1960, when only one third of the overall population had done so. A striking 85 percent of Cleveland's Jews, for example, had departed for the suburbs by 1959.[26] Though Jewish women had begun to leave wage labor during the period before immigration restriction in the 1920s, Jewish families were more likely than their Protestant or Catholic neighbors to rely on the family wage of a husband breadwinner during the immediate postwar era. In 1957, 27.8 percent of married Jewish women worked for a cash wage compared to 29.6 percent of non-Jewish white women.[27] And while Irish and other immigrant Catholic women of the nineteenth and early twentieth centuries were judged for their purported likelihood to stay single, work service jobs for a pittance, and have children outside of marriage, Catholics also embraced suburban, middle-class heteronormativity. By 1960, Catholics had surpassed the national average for income and educational achievement, and four inner-city parish churches a week were closing as Polish, Croatian, Italian, and other immigrant families left for the single-family homes of the suburbs.[28] Rather than a narrative about exclusion, then, the Catholic and Jewish journey through American metropolitan space in the first half of the twentieth century was a story about cultural whiplash, one in which proletarian and peasant families fled deprivation, hunger, and violence in Europe, briefly touched down in hardscrabble urban industrial neighborhoods of northern cities, and then landed in the government-backed abundance of the suburbs, all in two generations.

This sense of cultural whiplash explains why some people forwent the security of mid-twentieth-century corporate employment and embraced the unruliness of coin-operated vending machine business. The service industry, I argue, was a place to make a living for the descendants of Catholic and Jewish immigrants who were unwilling or unable to comply with the restrained cultural norms that defined the affluent suburban landscape. By the mid-1950s, those norms were a source of widespread discontent. In *Ambivalent Embrace*, for example, historian Rachel Kranson argues that the journey from shtetl to cul-de-sac forged not a progressive narrative of achievement, but rather a deep cultural ambivalence about how newfound affluence would transform a Jewish identity long defined by outsider status and cultural dissent.[29] The ambivalence that Kranson describes was particularly evident in the context of personal comportment.[30] People who left city neighborhoods for the suburbs had to adopt a new, regulated demeanor, one enforced by the pedagogy of the large corporation's personnel department, the grievance procedure of the industrial union, and the strict behavioral standards for suburban living. A quiet voice speaking standard American English, minimal physical gesticulations while speaking, restrained body language, subdued clothing styles, unadorned physical spaces, and the containment of desire within heterosexual domesticity were common markers of such comportment.[31] Those who came to the suburbs from the Catholic and Jewish central city had to quickly learn how to perform their newfound racial and class privilege, performativity that required them to cite and reiterate the appropriate middle-class regulation of their voices, their accents, their word choices, their bodies, and their desires to avoid conveying any sense of flamboyance or crassness.

The physical environment of suburbia stoked the cultural tensions surrounding the new comportment. Whereas unpredictability, architectural heterogeneity, linguistic complexity, and a wide array of conflicting sounds, smells, and interactions defined the environment of Catholic and Jewish central city neighborhoods, the simplicity and abstraction of the international style of modernism was the dominant idiom of suburban design. As Kranson demonstrates, many Jewish intellectuals, rabbis, and community activists saw the austerity of the international style as incompatible with the expressiveness of eastern European immigrant Jewish culture. *Commentary* magazine's Morris Freedman, for example, described what he saw as the emotional and spiritual emptiness of the newly built synagogues of 1950s Queens, calling one "a great white building that looked something like a bank" and comparing another to a "modern college auditorium."[32] Similarly, Rabbi Samuel Schafler argued that the modernist minimalism of postwar synagogues denied congregants the visceral experience of worship. In an essay for *Mas'at Rav*, a publication from the Rabbinical Assembly of the Conservative Jewish movement, Shafler relayed the observations of an elderly Jewish woman. "Everything is pretty, but you cannot cry here,"[33] the woman remarked in Yiddish, indicting what she saw as hollow, generic religious spaces that failed to provide a dignified venue for 1950s Jews to process the stinging discordance between affluent American suburban life and the horrors of the Nazi atrocities in Europe.

The coin-operated vending machine business and other service industries delivered a means to reconcile some of the ambivalence that Kranson describes. They did so by allowing one to work beyond the boundary of middle-class personal style. Rarely was there a personnel department at a small firm, and thus there was little oversight of grooming, clothing choices, or managerial techniques. Clients were often other people from Italian-, Yiddish-, Russian-, or Polish-speaking families who shared local ethnic- and class-inflected speech patterns. Instead of solving problems with the paperwork of lawsuits, grievances, or arbitration, people processed their differences with their voices and, if necessary, their fists. Shouting, waving one's arms, and storming out of the room were regular, respected components of the business process. And while industrial unions had forced many large corporations to pay family wage to husband breadwinners for their dependent wives and children, thus underwriting the nuclear family that defined the nineteenth-century Protestant ideal of bourgeois domesticity, in service businesses everyone contributed, as husbands, wives, children, parents, cousins, in-laws, friends, and neighbors helped build Jewish and Catholic family firms. The decision to work beyond the boundary of middle-class comportment was by no means a rejection of suburbia, as many proprietors took full advantage of the economic and cultural capital that suburbanization provided. Eugene Jacob indeed lived in an international-style modernist home in Levittown[34] as he helped his brother Herbert threaten Salvatore Caruso, whose business was also in this archetypical suburban location. Rather, service work helped people balance a yearning for an older, more dynamic world with a possessive investment in suburban whiteness and all of the resources it delivered.

Committed though they were to continuing to run their power laundries, pillow factories, beer distributorships, and jukebox routes, Catholic and Jewish business owners recognized that they needed additional resources to deliver the economic stability they had come to expect. While they may have dissented from the restrained cultural norms of suburbia, their newly stable whiteness led them to expect middle-class incomes, which the trade association system only sometimes delivered. Therefore, the proprietors of small shops turned to an institution that had played a pivotal role in many of their families' successful entry into the middle class: the labor movement. Small business owners such as the Jacob brothers used unions to help their firms deliver a middle-class wage while remaining beyond the boundary of the mainstream suburban culture of the 1950s.

"Cutting Off the Drink and Vittles": Labor Unions as Service-Sector Cartels

The broken ribs and the hacked-up pinball machines of the mid-twentieth-century service industry confound what scholars often teach us about the history and culture of trade unions. In his influential text *Citizen Worker,* for example, David Montgomery demonstrates that in the early nineteenth century, skilled craftsmen—hatters, spinners, cordwainers, plastermakers—politicized their status as wage workers to make claims for the full benefits of American citizenship, demanding access to privileges that had once been reserved for people who owned the means of production.[35] A century later, the industrial union movement of the 1930s pushed through a new federal law that helped unions win the economic resources that wage-worker activists had sought for a century. The Wagner Act of 1935 encouraged rank-and-file workers to identify a common set of interests on the shop floor, to bargain with corporate managers around those interests, and to use the power of the courts to enforce union contracts that governed pay, benefits, and work rules. Though historians have rightly illuminated the robust gains that this wage-work-focused unionism has delivered to millions of workers, we—and often the labor movement we write about—produce a series of binaries in our analysis: home versus work, neighborhood versus shop floor, worker versus owner, union activist versus business entrepreneur, and so forth.

Three decades before President Roosevelt signed the Wagner Act, a far different practice of trade unionism had emerged in the service, retail, and light manufacturing businesses in large industrial cities. The owners and the employees of small, family-owned proprietorships strove to build a system of regulation to curb the cutthroat competition that undermined their livelihoods. While large corporations demanded the right to regulate themselves and thus fiercely resisted both trade union and government oversight, small service businesses welcomed regulation to stabilize their businesses. Workers and managers collaborated to leverage scant resources: a shifting array of trade associations that helped firms set prices;

small, AFL-affiliated craft unions that stabilized wages; and administrative agencies that used their limited resources to control licensing, work hours, and safety procedures. Historian Andrew Wender Cohen calls this provisional, precarious regulatory apparatus a system of "craft governance."[36] In part because of that precariousness, violence plagued craft governance, as its participants lacked other legal and financial means to enforce the regulation they sought. Therefore, and as Cohen argues, union violence in the service sector emanated from workers' and owners' search for order and not from a pathological cultural acceptance of disorder.[37] By the time coin machine operators began to organize in the 1930s, then, two distinct forms of unionism defined labor relations in the industrial metropolis. One was built around formal collective bargaining outlined in the Wagner Act and most common at large firms in manufacturing. The other was an unruly unionism that had grown out of the service sector, one that in Cohen's words, "created a city within a city (that was) immodern and illiberal."[38]

Beatrice Richer's career exemplifies how this immodern, illiberal city worked in the 1950s. At first glance, one might have described Richer as an activist in the mid-1940s. A middle-aged single woman, Richer lived in a small but sunny apartment not far from the original Yankee Stadium in the Concourse neighborhood of the Bronx.[39] She was active in local labor politics. On October 7, 1947, for example, Richer was one of one hundred labor leaders who signed an advertisement in the *New York Times* that condemned the reactionary, antiunion agenda of the Republican-controlled 80th Congress and that asked for the public's embrace of the joint AFL and CIO initiative to support New York's Liberal Party. Her name appeared next to David Dubinsky, A. Phillip Randolph, and many other influential trade unionists.[40] Similarly, on November 7, 1949, Richer joined forty union higher-ups in a full-page election day advertisement for Newbold Morris, the Liberal-Fusion candidate for mayor who ran as an open critic of the Irish political machine in Tammany Hall.[41] Like many other activists in a labor movement at the peak of its financial stability, Richer made a living through a job as a union staff member, working as the secretary-treasurer of the Amusement Clerks and Concessionaire Employees Local 1115c.[42]

While Beatrice Richer clearly sought to advance labor's cause, the day-to-day details of her affairs diverge sharply from the methods outlined in the Wagner Act. The discontinuity stems from Local 1115c's involvement in shadowy spaces on the margins of New York's service economy: the grindhouse movie theaters of Times Square. In 1937, Mayor Fiorello LaGuardia had banned burlesque performance as part of a wider, good-government effort to root out vice. No longer could people bend gender and entice desire in scant leather and velvet costumes on the stage. The reform triggered a commercial real estate crisis for Times Square, the Manhattan neighborhood that was the epicenter of the burlesque scene. In the economic upheaval, a Jewish entrepreneur named William Brandt saw an opportunity. He began to buy up closed burlesque theaters on the cheap, to convert them into movie houses, and to set up a system to maximize revenue while aggressively controlling costs.[43] Rather than show first-run blockbusters that required expensive payments to Hollywood studios, Brandt recycled movies that had left the screen years ago, and he paid little for their licensing. Rather than offer big-budget features, Brandt screened movies that were cheap to make and thus cheap to run. And rather than limit screenings to the peak demand hours like more respectable venues did, Brandt used his real estate to the fullest, running films all the time.[44] In the city that never slept, Brandt knew there would be plenty of people willing to stumble in at 3 a.m. and watch a 1930s classic or a blood-soaked slasher film. The process was a grind, churning out product day and night like a factory. Thus, these theaters in New York and many other industrial cities were known as grindhouses.

New York City's grindhouses were popular, attracting large audiences with content that flagrantly violented mid-twentieth-century norms of gender, sexuality, and race. Among the highest grossing grindhouse films of the 1950s was *Glen or Glenda*, a cheaply made one-hour-and-eight-minute film that was released in 1953. *Glen or Glenda* was the work of Ed Wood, who decades later would become a cult hero because of the campiness of his films' abrupt transitions, unconvincing special effects, and breezy dialogue, and because we later learned that Wood struggled to express his own queer and transgender affinities. In this film, the main character appears to be a young white man named Glen who lives in a comfortable suburban bungalow. Viewers soon learn, however, that Glen often commutes to a gritty central city fashion district, where he peruses makeup, lingerie, and women's formalwear, and where he adopts the name Glenda to express a personhood that a contemporary audience would understand as transfeminine.[45] Glenda's story enables documentary-style interviews with purported scientists, doctors, and police about gender nonconformity. Given the popularity of the film and the absence of mainstream representation of queer topics, we could guess that it drew a wide variety of viewers. Some people may certainly have used *Glen or Glenda* as a source of information about their own transgender experience or those of their friends and loved ones. Others could have watched it to fashion themselves dissidents in society that repressed queer culture. Still others could have gawked, hatefully scorning a queer narrative as a freakshow. Or they could have just walked in, bought some sweet treats, and watched *Glen or Glenda* because it was the thing everyone was doing.

It was those sweet treats, and not Glenda's transgender expression, that put the grindhouses—and Beatrice Richer—on the cover of New York's newspapers in the early 1950s. To keep costs to a minimum, Brandt and other grindhouse owners outsourced the candy business, allowing entrepreneurs to set up concession stands in the theaters. In 1947, Jacob Bernoff—who sometimes went by Jack Cohen or Jewey Cohen[46]—became one of those entrepreneurs. Bernoff had ties to Lepke Buchalter in the 1930s, the infamous member of the "Murder Inc" underworld hit squad, and had served prison time for extorting millions of dollars from milk delivery companies during the Great Depression.[47] Bernoff sometimes worked with his brother Charlie, a businessman whose dealings were understood to be legitimate and who had financed the construction of Vernon Hills Estates, a tony, segregated housing development in suburban Eastchester, New York.[48] Sometime after Jacob Bernoff's parole, it appears that he invested in a company called ABC Vending, which was in the process of taking over small, disparate, and undercapitalized concession stands in the grindhouses and connecting them into a single umbrella organization.[49] But because scores of entrepreneurs were selling candy cigarettes, Dots, and Charleston Chews at the movies, Bernoff's group was constantly vulnerable to being undercut by new companies with lower costs, much like jukebox operators faced the incessant threat of jumping.

To neutralize this threat, Bernoff turned to Beatrice Richer's union. Bernoff and Richer signed up everyone who did business with ABC Vending as members of Local 1115c, both rank-and-file workers who hocked candy in the grindhouse aisles and the entrepreneurs who actually owned the concession stands that had become part of the ABC Vending umbrella. Since union contracts included job security provisions, they made it more expensive, legally onerous, and time-consuming for a grindhouse owner to change concessions companies, thus providing an extra layer of protection for Bernoff's business. The pact between ABC Vending and Local 1115c functioned as a cartel, one that set consistent wages and prices and that blocked other firms from entering the marketplace. It is not clear if front-line concession workers even understood that they were members of Local 1115c, as the union's main purpose was to protect the cartel that ABC Vending had established, and not to rally rank-and-file activists around workplace grievances.

Beatrice Richer physically ran the cartel, visiting every grindhouse each week to verify that all concessions staff were union members and collecting commission payments from the stands' owners that would go to ABC Vending.[50] Richer reaped significant financial benefits from this system. Not only did she collect a paycheck from Local 1115c, but she also appears to have been Jacob Bernoff's hidden partner in ABC Vending, a stockholder who was entitled to a cut of the fees she obtained from the concessionaires each week.[51] Rather than understand Richer as a union activist or a businesswoman—though it appears that she was both—law enforcement saw her as a criminal, alleging that the payments she gathered each week for ABC Vending amounted to extortion, money that was forcibly extracted from concessions managers for nothing in return. On April 26, 1951, the *New York Times* announced that Beatrice Richer had been indicted for orchestrating what the New York Police Department called the "candy kickback racket."[52]

While Beatrice Richer's affairs blurred the line between licit and illicit, and between activism, entrepreneurship, and fraud, union cartels like the one she helped build were widespread in New York's service economy by the mid-1950s. The affairs of Charles Guerci illustrate how the coin-operated vending machine business made use of a similar system. In 1952, Guerci joined the labor movement not as a rank-and-file union member, but as an upstart entrepreneur. He was living in Murray Hill, a working-class neighborhood in northeastern Queens where Jews, Italians, and eastern European Catholics had moved as they became whiter and more middle class and as they left behind older, less resourced neighborhoods in Brooklyn and the Bronx. Guerci had run a speakeasy called the College Inn as a young man, and he moved into above-board hospitality after Prohibition was repealed. One evening, he was talking with a customer at the Villa Grove, the restaurant he managed in Flushing, Queens. The customer told Guerci to leave the hospitality industry behind and get into trade unionism, as the pay and working conditions were far better than on the front lines of the service business. Based on the customer's suggestion, Guerci called the Retail Clerks Union-AFL. Like many unions in the American Federation of Labor, the retail clerks union was less mobilized and less centralized than its politically active cousins in the CIO. While they were often conservative in outlook, AFL unions did organize. International presidents would issue "charters"—founding documents for new locals—to individual operatives who would be tasked with recruiting new members. The union assigned Guerci just such a task, making him president of the newly chartered Retail Clerks-AFL Local 433. Guerci's job would be to cross the Nassau County line and canvass the suburbs, filling up Local 433 with members from the coin game business who operated pinball machines, pool tables, and bowlers. As more operators paid initiation fees and monthly dues, Guerci would be able to pay himself a salary, effectively turning Local 433 into a small business of which Guerci would be the sole proprietor.[53]

Unlike most unions that followed the Wagner Act's strictures, Guerci's local did not limit membership to rank-and-file workers. Instead, the union worked in tandem with trade associations to stabilize the coin game business for both owners and workers. In 1955, Local 433 signed a contract with the coin game trade association AAMONY. Each small business that was a member of AAMONY became a "worker" under the union contract, and the proprietor of each firm would pay monthly union dues for themselves and for all salaried and hourly employees. In exchange for the dues, the union distributed stickers to be displayed on the machines that the company operated. Local 433 staff would regularly visit every bar and tavern in the Long Island suburbs to check for Local 433's stickers. If they found a machine without one, the staff would call Guerci, notifying him that the location needed "service." Local 433 would then mobilize against the bar or restaurant just as a traditional union would when a worker had a grievance against a manager.[54]

Upon receiving a "service" call, Guerci would deploy pickets to enforce the cartel that AAMONY and Local 433 had built. These were not the conventional, Wagner Act picket lines where union members angry at an injustice in the workplace would put down their equipment, march outside, and carry signs that notified the public of their dispute. Instead, the union would hire picketers off the street, often with no involvement in the bar or laundry or lampshade factory with the problem.[55] When the union mobilized against Salvatore Caruso's restaurant, for example, the sole picketer was a dockworker from Brooklyn named Kenneth Ciazzo, who had no connection to Caruso or to Levittown. When passersby asked about the conflict, Ciazzo admitted he knew little about the nature of the grievance other than that it involved a Wurlitzer jukebox. Ciazzo was paid a one dollar per hour, which was minimum wage in the 1950s.[56]

Unorthodox though it was, paid pickets like Ciazzo were highly effective because they packed both a material and ideological punch. In material terms, a single person holding a union-endorsed protest sign could cut off a business from its supply chain, as Teamster truck drivers often refused to cross picket lines to deliver goods. For example, in March 1958, the Barbers Union-AFL Local 760 escalated a dispute with the Terminal

Barber Shop, a company that provided high-end grooming services for businessmen in hotels, office buildings, and railroad stations. After Terminal refused to recognize the union, activists dispatched a picket to the Fiftieth Street loading dock of Manhattan's Waldorf Astoria hotel, the barber shop's highest-grossing location. Every Teamster truck driver—those who hauled meat, vegetables, liquor, uniforms, and linen among many other essential supplies—honored the picket line. After two days without food and beverage deliveries or garbage and linen pickups, the Waldorf and its guests claimed they were in crisis. Managers repeatedly made the colorful, breathless claim that the picket had "cut off the drink and vittles"[57] as they described the squalor inside the hotel.[58]

Pickets also had an ideological impact. For many descendants of Catholic and Jewish new immigrants, and especially for Italians and eastern European Jews, socialist and anarchist radical traditions had guided their journey as immigrants. As historian Peter Vellon demonstrates, since the overwhelming majority of Italian immigrants could not read English, the Italian-language press disproportionately shaped the worldview of the Italian American population in the early twentieth century. Although the Italian newspapers with the largest circulation were often openly antiradical, most Italian immigrants also read leftist newspapers in which stories about unions and strikes dominated the front pages. Coverage of the labor movement helped solidify the affinity between many Italian Americans and the left.[59] Meanwhile, though American Jews became more religiously observant after the move to the suburbs, many in the immigrant generation had expressed their Judaism through secular radicalism and had made socialist and anarchist critiques the core of their outsider identity.[60] Even as ethnic particularism waned after World War II, crossing a picket line remained anathema to people whose families and childhood neighborhoods had embraced trade unionism.

The coin-operated vending machine business took full advantage of the paid picketing system's effectiveness. It seems that the picket coordinator for the jukebox and pinball sector was Sylvia Goldberg, a union operative whose affairs, like Beatrice Richer's, defied categorization. On February 13, 1959, Chief Counsel Robert F. Kennedy called Goldberg to testify in front of the Senate's McClellan Committee, which by this time had been investigating ties between unions and organized crime for two years. Mystery surrounded Goldberg from the moment she began to speak. Although the press described her physical characteristics in granular detail—one of Rochester, New York's daily newspapers described her as "a brunette with heavily penciled eyebrows"[61]—her occupation remained in question.

She flatly introduced herself to senators, saying "My name is Sylvia Goldberg. . . . I am from Flushing, Queens, and I am a housewife."[62] Housewife was an odd way to describe Goldberg, as she had long worked for a wage outside of the home. During World War II, she was said to have been a model for a time, and she had definitely begun a career working in New York's nightlife. By the summer of 1953, Goldberg was living in a brick rowhouse in the Gravesend neighborhood of Brooklyn, about a mile north of the amusement park at Coney Island. She ran the hat check concession at the Town Hill Restaurant, a popular club on Eastern Parkway in Crown Heights where people ate, danced, and drank late into the evening. The work was tough, and it forced Goldberg to work with obstreperous drunks, leering men, and a cast of other pugnacious characters. One June 25 that summer, armed men whom the *Brooklyn Daily Eagle* newspaper called "submachine gun bandits" burst in at closing and forced Goldberg to lie splayed out on the floor while they took all the cash from the bar and the hat check and pistol whipped a few of her colleagues.[63] Soon thereafter, and perhaps because the demanding working conditions and late hours were less appealing as Goldberg aged into her mid-thirties, she changed careers and got involved with labor organizing, taking the helm of the United Industrial Union Local 531, a union that was building a cartel among jukebox operators.[64]

Nevertheless, and even though she proceeded to exercise her rights under the Fifth Amendment to protect herself from the self-incrimination related to her business dealings, she identified her profession to the senators as a housewife. We can speculate about why she did this. Did she call herself a housewife because Jewish women had long blurred the line between the public and private spheres, and had made room for marriage, motherhood, wage labor, and political activism within their femininity? Did she call herself a housewife because she thought of union work as activism and not as a job? Did she call herself a housewife because she hoped to align herself with middle-class white women's moral authority, which might have provided cover for union dealings that were illegal? Did she call herself a housewife to evade deep scrutiny from both Robert Kennedy and the police, who she would have known had discounted women's contributions to labor, business, politics, and economics? Regardless of the motivation, calling herself a housewife seemed to help Goldberg on the witness stand, as Kennedy and the senators largely ignored her, asking few of the probing questions they reserved for Charles Guerci, Jacob Bernoff, Eugene Jacob, and other men who worked alongside her.

Rather than distill the essence of Sylvia Goldberg's work or pin down the way she understood herself, I argue that the nature of the cultural world that Sylvia Goldberg's story brings into view is much more important. She, Beatrice Richer, Charles Guerci, and many of their colleagues had come of age enhancing and monetizing working people's pleasures through service work.[65] They distributed and served alcohol both when it was legal and when it was illegal. They owned, worked in, and socialized in speakeasies, night clubs, dance halls, and bars. They managed venues that played live or recorded music and created networks to distribute that music. They sold fountain drinks that made the floor sticky in grimy theaters where workers amused themselves after long days on the job. As they remained in the service industry while the decades passed, they claimed the full spatial privilege of their increasingly stable Catholic and Jewish whiteness, creating home and work lives both in old city neighborhoods and in the suburbs. Labor unions were a powerful mechanism to build a bridge between that nighttime culture of the immigrant industrial cities of the 1930s and the suburbanizing culture of the 1950s. The unions they built mirrored the hardscrabble world of the service economy, a world where work was often underpaid and disrespected, where workplace culture disregarded middle-class respectability, where there was no clear division between the indignant demands of political activism and the hustle of business, and where skirting the law was commonplace when margins were thin and resources were scant. Therefore, the unruly and sometimes unseemly unions that Goldberg and her peers built in the 1940s and 1950s bore little similarity to the democratic, professionalized institutions that the Wagner Act envisioned.

While the tumult of coin-operated vending makes it a colorful site for historical analysis, it is tempting to frame this unruly world as a vestigial remnant of the old industrial city that would fade away with the transition to suburban mass consumption and gentrified downtowns. That, however, would be a mistake. Beginning in the mid-1950s, and in a search for stability that remained elusive in the service sector despite the presence of union cartels, Goldberg and other union operatives began to link their small, disparate unions to a juggernaut: the International Brotherhood of Teamsters in the age of Jimmy Hoffa. Hoffa believed that to deliver standardized, living-wage, industry-wide contracts in the transport and logistics industries, the Teamsters would have to organize all the businesses that truckers touched, from small industrial lofts to corner grocery stores to neighborhood bars with Wurlitzer jukeboxes and shuffleboard alleys. The gritty service businesses where Beatrice Richer, Charles Guerci, and Sylvia Goldberg organized would thus become a centerpiece of Hoffa's rise to power in the Teamsters. Through this alliance between Jimmy Hoffa and the proprietors of Catholic and Jewish immigrant family businesses, a new spatial formation—that I call the Teamsters metropolis—came into being.

Teamsters Metropolis: Jimmy Hoffa's Service-Sector Unionism

Jimmy Hoffa's interest in the service industry grew alongside his rapid ascension in Detroit's labor movement during the economic disorder of the Great Depression and World War II. Hoffa had joined the full-time staff of the International Brotherhood of Teamsters just after his twentieth birthday in 1934. Since his first assignment was to organize for truck drivers' Local 299, and because he had discovered his passion for trade unionism while working with truckers on the loading dock at a Kroeger grocery warehouse in the early 1930s, the transport industry was Hoffa's primary concern for his entire career in the Teamsters. In 1937, Hoffa took the helm of the Detroit truckers' local, and by the time he turned twenty-eight in 1942, he had become the president of the Michigan Conference of Teamsters, the umbrella group for all the union's members in the state.[66] With Hoffa's new responsibilities came a wider perspective on the regional economy, one that intensified his interest in services and retail. He recognized that while large-scale manufacturing was the core of the midwestern economy, hundreds of thousands of people still worked in mom-and-pop shops on every city block. The unceasing volatility of those small businesses was, in Hoffa's mind, an organizing opportunity, one that would help him build a larger, stronger social movement that would touch people not just at work, but in the places where they washed their cars, bought their bread, drank their beer, and sang and danced after a hard day on the job.[67] But for the new surge in organizing to be effective, Hoffa believed that he would need to harness the unruly forms of trade unionism that already existed along the blocks of this immodern, illiberal city within a city.

Detroit's coin-operated vending machine industry provides an early example of how Hoffa took full advantage of the illicit unionism that defined the service sector. The business had been wildly erratic for a decade, with war-era parts shortages throwing machines out of service and with operators' revenue surging and cratering as new entrants jumped established companies' locations. In 1944, the local operators' association called a meeting at the Hotel Detroiter to address these problems. The stately, Italianate renaissance tower had been a site of intrigue since it opened in 1926. Jerry Buckley, the famous Detroit radio host, was gunned down in the lobby in 1930 after an on-air plea for a crackdown on organized crime.[68] First up on the agenda in the Detroiter's storied dining room was Bill Bufalino, who co-owned a jukebox company called Bilvin Distributing that was aggressively jumping its competitors and that had stripped 1,200 locations away from other members of the association. Bufalino co-owned Bilvin with Vincent Meli, the nephew of Angelo Meli, who was among the most powerful figures in the Detroit underworld of the 1930s. Afraid of provoking the Meli family and its heavily armed allies in the Italian syndicate, the jukebox association shied away from dispatching the union pickets that helped thwart jumping in other cities.[69] Because of that constraint on enforcing their cartel, jukebox operators faced the constant threat of losing their customers to Bufalino and Meli.

It appears that Jimmy Hoffa arranged a détente to quell the unrest while bringing the Teamsters into the jukebox niche of the service industry. Hoffa sent his associate Bill Presser to the meeting at the Detroiter, and he helped convince the other jukebox operators to take up a collection and make a cash payment of $5,000 to Bufalino and to permanently cede the 1,200 locations that he and Meli had already jumped. In return, all association members would join Teamsters Local 985, which would operate a cartel to protect their businesses as well as Bufalino and Meli's. Members would receive the full protection of both the Teamsters and the Meli family, who would enforce grave physical consequences on any operator who broke the new, stronger cartel. The deal seems to have paid off. When jukebox association president Morris Goldman answered a letter from his counterpart in Los Angeles in August 1947, Goldman wrote back saying that a contract with the Teamsters was the best means to fend off jumping. According to Goldman, Detroit operators had protected 98 percent of their locations after they joined Local 985. Newfound stability in the coin machine business benefited Goldman personally.[70] By the late 1950s, he had used the proceeds from his jukeboxes, bowlers, and pinball machines in working-class taverns across Detroit to move to the leafy suburb of Oak Park and to buy a newly built three-bedroom, two-bathroom ranch house for his family.[71] The détente in Detroit's coin game business also benefited the Teamsters. Sometime in late 1947, Hoffa had picked Bill Bufalino to lead Local 985. Bufalino's organizers had fanned out across Detroit and signed up thousands of new members from car washes, laundries, and other small service companies, which expanded the union's reach far beyond coin gaming.[72]

Bill Bufalino's control of Local 985 raises the question of why Jimmy

Hoffa's campaign to organize service and retail workers often involved the institution that outsiders referred to with the Sicilian term "Mafia," and that participants more frequently called "the family" or "the corporation" or "La Cosa Nostra": "our thing." Many popular historical narratives about the Mafia date to 1957, when law enforcement interrupted a meeting of syndicate leaders at a private home in the small town of Appalachian, New York. Inflammatory media coverage of FBI sources claimed that the Mafia was a nationwide, tightly organized Italian criminal conspiracy with a single, military-style hierarchy.[73] Two decades later, Hollywood amplified and embellished the Mafia story. After social movements from Black power to gay liberation had politicized marginalized people's stories, many middle-class white people discovered an interest in their own ethnic particularity. Scores of 1970s blockbusters told gritty stories about how, just like the Black and Brown people and feminists and gays protesting in the streets, people from European immigrant roots also had authentic history that was rooted in overcoming adversity. For white people of Italian descent, and as the massive popularity of *The Godfather* films shows, the Mafia was the most important plot device in that genre. By 1980, and after they had gone to the movies, everyone seemed to know that there was a single Mafia with dons, underbosses, and caporegimes, and that included everyone from Al Capone to Marlon Brando's Vito Corleone.

Decades of historical analysis shows La Cosa Nostra to have been a more decentralized, far less cinematic network than the one portrayed in *The Godfather*, a local institution that, just like union cartels, aimed to deliver stability to immigrant-owned family businesses. In the Detroit case, Sicilian immigrants had built small companies in scrap hauling, waste handling, and other services during the first three decades of the twentieth century. With the onset of the Great Depression, labor unrest was common in those industries. Some Sicilian business owners started side hustles hiring and training strikebreakers to harass, assault, and in some instances kill workers on the picket line, and they coordinated those side hustles through an underground network that—like Italians in other cities on both sides of the Atlantic—they sometimes called La Cosa Nostra. This violence was a hindrance to the Teamsters, who were increasingly interested in organizing people who worked at small businesses whose owners were often involved with La Cosa Nostra.[74] Rather than fight fire with fire in a pitched battle with underworld operatives who were well-armed and fearless, it appears that Hoffa pursued détente with the Italian networks. Historical scholars disagree about when this happened; some say it was during the Teamsters turf war with the CIO in Detroit in the late 1930s,[75] others say it occurred through Hoffa's Sicilian friend Sylvia Pagano in the early 1940s,[76] and still others claim Hoffa had no connection to La Cosa Nostra until the late 1940s.[77] But as Hoffa's dealings with Bill Bufalino in the jukebox business show, he clearly worked to get the Teamsters and the underworld rowing in the same direction, collaborating to build the cartels that brought order to the unruly world of the service industry.

Hoffa could have avoided this relationship. If he would have stayed far away from the coin game operators, beer distributors, bakeries, or other businesses made up of small firms and had reoriented Teamster organizers toward large companies in the manufacturing, petrochemical, or food-production sectors, he may have been able to steer clear of La Cosa Nostra. But Hoffa leaned into the service economy, as the hardscrabble world of the Jewish and Italian shops seems to be where he was most comfortable, where his cultural attributes most clearly resonated, and where he could resist the button-down world of big business that he and his self-consciously working-class Teamster peers openly scorned. By deciding to build the Teamsters metropolis, to organize the workers in every store that truckers touched, Hoffa made the decision to operate in an environment where the underworld was one of many tools that helped business entrepreneurs and labor organizers bring order to the metropolitan world.

Jimmy Hoffa used that tool as he began to intervene in the service, retail, and light manufacturing industries in other cities. In the New York case, Hoffa stepped up his involvement in local affairs during a conflict over a citywide campaign to organize thousands of taxi drivers in the early 1950s. Union mobilization was particularly difficult in that business, as drivers reported to hundreds of small, privately owned cab companies and as communication was difficult when workers drove alone and lacked a central workplace. Organizing, thus, would require an expensive, well-staffed, disciplined operation. Two groups were vying to run the campaign, each rooted in a different New York European immigrant genealogy. In one camp, the Teamsters had built a network of two hundred volunteer grassroots organizers who reported to International vice president Thomas Hickey, a truck driver from Brooklyn who had become president of drivers' Local 807 in 1937. The overwhelming majority of Teamsters leaders in the early 1950s, both in New York and nationally, were Irish American men from families like Hickey's who had immigrated in the second half of the nineteenth century.[78]

In the other camp was John Dioguardi, whose kin had immigrated from Italy in the first two decades of the twentieth century. Dioguardi had put up $200,000 to hire activists to recruit drivers into a local of the United

Automobile Workers-AFL.[79] The overwhelming majority of UAW locals were members of Walter Reuther's relatively progressive Congress of Industrial Organizations. In a few cities with a preponderance of small, family-owned manufacturing shops like New York, however, some UAW locals had split off from the parent organization and aligned themselves with the AFL, a linkage that came in part from the AFL's willingness to condone the union cartels. By the early 1950s, Dioguardi—who was a relative of the Luccheses, one of the "five families" who controlled La Cosa Nostra in New York and New Jersey—ran fourteen of these UAW-AFL locals. He had first gotten involved in labor dealings in the late 1930s during a particularly rough campaign to organize truck drivers in New York's garment industry. Dioguardi was regarded as a violent, unpredictable rogue, especially after he got caught orchestrating a debilitating acid attack that left the well-known labor journalist Victor Riesel blind.[80]

As the campaign intensified, Hickey told the Teamsters' then-president Dan Tobin that he thought the union should continue grassroots organizing, ignoring Dioguardi's underworld-controlled operation, and attempting to win a representation election on its own. Hoffa, however, believed otherwise. Despite Dioguardi's infamous reputation, Hoffa thought he was a good organizer. Hoffa once told Hickey how impressed he was that Dioguardi had "tied up the barn" at a local transport company while Hoffa was in town, shuttering the rogue employer with surprise strike. By early 1953, Hoffa appears to have thought that Dioguardi's structure among cabbies was stronger and better organized than Hickey's. He flew to New York, and sat down to meet with Hickey, Dioguardi, and Dioguardi's underworld associate Paul Doria. While he eschewed the luxury cars, the showy attire, and the rolls of bills that often marked the culture of the midcentury Teamsters, Hoffa strongly believed that a formal lunch at a luxury hotel in a prime, downtown location—which would have defined opulence in the industrial metropolis of Hoffa's youth—was the principal means to show respect and to get business done. For this meeting, he chose the Hampshire House, a 1929-built art deco high-rise on Central Park South with a gorgeous view of the park's gardens and pond. Over lunch, it appears that Dioguardi proposed doubling his investment in the campaign for a total of $400,000, the equivalent of $3.8 million today. In exchange, Hoffa would get Dioguardi a charter for a new Teamsters local for the cab campaign. The tradeoff laid the groundwork for the Teamsters to drastically expand their New York footprint by bringing the cab union and other Dioguardi-aligned union locals into the Teamsters. While Hoffa, Dioguardi, and Doria worked toward a deal, Hickey was unmoved, and incensed that a midwesterner like Hoffa would attempt to challenge a Brooklynite's authority over a local union that had always valued decentralized, neighborhood-scale leadership.[81]

The Teamsters' top brass initially sided with Hickey, apparently bowing to pressure from AFL president George Meany, who, as a law-and-order Cold War conservative, discouraged entanglements between labor and La Cosa Nostra. Hoffa nevertheless continued to push the Teamsters into New York City's service industry and to solidify his relationship with John Dioguardi. The *New York Times*, for example, reported in April 1954 that Hoffa had publicly offered Dioguardi a full-time job with the Teamsters.[82] Though Dioguardi did not accept the overture, he clearly benefited from a new batch of service and light manufacturing locals that Dave Beck—who was elected general president of the union in 1952—and Jimmy Hoffa chartered. Prior to Beck's presidency, the initiation process for a new Teamsters local was guided by the regional "general organizer," which in early 1950s New York was none other than Thomas Hickey. After Beck assumed the reins of the union, however, he usurped that power, issuing charters directly from the president's office, often at Hoffa's behest. By late 1955, Beck and Hoffa had authorized the creation of six new Teamsters locals for Dioguardi. It appears that Dioguardi's network of organizers was filling these locals with members from the service industry, which helped Hoffa build a new network of allies for his effort to push New York's Teamsters away from the localized, autonomous, and often parochial unionism that Hickey favored and toward the centralized, national system of collective bargaining that Hoffa hoped to introduce in both the transport and service sectors.[83]

Through this push for large-scale bargaining and via the alliance with John Dioguardi, Jimmy Hoffa dug into the New York City coin machine business. Despite the success of the pickets that Sylvia Goldberg and other activists deployed, the stability that Detroit's jukebox and pinball operators had achieved in the mid-1950s remained elusive in New York. As Hoffa drove the Teamsters further into New York's service industry, the union intervened to remedy that volatility. In the spring of 1958, John O'Rourke—an Irish Teamster and Hoffa ally who had recently won the presidency of the umbrella organization for all Teamsters in New York—issued a charter for Teamsters Local 266. With Hoffa's blessing, O'Rourke tasked Joseph DeGrandis, a local labor entrepreneur with underworld ties, with filling up Local 266 with members from the jukebox and pinball business. Recognizing the power of the insurgent, rapidly expanding Teamsters, and perhaps guessing that Hoffa's openness to La Cosa Nostra signaled a wider willingness to accommodate unruly tactics, many coin game labor entrepreneurs soon aligned themselves with Local 266.[84] Therefore, when Kenneth Ciazzo got out of his car to earn a dollar an hour as a picket in front of Caruso's restaurant that day in July 1958, his sign bore the insignia of Local 266, International Brotherhood of Teamsters. Rows of cars lined up in a Levittown parking lagoon would seem to have exemplified the clean affluence of the new suburban mass consumption economy of the 1950s. But after he decided to cancel that jukebox contract and buy the brand-new Wurlitzer with the gleaming red, orange, and green neon lights, Salvatore Caruso faced the full wrath of Jimmy Hoffa's foray into the service economy. The old, tough, inner-city networks of small-time entrepreneurs, aggressive labor activists, and scheming underworld operatives were making their marks on the booming suburban landscape of the Teamsters metropolis.

Conclusion: The Teamsters Metropolis and Its Discontents

Jimmy Hoffa's bid to organize every worker at every small business on every city street corner and in every suburban strip mall had produced two trends by the end of the 1950s. The first involved the union's spectacular growth among marginal workers, a story that has much to teach twenty-first-century scholars and activists who argue that the service sector is pivotal to the future of the labor movement. Hoffa built an organizing juggernaut that recruited in restaurants, bakeries, and beauty salons, gains that offset some of the wider labor movement's losses. From a high-water mark of 34 percent of the private-sector workforce in 1954, overall union membership slipped to 31 percent by 1957, in part because the large manufacturing firms where the industrial unions of the CIO had been most effective had already begun replacing people with automation.[85] The Teamsters bucked this trend. The union claimed approximately half a million members when Hoffa secured his first regional leadership position in 1940. But as he, Dave Beck, and other Teamster activists compelled the union into the service, retail, and light manufacturing trades with a tenacious commitment to organizing the unorganized, the Teamsters crossed the million-member mark in 1950, a number that rose to 1.4 million by the time Hoffa became general president in 1957. And while the 500,000 long-haul truck drivers were the union's best-paid members by the mid-1960s, the bulk of the union's million other members were in more marginal trades, from local delivery driving to warehousing to the hundreds and thousands of workers in small service businesses.[86]

Vigorous, successful organizing brought robust material gains for the Teamsters' members. By 1960, Hoffa had begun to deliver on the centralized bargaining system that he insisted would maximize worker power. The union won a standardized, regional contract for all truckers in New York and New Jersey in 1962, a project that Hoffa had worked on for a decade. Two years later, the Teamsters ratified the National Master Freight Agreement, a single, uniform contractual framework for every long-haul trucker in the United States, a deal that was the crowning achievement of Jimmy Hoffa's career as a union activist. Wages soared with the union's organizing momentum. A 1965 compensation study by the labor economists Estelle and Ralph James found that workers in Hoffa-aligned Teamsters locals in all sectors of the economy averaged a 70 percent pay increase over the course of the decade, a far larger raise than manufacturing workers, who saw their pay increase 55 percent over the same period. Gains were particularly impressive on the periphery of the economy. Teamster members in the South, for example, saw their pay rise 91 percent during the 1950s, a rate that outpaced any other region of the United States.[87] Teamster leaders secured company-paid pension plans in 1955, which provided a monthly Social Security supplement that made retirement more pleasurable and secure.[88]

The central argument of this chapter is that Teamster activists won these lucrative economic gains not despite the unrestrained culture of the union but because of it. Teamster membership brought hundreds of thousands of people access to quiet, verdant, spacious suburban landscapes while keeping them connected to the heterogeneous, tumultuous spaces of their parents' and grandparents' central city neighborhoods. The Teamster operatives who appear in this chapter often strove to be normal. Yet they were also willing to transgress those norms. Sylvia Goldberg swore under oath that she was a housewife in a middle-class neighborhood that was a stepping stone to the suburbs. But she had also made a career out of checking the mink coats and fedoras of people who smoked, drank, danced, and cavorted all night long, work that was apparently disreputable enough to have convinced her to plead Fifth Amendment protection when testifying about it. Eugene Jacob built a brand-new, tidy, modest home in Levittown, joining hundreds of thousands of American Jews who moved to the suburbs after World War II. But he also helped run a cartel system that vaporized pool tables in steaming clouds of acid and that used giant hacksaws to reduce pinball machines to piles of shimmering rubble. Jimmy Hoffa succeeded as an organizer because he accommodated—and perhaps even embraced and identified with—the unpredictable, extralegal dealings like Goldberg's and Jacob's, dealings that defined day-to-day life in the Teamsters metropolis.

It is precisely these heterodox, aggressive, and sometimes violent and duplicitous organizing strategies that reveal a second, countervailing trend that faced the Teamsters in the 1950s. Jimmy Hoffa and his allies made scores of enemies as they built their union outside the legal framework of the Wagner Act. Those enemies provoked an aggressive, antiunion, and antiworker response from a federal government at the peak of its Cold War authority. Such conflicts often stemmed from local-scale disputes in the service sector. In the spring of 1958, for example, Milton Green attempted to rebuff his colleagues' effort to align New York's coin game trade association with Teamsters Local 266. Green had come of age running slot machines in New York and Miami during an earlier era when they were still legal and had been a 112-pound Golden Gloves boxer in the 1920s. Now living in a working-class, Catholic and Jewish section of Brighton Beach in southern Brooklyn, Green operated jukeboxes, pool tables, and shuffleboard machines in bars across Brooklyn and Queens. Green appears to have thought that alliance with Local 266 was a scam, one that would turn the coin game business into a front for La Cosa Nostra or other nefarious networks. Predictably, Teamster operatives intervened to thwart Green's intransigence. One afternoon in March, Green went to a trade association meeting at the Park Sheraton, a lavish Midtown hotel from the 1920s where coin machine operators did business. Herbert and Eugene Jacob—the same people who had the fight with Salvatore Caruso in Levittown—intercepted word of what they saw as Green's troublemaking and sent muscle to the hotel in advance of his arrival. Two men waited for the meeting to end, then tailed Green as he left the Park Sheraton and drove southward across Brooklyn on Ocean Parkway. They attacked Green in the driveway of his home when he got out of the car, sending him to the hospital, giving him a concussion and cuts that needed thirty stitches, and leaving him out of commission for several months.[89]

Green remained undeterred despite the disfiguring injuries, and he struck back against the Teamsters with a forceful blow that took the conflict far beyond the parochial boundaries of Brooklyn's jukebox business. He made contact with the FBI and agreed to tell his story to the United States Senate Select Committee on Improper Relations in the Labor or Management Field. For twenty-seven months beginning in the spring of 1957, the committee employed 104 staff people and served 8,000 subpoenas to 1,526 witnesses, who described corruption in labor unions, chief among them the Teamsters. The networks broadcast the investigation on live television, creating a media spectacle for millions of households who were fascinated with the new communications medium. The overwhelming majority of Chief Counsel Robert F. Kennedy's relentless interrogation focused on identifying, cataloguing, and castigating the unregulated bodily comportment of Teamster operatives: the yelling, the threats, the underworld payoffs, the beatings, and the stink bombings. During a decade when eastern and southern European Catholic and Jewish immigrant families were moving to the suburbs, sending their children to college, and learning to perform middle-class American whiteness, Kennedy framed the Teamsters—and, in deeply personal attacks, Jimmy Hoffa—as suburbia's vulgar antithesis. Over the coming decades, Kennedy's stigmatizing narrative about a pathological union culture would undermine the credibility of the Teamsters and of the entire labor movement with wide swaths of the public. To the federal government's vivid excoriation of the Teamsters metropolis chapter 2 now turns.

CHAPTER TWO

Blackmailers, Safecrackers, Dope Peddlers, White Slavers, and Sodomists
Regulating Teamster Culture at the McClellan Committee Hearings

On the icy morning of February 6, 1956, George Connolly left Minneapolis. Just past nine in the morning, he climbed the mobile stairway to board the Eastern Airlines Douglas DC-7B that would carry him to the warm waters of Miami Beach via Chicago Midway Airport and Atlanta. Connolly traveled in style, paying the equivalent of $2,000 today for a one-way first-class ticket on a state-of-the-art airliner. General Motors' Cadillac Division designed the plane's interior, which featured rich, sparkling-gold and navy-blue fabrics for the seats, curtains, and carpets and included a semicircular cocktail lounge at the rear of the aircraft where passengers could smoke and socialize away from the noisy propellers. In Woodridge, New Jersey, Curtis-Wright built the turbo-compound engines that made the DC-7B the fastest airliner of the mid-1950s. Cruising at nearly 350 miles per hour, Connolly could have brunch aloft and still make it to the beach for a swim before dinner. After landing, Connolly checked into the Waves, a quaint, art-deco hotel styled with mirrors and pastel neon just off the oceanfront at Eighth Street and Collins Avenue. He took his secretary out to an opulent dinner, spending $25—the equivalent of $241 today—on cocktails and fresh Florida seafood.

While it appears he enjoyed the journey, George Connolly had to expedite his departure from Minneapolis. Three nights later, in the wee hours of the morning on February 10, Connolly had arranged to have dynamite placed in the car and the home of Tony Felicetta, an activist in the International Brotherhood of Teamsters. It seems that Connolly intended to terrorize but not to kill Felicetta, as he consulted a local ballistics expert in an effort to amplify the audio and visual impact of the attack while minimizing its lethality. The blasts were payback for Felicetta's failure to support the organizing work that Connolly was conducting for his job as secretary-treasurer of Teamsters Local 548. Connolly ran his local like an entrepreneur, filling it up with the proprietors of liquor stores, with workers in local barrel-making plants, and with others at small-scale firms, and living off the dues his members paid. Felicetta had condemned Connolly for "raiding" AFL-aligned locals, for building his ranks by stealing members from other unions in Minneapolis. To discourage Connolly's raiding practices, Felicetta urged Teamster truck drivers to ignore the pickets that Connolly would send out to venues he was trying to organize. Recognizing that his operation would collapse if local truckers were unwilling to cut off businesses from their supply chains, it seems that Connolly turned to another form of muscle—dynamite—to demonstrate his resolve to Felicetta.[1]

As he departed Minneapolis to avoid the shock wave of his most recent organizing strategy, George Connolly worked on the margins of an otherwise robust economy. The rapidly suburbanizing Minneapolis-Saint Paul metropolis was booming. Construction was just about finished in the ritzy suburb of Edina on Southdale, the first indoor shopping mall in the United States, with anchor department stores, scores of boutiques, and parking lots massive enough to accommodate every car on the busiest day of the year. Despite ample above-board employment opportunities for white men in agribusiness, banking, insurance, real estate development, transportation, and many other sectors that defined Minnesota's diversified, dynamic economy, Connolly opted to work in the shadows.[2] Upon arrival on Miami Beach, he stayed in adjoining suites with Ben Dranow, who had recently gotten a $1 million loan from Jimmy Hoffa to buy the Thomas Department Store on downtown Minneapolis's bustling Nicollet Avenue. It seems that Dranow was also part owner of the Waves Hotel, which claimed to have lost all the records of his and Connolly's stay on the beach. Sometime during the Miami trip, Connolly began going by George Cohen, shifting away from the Irish American identity that many Teamster higher-ups shared and choosing a Jewish surname common among local Teamster operatives in the service industry.[3] Over drinks and lavish dinners in the tropical breezes of Miami Beach, and as he waited for his plan to detonate, Connolly/Cohen clearly rejected the suburban, middle-class comportment that many other white Minnesotans—at least on the surface—

embraced as they moved to the suburbs and shopped at Southdale.

While George Connolly or George Cohen's world would have been familiar to some people who worked for trucking companies, warehouses, laundries, and taverns in Minneapolis in the 1950s, it remained hidden from those with jobs in the licit economy at Honeywell, 3M, General Mills, Northwest Airlines, and other large firms that the midcentury federal bureaucracy regulated. A year after he arranged for the dynamiting, however, the curtain that had obscured Connolly/Cohen's unruly unionism from the middle-class public began to fall. On Tuesday, February 26, 1957, Arkansas senator John McClellan convened the first day of hearings before the Select Committee on Improper Activities in the Labor or Management Field. Over the next three years, McClellan's committee would use a wildly popular new communications medium—television—to broadcast its version of the affairs of George Connolly/Cohen and thousands of other trade unionists directly into the living rooms of millions of American families. The level of detail is difficult to overstate. Connolly/Cohen's story emerged in two and a half hours of testimony from three witnesses on the morning of Wednesday, September 25, 1957. Their recollections contributed forty pages to a transcript that eventually included twenty-five thousand pages of testimony and 125,000 pages of corroborating documents. Television viewers would not only hear the speculation about how Connolly/Cohen obtained the dynamite, but they would see enlarged images of the airplane ticket for which he paid $214.70, of his bill from the Waves Hotel where he spent $77.25, and of the checks that the Thomas Department Store wrote to cover those expenses.[4]

The previous chapter explained how the jukebox, pinball machine, and pool table business helped give rise to a new spatial formation that I call the Teamsters metropolis, one where eastern and southern European Catholic and Jewish family businesses helped make the International Brotherhood of Teamsters the fastest-growing labor union of the 1950s. This chapter is a history of the tale that the United States government told about that union movement. Historians have written widely about the McClellan Committee and have shown that Chief Counsel Robert F. Kennedy made particularly effective use of media during the proceedings.[5] Kennedy regularly gave advance notice of salacious testimony to newspaper reporters, and committee members wrote feature articles in the era's most popular magazines: John McClellan in the *Saturday Evening Post*, Kennedy in *Life*, and with multiple members siphoning information to John Dos Passos for his series in *Readers Digest*. Thus, as David Witwer argues, "Although the outward trappings of congressional hearings mimicked a criminal trial and purported to uncover hidden truths, the reality of the proceedings more closely resembled a carefully managed media event."[6]

While these insights help us recognize the spectacle that the McClellan Committee staged, they tell us less about the ideas that the senators used to inflame the public. This chapter offers such an explanation, showing that the McClellan Committee created a media clamor by elaborating, repeating, and embellishing what they saw as the aberrant culture of the Teamsters metropolis. For thirty-seven months, Kennedy, McClellan, and their colleagues were consumed with the ways that Teamster operatives violated bourgeois standards of comportment. By hyperbolizing Teamster speech, dress, desires, and deportment, Kennedy and the other committee members strove to control activists' conduct by shaming what they saw as the union's unruly culture.

The McClellan Committee's regulation, I argue, aimed to transform mid-twentieth-century cities, pushing Jewish and Catholic eastern and southern Europeans away from the undisciplined spaces of the Teamsters metropolis and toward a sanitized suburban lifeworld.[7] Kennedy and his colleagues strove to fully align eastern European Jews, Sicilians, and other second- and third-generation immigrants whose whiteness had once been ambiguous with the foundations of the suburban political economy of the 1950s: racial segregation, heterosexual domesticity, the nuclear family, large-scale industrial production, and mass consumption within the single-family home. An alliance between northern Cold War liberals and southern white supremacists at the twilight of the Jim Crow era, the McClellan Committee pushed truckers, barkeeps, car wash workers, fruit distributors, and other white workers on the margin of the midcentury economy toward the center of the system of racial Fordism that was dominant during the years that the hearings took place. This chapter, then, takes up the public struggle between union activists, Teamster leaders, and public officials over working people's cultural and spatial role in the US cities of the mid-twentieth century.

The Shakedown Ride: Regulating Teamster Comportment in Metropolitan Space

The United States Senate would collide with Jimmy Hoffa and with the International Brotherhood of Teamsters as it struggled with the consequences of the rapid expansion of the power of the federal government in the wake of the New Deal. In 1954, the Senate censured Joseph McCarthy, the chair of the Permanent Subcommittee on Investigations of the Committee on Government Operations, for conduct associated with his probe of alleged communist subversion. Senators condemned McCarthy's draconian use of government infrastructure—the FBI, the IRS, and the committee's own staff—to invade privacy, violate civil liberties, and level uncorroborated allegations that devastated personal and professional lives. After the Democrats gained control of the Senate in the 1954 midterm elections, the committee adopted what most of its members hoped would be a less controversial mission: performing due diligence to ensure that the federal bureaucracy was efficient, responsive, and ethical.[8]

One of those seemingly mundane functions was assigned to Robert F. Kennedy, who had joined the Committee on Government Operations as a staff attorney fresh out of Harvard Law School not long after his brother John was elected the junior senator from Massachusetts in 1952. Kennedy's initial assignment was to examine suspected racketeering in the military's uniform procurement process. During that work, Kennedy stumbled upon John Dioguardi, who federal prosecutors believed was obtaining charters for new locals of the Teamsters union, operating the locals outside the process delineated in the Wagner Act, skimming money off the contracts the locals administered, and taking kickbacks from separate deals for military uniforms with corrupt vendors. The growing cache of documents that his associates compiled rattled Kennedy, who began to worry that the union was running a coordinated, malignant effort in conjunction with organized crime to defraud their members and scam the American people. Recognizing that many unions' tax-exempt status gave the federal government the authority to scrutinize their dealings, Kennedy asked Carmine Bellino, the committee's top accounting specialist, to "conduct a national investigation of the labor scene."[9]

Senators, however, balked at a bold action by a young staffer. Members of the Committee on Labor and Public Welfare insisted that they and not the Committee on Government Operations were the stewards of the relationship between the government and the labor movement, a partnership that was highly valuable to elected officials given widespread public support for unions and the movement's immense membership rolls. To break the stalemate, senators agreed in January of 1957 to let Kennedy move forward but required that he do so under the supervision of a new, bipartisan group that would have equal representation from both the Government Operations and Labor Committees. They chose Arkansas Democrat John McClellan as chair and Bobby Kennedy as chief counsel, and called the freshly minted group the Senate Select Committee on Improper Activities in the Labor or Management Field.[10]

The senators on McClellan's new committee were a motley crew. Although its members spanned the full ideological spectrum for midcentury white American men, they shared the common traits of strong personalities and passionate political commitments. Like Chairman McClellan, North Carolina senator Sam Ervin was a southern Democrat and an ardent segregationist. A signatory to the "Southern Manifesto" that spurred the resistance to the Supreme Court's *Brown v. Board of Education* desegregation decision, Ervin went on to vocally oppose both the 1964 Civil Rights Act and the 1965 immigration liberalization. During his spare time, Ervin recorded his own renditions of the era's popular songs, including an apparently unironic cover of Simon and Garfunkel's "Bridge Over Troubled Water" for CBS Records in 1973.[11] Other conservatives on the committee included Barry Goldwater, the Arizona Republican whose far-right 1964 presidential bid would galvanize grassroots anticommunists, conspiracy theorists, and racists, and Joseph McCarthy, who, despite his 1954 censure, remained on the committee until his death in May 1957. Among the liberal wing was John F. Kennedy, whose family had landed in East Boston from Ireland in 1849 and who would soon become the nation's first Catholic president. Michigan senator Pat McNamara was also from an Irish immigrant family, though one that arrived later and remained far poorer than the Kennedys, and had been president of the Detroit pipefitters union during the 1930s. McNamara resigned from the committee on March 31, 1958 to protest the harsh treatment of union witnesses, and was replaced by Frank Church, the Idaho senator best known for the select committee he led in 1975 that exposed the abuses that the CIA, NSA, IRS, and other agencies perpetrated in Latin America and Southeast Asia the context of global anticommunism.

Despite the senators' ideological heterogeneity, Robert Kennedy put the McClellan Committee on a collision course with the Teamsters from its outset. By his own admission, Kennedy knew next to nothing about organized labor when he became the committee's lead attorney and had "only a vague impression that (the Teamsters union) was big and tough."[12] Rather than reading labor history, talking to rank-and-file workers, or meeting union activists, Kennedy leveraged his own network of elite professionals—most of whom worked in the legal system, in law enforcement, or who were journalists who covered law enforcement—for information about trade unionism. For example, Kennedy regularly had lunch with his friend and colleague Edward Bennett Williams, a prominent Washington lawyer known for taking the most contentious labor cases and who had represented Teamsters from Jimmy Hoffa to George Connolly/Cohen. He enlisted James Hamilton, who led the Intelligence Division of the Los Angeles Police Department, an organization with a long, violent history of repressing all forms of workplace activism in a city that was among the most staunchly antiunion in the United States.[13] Kennedy was also in regular touch with Clark Mollenhoff, the Washington bureau chief for the *Minneapolis Tribune*, whose crime beat coverage of Teamster corruption had introduced the public to George Connolly/Cohen's violent dealings.[14] Perhaps because of the advice he took from Hamilton and Mollenhoff, most of the people Kennedy hired to fill open McClellan Committee staff positions came from law enforcement, with experience in the military, at the FBI, and in local police departments.

Armed with a trove of incriminating information from his law enforcement contacts, and absent a coherent historical or sociological understanding of the culture of labor unions, Kennedy defaulted to his own ideas about morality, democracy, business, and activism as he built his case, notions that were forged in the most elite networks in the United States: Harvard University, his father's associates from Wall Street investment banks, his brother's Washington connections, and the social world of the Hamptons on Long Island's easternmost tip. Kennedy's ideas stood in stark contrast to a Teamster culture that stemmed from the immigrant industrial metropolis of the 1930s and that was shaped by the police violence, food insecurity, xenophobia, antisemitism, and antiradicalism to which many workers were subjected. Therefore, while Kennedy revealed a wealth of information about operational practices of many unions, it was the culture of the International Brotherhood of Teamsters—that which diverged most starkly from his own firmly held notions about appropriate conduct and comportment—that would absorb the majority of Kennedy's attention as he built the McClellan Committee's investigation.

Throughout the hearings, Robert Kennedy framed culture not as an abstract set of ideas or values, but rather as an embodied practice in metropolitan space. The overwhelming majority of the witnesses Kennedy called were Jewish and Italian men whose whiteness was uncontested by the 1950s. The cultural power associated with whiteness, manhood, and conventional domesticity entitled these men to sexual privacy, and Kennedy thus kept most information about adultery, intimate partner violence, unwanted pregnancy, and other sexual transgressions out of the Congressional Record.[15] The core of Kennedy's case was instead about public comportment, about Teamster men who were too loud, too explosive, too violent, and too unwilling to control their bodies in the restaurants, retail establishments, financial venues, shop floors, and suburban subdivisions of the mid-twentieth-century metropolis. The McClellan Committee's attempt to regulate Teamster bodies was thus a spatial one, an effort that condemned union activists for transforming productive urban and suburban places into the vulgar, unrestrained Teamsters metropolis. To correct these transgressions, Kennedy aimed to persuade his television audience—which would presumably include scores of rank-and-file union members—to respect the upstanding use of metropolitan space: downtown for men's respectable public life in business, manufacturing, and finance, and suburbia for heterosexual domesticity.

James Caggiano's purported brush with death illustrates the central role that central city spaces played in Bobby Kennedy's theatricalization of aberrant Teamster comportment. Early one afternoon in November 1947, Caggiano walked into the Lazarus Building on the corner of Fifty-Seventh Street and Broadway in an elite commercial district just south of Central Park in Manhattan.[16] The esteemed architects Edward and George Blum designed the twenty-five-story neogothic skyscraper that first opened its doors in 1927. The Blum brothers had studied at the École des Beaux-Arts in Paris at the turn of the twentieth century and were most famous for the art nouveau apartment buildings they built in Manhattan in the 1910s. The Gramercy House just north of Greenwich Village, for example, was adorned with striking navy, teal, pink, and peach chevrons on the lower façade of the ten-story complex. And for the Gramont on the Upper West Side, the Blum brothers designed the entry to resemble the Paris arcades. The Lazarus Building was less ornate, but its lobby would nevertheless have felt stately as Caggiano waited for the elevator.[17]

The doors opened on the eighth floor, and Caggiano proceeded to the office of Frank Calland, the business manager of Local 786 of the International Brotherhood of Electrical Workers. Among the many employees Calland represented across New York City were mechanics who fixed jukeboxes in bars, taverns, and nightclubs. Calland called Caggiano to his office because he learned that Caggiano and his associate Charles Lichtman had started a union that was also recruiting members from jukebox companies, employees Calland believed he deserved to represent. Well aware that uninvited competitive organizing often brought violent reprisal from already-established unions and trade associations (see chapter 1), Caggiano was prepared for Calland's rage. Yet he was unworried, as Caggiano had been a driver for the prominent Jewish underworld figure Meyer Lansky in the 1930s, and he remained connected to some of the most infamous muscle in New York. Calland, he assumed, would never cross Meyer Lansky's muscle.

When he felt the frigid November wind blowing through Calland's wide-open office windows, Caggiano knew his assumption was wrong. Calland started toward him but stopped abruptly when Lichtman came in the door behind Caggiano. As Lichtman dramatically told the McClellan Committee's television audience, Calland later admitted that he set up the meeting to kill Caggiano. Hearing the knock on his door, Calland planned to attack Caggiano, to drag him across his office, and to throw him out the eighth-floor window. His body would have careened through the air past the lower offices and smashed on the sidewalk, sending horrified shoppers scattering. Only when Calland saw that Caggiano was with Lichtman—a witness to a crime and an additional body to fight—did he abandon the plan, or so Lichtman told an aghast McClellan Committee.[18]

Although Calland calmly closed the windows and continued the meeting without further incident, Caggiano would not escape unscathed. During their discussion, Calland picked up the telephone and called the Manhattan office of Albert Denver, the president of the trade association for jukebox operators. He asked if the men could meet Denver at his Brooklyn machine shop at 5 p.m. Denver was immediately suspicious, as he knew that Calland was calling from the Lazarus Building, which was directly across the street from Denver. Why, Denver anxiously wondered, did Calland want to drive all the way out to Brooklyn when they could all walk down the block and meet in the bar at the Park Central Hotel? The twenty-five-story renaissance revival hotel opened in 1927 and had an illustrious past. Mae West and Jackie Gleason had lived there soon after it opened, and Eleanor Roosevelt had moved in for a stint in 1950. Its cocktail lounge—called the Mermaid Room in a reference to exoticized, tropical design themes common in Gilded Age hotels—was widely popular and was home to the Irving Fields jazz trio throughout the 1950s.[19] Ordinarily, jukebox operators settled their disputes over drinks in the Mermaid Room, and Denver recognized that Calland's departure from that tradition could come at Caggiano's peril. Denver's suspicion proved prescient, for as soon as Caggiano got out of his car in Brooklyn, two heavies attacked him, brutally beating him and leaving him hospitalized for an extended period.[20]

By calling Charles Lichtman to testify, Robert Kennedy strove for maximum cinematic impact and not to prove his case beyond a reasonable doubt. The riveting story of the foiled attempt to throw James Caggiano out of the eighth-story window of the Lazarus Building came from a private conversation between Lichtman and Calland that had no witnesses and no corroborating evidence. While Kennedy led Lichtman through the story with encouragement, there is no opposing counsel in a Senate committee hearing, and no cross-examination that could disrupt a fact pattern or cast doubt on evidence. Moreover, a Senate committee hearing is not a trial. Although the witnesses are under oath, the purpose of the hearing is to move the public to push Congress to pass legislation. Mobilizing the public requires strong narrative, and Kennedy saw storytelling as the hearings' central purpose. The 1954 film *On the Waterfront* had already linked trade unionism, violence, and organized crime to the cinematic realm in the mind of the US middle class. Leveraging Hollywood's groundwork, Kennedy turned to the cinematic in a bid to save downtown from unruly unionism. Furthermore, Kennedy took his audience on wide ellipses, staging weeks of cinematic testimony from operatives who engaged in the violent, underhanded practices common in service-sector unionism for half a century but who had little or no connection to the Teamsters. None of the above descriptions of urban or suburban malfeasance involved the Teamsters, but instead implicated the Laundry Workers Union, the International Union of Electricians, and the International Brotherhood of Electrical Workers. Kennedy nevertheless called these witnesses to dramatize a wider, embellished narrative that always circled back to the aberrant culture of the International Brotherhood of Teamsters.

Most vulgar about that culture was the wildly unrestrained body. Frank Calland was ready to kill a man rather than rationally talk through a disagreement, and he was ready to subject the consuming public to his gruesome plans. Caggiano's body would have hit the pavement in the middle of a pre-eminent New York neighborhood, with the renowned Plaza Hotel just three blocks away on Central Park South, with the Waldorf Astoria a bit further down on Park Avenue, and with the Rockefeller Center seven blocks to the south. Opulent though it certainly was, this central city neighborhood had long been disorderly. Arnold Rothstein, the infamous New York bookmaker who helped rig the 1919 World Series, was fatally shot inside the Park Central Hotel in 1928. Sicilian underworld figure Albert Anastasia was also gunned down in the hotel, a killing that took place during the McClellan Committee hearings in 1957.[21] For Kennedy, calling Lichtman to the witness stand and bringing Calland's depravity to light was a chance to redeem the central city, to make it a place for productive consumption[22] where people could dine, shop, and stroll in Central Park while they conducted America's business. The regulated body of the moneyed consumer and the hard-working businessman would replace the unmanageable bodies of Arnold Rothstein, Albert Anastasia, Frank Calland, and James Caggiano that had troubled Central Park South since the twentieth century's outset.

Robert Kennedy was equally vivid as he described the threat that unrestrained Teamster bodies posed to the suburbs. On Thursday, February 19, 1959, at 10:30 in the morning, Senators Ervin, Goldwater, Ives, and McClellan sat down to listen to Kennedy question a series of witnesses who described disturbing events that had shaken the leafy bedroom communities north and west of Chicago. The first sworn in was Donald Moloney, who lived in a comfortable but modest 1,440-square-foot colonial-style home built in 1955 in Wilmette, a suburb between upscale Evanston and Winnetka.[23] Moloney and his brother owned the Donan Distributing Company, which operated eighty coin game machines in bars and restaurants in the north shore suburbs. In 1958, Moloney expanded his business by acquiring the right to maintain fifty jukeboxes in similar establishments. Not long after the purchase, Fred Smith, the business agent for International Brotherhood of Electrical Workers Local 134, approached Moloney and gave him notice that he would need to join his union and the trade association for jukebox operators if he wanted to continue with the purchase. Moloney balked, unwilling to further diminish his already slim profit margins. Smith cursed Moloney's intransigence, ordering him to join the union and threatening Moloney with physical harm if he continued to refuse. A few nights later, Smith made good on his threat. James Rini, who provided muscle for Smith, followed Moloney home from work. Before he could close his garage door, Rini charged inside and attacked Moloney, hurling his body against the car, the lawn mower, and the snow blower and interrupting the tranquil quiet of a suburban neighborhood with the smashing of fists, with moans, and with gasps.[24]

The violence was not limited to Moloney's company. After Moloney finished his testimony, Bernard Poss took the witness stand to describe a physical attack he had endured. Poss lived thirty-five miles west of Moloney in Aurora, a former small town that was in the process of becoming a suburb of Chicago, and operated two hundred game machines in the area. One evening, Rocco Pranno appeared in Poss's office, cajoling him to add pull-tab machines to his lineup of games. Well aware that many municipalities had banned gambling in bars and unwilling to take the risk of purchasing equipment that new laws could idle, Poss declined Pranno's overture. Pranno exploded in anger and forced Poss into his car. He took Poss on what Poss described as a "shakedown ride," terrorizing him and threatening to kill him as they sped through the dark, empty streets. Poss claimed that Pranno drove him down an abandoned road where, as Poss switched to an oddly omniscient passive voice, "it had been reported" that the Mafia "hung bodies from fence posts." Meanwhile, Pranno's muscle attacked the locations where Poss operated his equipment, storming into a bar in a peaceful residential neighborhood of Aurora, holding all the patrons at gunpoint, and using an axe to demolish the pool table, the shuffleboard alley, and the pinball machine in front of the terrified, captive audience. Pranno also assailed Poss at his home, making constant, harassing phone calls and threatening to kill his wife.[25]

Several witnesses described Pranno's alarming stalking of Ralph Kelly, another coin machine operator in Chicago's west suburbs. Pranno had tried to intimidate Kelly into the same pull-tab scheme. After he refused, Pranno threatened to tie cement blocks around Kelly's legs and throw him off a bridge into the Fox River. When the threat of drowning failed to yield results, Pranno began to follow Kelly as he serviced his machines, ominously waiting in his car outside of each establishment he visited. Bernard Poss editorialized to the McClellan Committee's television audience that Kelly was so shaken by Pranno's stalking that he considered doing the "dutch act," taking his own life to end the misery of Pranno's aggression.[26]

As he lined up witnesses to describe violent unionism in the suburbs, Bobby Kennedy elicited narratives of disturbingly unrestrained comportment that echoed those he presented about the central city. The legal facts of Kennedy's case were relatively unremarkable; operatives such as Fred Smith and Rocco Pranno were building fraudulent union locals with illegal tactics such as extortion and assault, and that some of these operatives were transferring their members into corrupt Teamsters locals that would throw their support behind Jimmy Hoffa's bid to take control of the union. The testimony that he used to tell that story, however, hung on the cinematic: the fence post yoked to a bloody, dead body after a mob hit; the paranoid, terrified man sweating as he drove past cul-de-sacs contemplating suicide; the body hurled over a bridge, splashing down into the muddy water, and vanishing beneath the surface as the cinderblocks pulled it down. As in the central city cases, few of these dramatic details were corroborated. The cinderblock threat story, for example, came from the testimony of an Elgin-based jukebox operator who only heard it from the alleged victim,[27] and Bernard Poss used the passive voice to avoid accounting for who knew about the bloody fence posts or how they knew it. Rather than prove these allegations, Kennedy compelled this testimony to illustrate the stakes of Teamster corruption for America's booming suburbs. Fred Smith and Rocco Pranno were turning newly built single-family homes, neighborhood restaurants, rivers, and parks into an anxious, film noir landscape of fear. By broadcasting Smith and Pranno's story into those same suburban homes, Kennedy aimed to mobilize the public to reorient the suburbs—and the unionized workers who lived there—toward their rightful cultural values: privacy, domesticity, and respectability.

The immense scale, duration, and cost of the McClellan Committee investigation raise the question of why Robert F. Kennedy cared so passionately about the bodily demeanor of activists associated with the Teamsters union. It is difficult to overstate the menace that Kennedy saw in Jimmy Hoffa's union. "Quite literally your life, and the life of every person in the United States is in the hands of Hoffa and the Teamsters," Kennedy wrote in *The Enemy Within*, his grimly titled book on the hearings. "As Mr. Hoffa operates it, this is a conspiracy of evil . . . an ugly influence and a threat to our nation."[28] I propose that the reason for Kennedy's alarm is he believed the International Brotherhood of Teamsters threatened the government's wider effort to stem the social disruption of the Great Depression and World War II and to meet the existential threat of the Cold War. Historian Elaine Tyler May famously argued that domesticity was the foundation of the US effort to win the Cold War on the home front. "In the domestic version of containment," May proposed, referencing George F. Kennan's geopolitical strategy to contain communism, "the 'sphere of influence' was the home. Within its walls, potentially dangerous social forces of the new age might be tamed, where they could contribute to the secure and fulfilling life to which postwar women and men aspired."[29] Suburbanization became the primary tool for the federal government to enact domestic containment, as state-backed mortgage loans to millions of white men allowed them to move their wives and children to brand-new, comfortable, single-family homes on the edge of the metropolis. And as literary theorist Julie Abraham has shown, the architects of suburbanization strove to discourage "problematic group attachments," the clannish, vestigial, and un-American connections to language, ethnicity, and religion that were enacted in the central city's public spaces. Moving to the suburbs cut those ties and replaced them with a single, homogenized, American affinity: the nuclear family.[30] The comfort and affluence of a lifestyle built around that new affinity would, in Robert Kennedy's words, neutralize "the enemy within."

The problem for Kennedy and other Cold War leaders, however, was that the architecture and landscape design of the suburbs undermined domestic containment. According to historian Clayton Howard, while real estate developers and their government backers encouraged people to hide their lives inside the protected spaces of the "bedroom communities" they built, the privacy that defined their work provided physical cover for transgressive desires and practices. With fenced-in yards, sunken living rooms with closed curtains, and master bedrooms hidden behind walk-in closets and en suites, suburban designers built a black box for the enemy within, one that allowed people to hide their dealings from neighbors, coworkers, relatives, and the police.[31] During the McClellan Committee hearings, I argue, Robert Kennedy aimed to shine a light into that black box, illuminating the nefarious dealings that the Cold War–era investment in the right to privacy had sheltered. Kennedy was well aware that not every Sicilian, not every Polish Catholic, and not every Russian Jew complied with the mandate to align their social networks, their kinship ties, their financial dealings, and their sexual desires with the bourgeois values that suburban design was supposed to inspire. For Kennedy, the International Brotherhood of Teamsters—and particularly Jimmy Hoffa— abetted that noncompliance. By exposing the vulgar culture of the Teamsters metropolis, Kennedy hoped to regulate the Teamsters' bodies, tastes, and styles, realigning them with the suburban culture at the center of US Cold War planning.

A Love Seat for a Rumpus Room: Overconsumption and Ethnic Flamboyance

Bobby Kennedy captured the public eye with the explosive McClellan Committee hearings, using jarringly violent narratives—such as George Connolly/Cohen's literal use of dynamite—to level damaging charges against the Teamsters. Once he had the attention of his audience, however, Kennedy turned to granular descriptions of Teamsters' daily affairs. Kennedy's questions were pedagogical, evoking information that taught viewers how to live in the suburbanizing midcentury metropolis: how to consume in a measured manner, how to embody ethnicity while shoring up middle-class whiteness, and how to make a living through hard work rather than via illicit ethnic networks. He taught this lesson, however, through negative examples, calling Teamsters to the witness stand who overconsumed, whose flamboyant Jewish and Catholic "problematic group attachments" set them apart from their Protestant neighbors, and whose business dealings transgressed the law.

Consumption practices garnered attention throughout the McClellan Committee investigation, and they were particularly notable in Kennedy's probe of the union's then-president Dave Beck during the first months of the hearings. Via the testimony of dozens of witnesses called to describe Beck's alleged financial misdeeds, Kennedy told a story of Teamster overconsumption, of Teamsters who bought too much, ate too much, relaxed too much, and played too much. By focusing on consumption, Kennedy aimed the investigation at the heart of the Cold War political economy of the 1950s. As Grace Hong persuasively argues in *The Ruptures of American Capital*, the "Fordist bargain"—the purported accord between labor and management that exchanged high wages for high productivity and labor docility—required people to become "good workers" and "good consumers," working hard to buy the products they would buy in mass. Hong demonstrates that the white suburban beneficiaries of the Fordist bargain were cast in racial terms against "bad workers" and "worse consumers": Asian immigrants, who underconsumed in the poverty of Chinatowns and Little Manilas, and African Americans and Puerto Ricans, who refused to work while overconsuming off the largesse of the welfare state.[32] I propose that Kennedy strove to locate eastern and southern European Jews and Catholics in the binary that Hong theorizes, stigmatizing Teamster leaders' crude consumption practices and pushing rank-and-file Teamsters toward their rightful position as white workers who were good consumers and who adhered to the Fordist bargain.

The discourse of overconsumption was most palpable when Kennedy interviewed Beck's associate Nathan Shefferman. Living in a downtown Chicago apartment with a view of Buckingham Fountain, Shefferman had run a management-side labor relations consulting firm with offices in New York, Detroit, and Chicago since the mid-1930s. The vast majority of Shefferman's three hundred clients were department stores, and the International Brotherhood of Teamsters was his only customer that was a labor union.[33] The crux of Kennedy's case against Beck was that Shefferman was using his connections in the wholesale and retail industries to obtain luxury items for Beck and disguising the union funds that paid for those goods as consulting fees for Shefferman's company. Unlike Jimmy Hoffa, who lived in a small, central city home, dressed modestly, and spent virtually all his time on the job (see chapter 3), Beck lived an indulgent life.[34] In an aggressive line of questioning, Kennedy suggested that Beck's lavish lifestyle depended on Shefferman's ties to merchants. The consumer products trade was heavily Jewish at the time, with two-thirds of both wholesale and retail businesses in New York, for example, being Jewish-owned in the 1950s. For Kennedy, the veiled networks of an underhanded Jewish businessman allowed a corrupt Beck to pilfer workers' union dues and spend them on glitter and gold for himself, his family, and his Teamster associates.

To theatricalize Nathan Shefferman's unscrupulousness for his television audience, Kennedy aimed his questions at the particular consumer products that Shefferman delivered to Beck. During a two-day interrogation that produced seventy-six pages of testimony for the Congressional Record, Kennedy touched only briefly on the arcane details that linked Shefferman's consulting firm to the Teamsters. Instead, he spent hours forcing Nathan Shefferman to read aloud lists of his purchases. "White nylons, golf balls, two dozen sheets, football tickets," Shefferman began just after noon on Tuesday, March 26, 1957. "Royal typewriter," Shefferman continued, "Jayson shirts—we are doing a lot of advertising here—Hathaway shirts, Shavemasters."[35] Kennedy's repeated prompts to read from a long inventory clearly jarred Shefferman, who protested an interrogation method that he believed would tarnish both he and Beck's reputation. "Gentlemen please," Shefferman plead to the senators as he looked past Kennedy. "The implication. I happen to know that Mr. Beck is a moral man, and so (the purchases) are alright."[36]

Kennedy cut him off and ordered him to resume reading aloud. "Five dozen diapers," Shefferman grudgingly continued, "a hose—I don't know if that is a garden hose or nylons. A Johnson outboard motor. A Hoover vacuum cleaner. Twelve pairs of Magna binoculars." Unsatisfied with a reading performance that he implied was insufficiently thorough, Kennedy escalated his demand of Shefferman, insisting that he backtrack and reread items along with their exact prices:

CHIEF COUNSEL KENNEDY: You are observing the amounts?
NATHAN SHEFFERMAN: The amounts?
KENNEDY: You are observing the amounts of those?
SHEFFERMAN: Yes; the Sulka ties and shirts were $192.65.
   And the two coats were $303.60.
KENNEDY: We did not get these others. Start up here with the
   bow ties.
SHEFFERMAN: It was $3.50.
KENNEDY: Now come down here to the Kaiser roofing sheet.
SHEFFERMAN: All right. Lamps, tables, Kaiser roofing sheet,
   $1,431.27. Custom made tie $14.[37]

As the minutes of Shefferman's reading stretched into hours, the five US senators present at that afternoon's hearing—Sam Ervin, John F. Kennedy, Irving Ives, John McClellan, and Karl Mundt—indulged Chief Counsel Kennedy's deep dive into the product list, often interjecting with their own, intricate questions. Mundt, for example, was particularly interested in an allotment of roofing material that Shefferman's operatives delivered to Beck:

> SENATOR KARL MUNDT: Could you explain a bit more about the Kaiser roofing sheet?
> SHEFFERMAN: I couldn't really, because I didn't know it. I can only imagine it could have been for some of the housing . . . I cannot say.
> MUNDT: That seems to be a pretty good item. It seems to be a building material of some kind?[38]

Shefferman seemed disconcerted and baffled by senators' apparent—though perhaps feigned as a pretense for rhetorical questioning—assumption that the chief executive of a consulting firm with three hundred clients would have had any recollection of individual transactions relevant to one account. Perhaps out of necessity, Shefferman diligently answered the exacting questions in some cases, engaging in a long back-and-forth with Bobby Kennedy about the specific function of a Fairbanks-Morse pump for Dave Beck's underground sprinkler system, for example, and speculating to John McClellan about whether or not love seats were appropriate furniture for a rumpus room:

> SHEFFERMAN: Chairs, tables, love seats for $1,242.45. I wouldn't know what those are for unless it might have been, and I am strictly guessing, what do they call those—a rumpus room?
> SENATOR JOHN MCCLELLAN: A love seat for a rumpus room?
> SHEFFERMAN: Well, it's a good combination, anyway. It's a good place to have a rumpus, anyhow.[39]

As the hours rolled by, and as Soviet expansion in eastern Europe and Black students' demand for educational access in Little Rock presented elected officials with simultaneous crises, five sitting US senators debated whether or not the president of the Teamsters had followed midcentury design trends and built a rumpus room in his basement, and whether Nathan Shefferman had helped him embezzle the funds to buy a love seat to furnish it.

Although the litany of purloined products provided intrigue for committee's television audience, the substance of the list was far less dramatic than the image of Nathan Shefferman forcibly reading it. The majority of Shefferman's purchases were not opulent, rare, or refined, but rather were unremarkable midtier dry goods. Shefferman, for example, spent $9.58 to buy five dozen disposable baby diapers for Beck. The price of the custom-made Sulka tie for Beck's business wardrobe was $14—or $134 when adjusted for inflation—which is half the price of the cheapest ties on today's department store designer racks. Shefferman delivered a winter coat to Beck for today's equivalent of $1,600. Nieman Marcus and Nordstrom are selling scores of coats for three times that amount in their current men's collections.[40] And while multimillion-dollar yachts have been the marker of elite excess for at least a century, the boat Shefferman obtained for Beck's fishing trips cost less than $10,000 in today's money and was powered by a small outboard motor.[41] The reprehensibility of Beck's apparent decision to steal from Teamster members aside, the total value of the goods Shefferman obtained for Beck—roughly $790,000 in today's dollars[42]—fails to register in comparison to the corporate malfeasance that the Senate has investigated at other times: the $132 billion that Michael Milken's junk bond business cost taxpayers[43] in the savings-and-loan crisis of the late 1980s, for example, or Bear Stearns' and AIG's reckless trade in mortgage-backed securities that required an $800 billion bailout in 2008. Thus, the Beck probe was notable for neither the gravity of crimes nor the quantity of misused funds that it exposed.

Instead, Kennedy's inquiry stood out because of the riveting details it provided its television viewing audience about the pathological attributes of the day-to-day culture of the Teamsters. In Shefferman's particular case, Kennedy leveraged a longstanding, transnational current of antisemitic discourse that conflated the Jew, financial exploitation, and sexual aberrance. According to historian Emily Rosenberg's compelling work on early twentieth-century finance, that current emerged in Aristotle's writing, where he argued that although the production of goods for household use creates a moral benefit, commerce for pure profit, and especially lending money for interest, has an unnatural character. For Aristotle, interest payments represent gain without labor, which is nonproductive and immoral. Aristotle's thinking migrated into medieval Christianity through Thomas Aquinas, who claimed that usury and sodomy are equivalent, as both stood in opposition to natural—and thus morally sound—methods of increase. Usurers were cast outside of medieval Christian society and were refused social rights such as communion. As Rosenberg shows, "the semiotics of the Jew, the usurer, and the outsider became overlapping cultural referents in this symbolic system."[44] Over the coming centuries, ideology that linked evil, aberrant sexuality, the Jewish outsider, and profiteering remained prevalent across the West, and it pervaded US critiques of finance from Andrew Jackson to the People's Party to Henry Ford.[45]

By the mid-twentieth century, Aristotle's formulation of household production had given way to mass consumption as the principal economic signifier of moral goodness. Yet Aristotle and Aquinas's insistence that labor is the necessary foundation for material gain remained. Robert Kennedy leveraged that prowork discourse as he forced Shefferman to read lists of banal consumer products. Kennedy condemned Shefferman for procuring a trove of goods—golf balls, designer shirts, sprinkler systems, fishing boats—without work, stealing union members hard-earned dues, embezzling them through a murky underworld of Jewish merchants, and filching some of the proceeds for his own decadence. Shefferman's dealings were, in Aquinas's terms, as unproductive as sodomy, severing mid-twentieth-century mass consumption from the hard work that would have made such consumption a morally appropriate mode of accumulation. Indeed, while buying a love seat would ordinarily have proven one's congruence with the suburban heterosexual domesticity that drove the 1950s economy, Kennedy's revelations about Dave Beck's rumpus room condemned the Teamsters as bad workers and worse consumers, which cast the nation's largest labor union outside the boundary of legitimate economic life and of acceptable cultural expression.

While the thinly veiled antisemitic logic that surfaced in the Shefferman interrogation was less noticeable during subsequent questioning, Kennedy continued to rely on derogatory ethnic tropes to illustrate his point about Teamster culture. He was particularly concerned, for example, with the nicknames that members of the Sicilian syndicate—and a few in the Jewish underworld—used to identify themselves in some contexts. Instead of connecting Italians and Jews to the universal suburban whiteness that Kennedy hoped to instill in ordinary Teamsters, nicknames accentuated ethnic differences, and they did so in a way that Kennedy clearly understood to be crass. Most troubling were the names that directly linked a person's identity to criminality: Anthony "Tony Ducks" Corallo was named for his ability to duck criminal charges, Joseph "Scarface Joe" Bommarito for the wounds that came with illegal acts, Michael "Trigger Mike" Coppola,[46] and Charles "Charlie the Blade" White[47] among scores of similar monikers. Other names that Kennedy reiterated described bodies that deviated from the norms of bourgeois masculinity: "Skinny Ray," "Fat Freddy," or "Cockeyed Mickey."[48] Some names just sounded like stereotypes of Italian gangsters from Hollywood cinema. Kennedy histrionically repeated the name John "Peanuts" Tronolone[49] during questioning, seemingly for the amusement of himself and his television audience.

Kennedy often interrupted his interlocutors to identify and accentuate what he understood to be the nicknames of people referenced in testimony and to insert such names into the Congressional Record. Interjections with the apparent intent of highlighting flamboyant, indecent performances of ethnicity often confused Kennedy's witnesses. For example, when Kennedy questioned Albert Denver about the events that led up to Frank Calland's purported attempt to throw James Caggiano out the window of the Lazarus Building, Denver mentioned a man named Ernie Rupolo.

> CHIEF COUNSEL KENNEDY: Who was the party that came to
>   see you?
> ALBERT DENVER: A man by the name of Ernie Rupolo.
> KENNEDY: Ernie "The Hawk" Rupolo?
> DENVER: I didn't know "The Hawk." I knew him at that time as
>   Ernie Rupolo. I knew he had been in the business, but I had
>   never met him before that time.[50]

Perhaps because nicknames were less pervasive among Sicilian Teamster operatives than Kennedy imagined them to be, or because Denver was careful to avoid perjuring himself by claiming to know something that he did not, Denver seemed flustered by Kennedy's repeated interruptions that restated the name Ernie "The Hawk" for his television audience.

Samuel Carnival and Samuel Zakman were also thrown off by Kennedy's invocation of nicknames. Carnival's testimony was steeped in ethnic misunderstanding from the outset. The proprietor of a family spray painting business located in a warehouse in Manhattan's Chelsea neighborhood called Carnival Spraying, the Senate's clerk recorded his name as "Conoval" throughout his testimony, perhaps because of the way the common Italian surname sounded to the clerk when Carnival, a second-generation Italian American from Murray Hill, Queens, pronounced it. Kennedy was probing Carnival about why he registered himself, his wife, his sister, and his three employees as members of the fraudulent Teamster local of John Dioguardi–associate Benjamin Ross. Carnival balked at Kennedy's use of a nickname to describe Ross:

> CHIEF COUNSEL KENNEDY: That was the local that was formed
>   by Johnny Dio. You were approached by Benny the Bug Ross,
>   were you?
> SAMUEL CONOVAL [sic]: I knew him as Benny Ross.
> KENNEDY: Well, he is Benny the Bug.

CONOVAL [*sic*]: So I found out.[51]

Ross's colleague Samuel Zakman was more explicit with his displeasure with Kennedy's ethnically charged rhetoric, and used an interjection by committee member Senator Barry Goldwater to provide historical context that framed Ross as an activist that, despite his flaws, was a good organizer:

> CHIEF COUNSEL KENNEDY: Did you object to Benny the Bug, Benny the Bug Ross?
> SAMUEL ZAKMAN: There is a fellow that did everything wrong and organized better than the rest of them.
> KENNEDY: You didn't object to (organizing with) him?
> ZAKMAN: No, not after I saw what he did.
> SENATOR BARRY GOLDWATER: Mr. Zakman, you said that Benny the Bug had a little different method of organizing and that he brought in quite a few members?
> ZAKMAN: Well, Benny, as we call him, used methods that were used about 40 or 50 years ago. He would just walk into the shop and pull the switch and say "Everybody out on strike." That is all there was to it. Everybody thought he was crazy and they would walk out and the boss would sign a contract. It was as simple as that. I know it sounds unbelievable, but he organized many shops by the same method. He was a hard worker. He just ran from shop to shop.[52]

With the nickname Benny the Bug, Kennedy trivialized Ross's activism as that of a Jewish crook who made money for a Sicilian Mafia capo by flimflamming ordinary Teamsters. Zakman recognized Kennedy's sleight of hand and challenged it, renaming Ross as Benny and not Benny the Bug and describing him as an adept activist who made frequent use of the strike for recognition, which was the most effective organizing tactic prior to the passage of the Wagner Act.

Nicknames seemed to disturb Kennedy not just because of their flamboyance and their tendency to accentuate rather than minimize ethnic differences, but also because they allowed rogue Teamster operatives to adopt multiple identities. By the 1950s, suburbanization had given eastern and southern European new immigrants access to a whiteness that was stable, unambiguous, and universal. Some Teamster operatives took advantage of that homogenizing process and adopted street names that helped them shapeshift between white-coded ethnicities to evade authorities. When authorities caught up with Rocco Pranno for terrorizing coin machine operators in suburban Chicago, for example, he used the name Rocco Martel, perhaps to hide an Italian surname that police may have assumed was evidence of a connection to La Cosa Nostra.[53] In other cases, unruly unionists amplified ethnic particularities. When Teddy Ray, who also went by Skinny Ray, was arrested for abetting the John Dioguardi–ordered acid attack that blinded the labor journalist Victor Riesel, he used the also ethnically-ambiguous name Mike Ray. But in other cases, Skinny/Teddy/Mike Ray went by Samuel Arenson, perhaps to trick authorities into believing that he was part of the Jewish syndicate.[54] Still in other contexts, Teamster operatives shapeshifted between clearly marked particular ethnicities. The obviously Irish George Connolly became the Jewish George Cohen the day the dynamite attack took place in Minneapolis. His son, meanwhile, changed from one Irish name to another, swapping Connolly for Kelly while he worked for Connolly/Cohen's Jewish associate Ben Dranow.[55]

Ethnic shapeshifting was, for Kennedy, evidence of a wider Teamster phantasmagoria. Throughout the hearings, Kennedy would use Jewish and Italian surnames—whether given or false—to introduce long lists of depraved crimes committed by the operatives he referenced. Joseph Bona, for example, was a "known associate of prostitutes, arrested for prostitution, and for assault to kill."[56] "Vagrancy, conspiracy, white slavery, grand larceny, armed robbery, and concealed weapons," Kennedy railed to his audience about Joe Ferrara's arrests.[57] Kennedy was particularly interested in the crimes Joseph Bommarito, whom he continually referred to as "Scarface Joe." One of Bommarito's business partners was, Kennedy argued, "a known procurer of women, fined for beating a news reporter, fined for prostitution, and placed his wife in a bawdy house."[58] And in his book *The Enemy Within*, Kennedy introduced Bommarito as someone who lived in a world of "blackmailers, safecrackers, dope peddlers, white slavers, and sodomists."[59] In these and many other accounts of brothels, white slavery, and houses of ill repute written with language that sounded more like Anthony Comstock's infamous antivice crusades of the 1870s than a hearing in the chastened, post-McCarthy Senate, Robert Kennedy highlighted Jewish and Italian men's aberrant relationship to business, to the family, and to the mid-twentieth-century city.

The absurdity of many of his words aside, Kennedy made a clear point about what he saw as the normative relationship between ethnicity and racial formation in the 1950s. As historian Mae Ngai argues, ethnicity gave eastern and southern Europeans access to the full benefit of American whiteness in the wake of the 1924 Johnson-Reed immigration restriction. Although the act's national origin quotas reduced the number of eastern and southern Europeans who could enter the United States, some people from Italy, Greece, Romania, and Ukraine were nevertheless admitted, and those immigrants soon became Italian Americans, Greek Americans, and Jewish Americans. People from Africa and Asia, however, were categorically excluded, denied entry on racial grounds and never given access to the ethnic particularity that the act granted to Europeans as it welcomed them into the United States.[60] A decade after the act, the Federal Housing Administration began to move white people—including Italian Americans, Greek Americans, and Jewish Americans—to the suburbs, where ethnic particularity gave way to white homogeneity. Through his exhausting interrogative argumentation, Kennedy demonstrated that George Connolly/Cohen, Rocco Pranno/Martel, Teddy/Skinny/Mike Ray/Samuel Arenson, and so many other Teamster operatives were interrupting historical progress by failing to perform the suburban, homogenized whiteness that was expected of second- and third-generation European immigrants in the 1950s. The McClellan Committee hearings, thus, served as a warning to other Jews and Italians to row with the current of history, to leave behind the flamboyant ethnic particularity that defined the immigrant industrial metropolis of the early twentieth century, and to disavow Teamster unruliness in order to access the full benefits of the suburbanizing metropolitan economy.

An Elusive Trek to the Altar: The Trace of Dissident Culture at the McClellan Committee

While the meticulous questions of the McClellan Committee revealed much about the Senate's idea of the normative role of Jews and Italians in mid-twentieth-century US society, Bobby Kennedy's unflagging attention to the physical comportment of second- and third-generation European immigrants covered up far more than it revealed. The cascade of stories about overly indulgent steak dinners at cigar-smoke-filled chophouses; tickets to boxing matches obtained with embezzled union funds; and beatings, stabbings, stink bombings, and brass knucklings crowded out other descriptions of the ways Teamsters lived at the intersection of racial formation, immigration history, and kinship in the 1950s. Because Kennedy was so focused on delivering what he understood to be a coherent, comprehensive narrative about Jewish and Italian unruliness, he seemed not to notice—and perhaps not to understand—the evidence of cultural practices within the Teamsters metropolis that contested a mid-twentieth-century suburban culture grounded in white privilege and heteronormativity. Despite Kennedy's effort to control the plot line of this thirty-seven-month media event, a dissident union culture nevertheless surfaced in the hearings, one that would challenge both the segregated, suburbanized metropolitan economy that the McClellan Committee was working to stabilize and the role of the Teamster hierarchy within that system.

The testimony of Lenny Baitler is a noteworthy example of how the trace of nonconformism operated in the McClellan Committee hearings. Kennedy subpoenaed Baitler in one of his many ellipses, which in this case involved sensationalized testimony about events in the upholsterers and textile workers unions that had no connection to the Teamsters, but which audiences could easily conflate with the broader portrayal of Teamster malfeasance. While working as a mechanic who fixed jukeboxes in Miami in the early 1950s, Baitler became chair of the coin machine unit of International Brotherhood of Electrical Workers Local 349, where he advocated for shorter work hours.[61] Overwork had been common among coin machine mechanics, who were expected to perform scheduled maintenance during the standard business day and to be on call on nights and weekends when bars were busiest and most likely to require emergency fixes for their machines. As the push for shorter work hours intensified, Baitler was drawn into a confrontation with Charles Karpf, whom Kennedy accused of running a fraudulent local of the Upholsterer's Union-AFL.[62] After Baitler ignored Karpf's demand to cease organizing, Karpf responded with muscle. Baitler and his colleague Donald Helow were walking out of a sales event for the 1955 Rock-ola jukebox on Miami Beach when one of Karpf's heavies—a former boxer from New York who was a strikebreaker in the building trades—attacked them, injuring both and sending Helow to the hospital.[63]

By presenting Lenny Baitler as an honest trade unionist who was wronged by an unruly service-sector unionist, Bobby Kennedy helped obscure Baitler's own unconventional past. Baitler was born into a working-class Jewish family in Boston in 1921 and had started a jukebox repair business by the time he was sixteen years old. In an era when heterosexual marriage and a husband's breadwinner wage defined normative Jewish manhood, Baitler never domesticated. Instead, he lived a highly mobile life, taking his business to Burlington, Vermont, then to Portland, Maine, and to Baltimore before moving south to Maimi,[64] where he began taking long trips to Panama, Colombia, and Venezuela as part of a jukebox exporting gig in the early 1950s.[65] While he worked tirelessly on organizing his International Brotherhood of Electrical Workers local during the struggle with Karpf, trade unionism seems to have been only one tool that Baitler used to build the life he wanted. After the physical altercation, Baitler left the labor movement and moved to Japan, where, despite his active role in Jewish organizations in Miami Beach,[66] he took a job as a Christian bible salesman in 1956.[67] By the time he testified in front of the McClellan Committee in 1958, Baitler was back in the United States, where he had re-entered the coin machine export business to Latin America and the Caribbean. In 1963, Baitler was living in Port-of-Spain, Trinidad, where he ran game arcades across the island.[68]

It appears that some people took notice of the unconventional aspects of Lenny Baitler's life. In 1952, for example, Baitler appeared in the "Coinmen You Know" section of *The Billboard*, the industry newspaper for jukebox and game machine operators. Dale Lee, who had formerly exported jukeboxes to Venezuela but who left to start an air freight company in Alaska, wrote in to say that he "telephoned Lenny to congratulate him on tying the knot, (but that) the felicitations were somewhat premature, as Lenny had not yet trekked to the altar."[69] There is no further text to explain how a man who also seems to have lived far away from Baitler obtained the mistaken notion that Baitler had married, or why he needed to convey that mistake to hundreds of Baitler's colleagues. It is clear, however, that at thirty years old, Baitler would have been very old for a first "trek to the altar," and there are no records to indicate that he ever married. Two years later, during the time he was building the union in Miami, Baitler again appeared in the press, this time in a local interest article in the *Key West Citizen*. It seems Baitler was a performer and had traveled to Key West to be the master of ceremonies for a men's night out that included a fish dinner on the patio at the Flame restaurant. The guests were employees of General Electric at a sales meeting whose wives attended a separate, women-only bridge party at a private home on the island.[70]

The details in these short news clippings are scant, and brief mentions of Lenny Baitler's domestic arrangements are even more ambiguous. Lenny Baitler testified to the McClellan Committee immediately prior to his colleague Donald Helow. Both men gave the same address as their residence,[71] which was a brand-new but modest three-bedroom, two-bathroom ranch house in northern Miami-Dade County near the Opa Locka airport.[72] The fact that the two men appear to have been roommates drew no comment from Kennedy or any of the senators, who instead focused on grilling Baitler and Helow about Karpf's attack after the Rockola jukebox event. It seems that Helow was married at the time he shared the address with Baitler, as he had disembarked from a ship that arrived from Nassau on October 5, 1959, with his wife Josephine, whom he had married in 1941,[73] and his sons, who were eleven and seven years old.[74] Not long thereafter, the customs declaration for Pan Am flight 503 from Havana listed Helow as a passenger and the house he shared with Baitler as his permanent address.[75] And though Helow had joined Lenny Baitler in the Miami jukebox export business by November of 1962,[76] the Opa Locka house was placed on the market for sale on June 12, 1964.[77] There are no other references to Lenny Baitler until notice of his death at the age of fifty in 1972,[78] and no records of any legal kin for Baitler. The only—very brief— obituary for Helow, from Florida in 2007, similarly mentions no kin.[79]

We may only speculate about the friendly and intimate relationships that created Lenny Baitler's spectral appearance in the historical record. There is, perhaps, innuendo in Dale Lee's account of a trek to the altar that never happened, but the exact source of the innuendo—about an older single man, about a man who never settled down, about a man who people presumed to be gay or have sex with men—is not knowable. Key West had long been a place for gay men to congregate, but there is no evidence that the island's queer history attracted Baitler.[80] International business travel was also a catalyst for male same-sex desire, but Baitler's relationship to that history is unknown.[81] And there are no documents that tell us if he lived with Donald Helow as a boarder, as many Jewish families would have taken on in the early twentieth century, or if a more complex form of kinship led Baitler to cohabitate with Helow and perhaps his family. All that is clear, however, is that for Lenny Baitler, trade unionism was one of a broad array of tools he used to live far beyond the boundary of conventional domesticity. Baitler got involved with the union because he wanted more time off at night and on the weekends. When Charlie Karpf made the cost outweigh the benefits of trade unionism, Baitler found other ways to dissent from the cultural norms of the 1950s, selling bibles in Japan, exporting jukeboxes to Venezuela, and relocating to Trinidad.

While Lenny Baitler used the labor movement to build a cultural alternative to suburban heteronormativity, other activists appeared in front of the McClellan Committee as part of an overt political movement to challenge the segregated metropolitan economy of the 1950s. At the twilight of the McClellan hearings, on the evening of July 13th, 1959, Ross Hill boarded an all-night flight from Los Angeles International to Friendship Airport in Baltimore. Hill was an operating engineer who lived in North Hollywood and had moved to California from Detroit in 1957 after he left his career as a truck driver. Earlier that afternoon, George Maxwell, a labor consultant from Cleveland, had unexpectedly testified that Jimmy Hoffa's home local, Teamsters 299 in Detroit, had been racially segregated in the early 1950s and had blocked Black truckers from accessing high-paying, over-the-road driving positions.[82] Maxwell's revelation startled Kennedy, as it was new to him and because it undermined Hoffa's frequent assertions that he opposed racial segregation. Kennedy's staff got a hold of Hill, a person they knew had tried to join Local 299 and had left the Detroit labor movement on bad terms. They asked him to get on an airplane to Washington and testify the next day.[83]

Hill laid out a damaging case against the Teamsters. In 1950, he started a job that required him to pick up steel in Youngstown, Ohio, and to drop it off at trucking terminals around Detroit. To secure full access to those facilities, one had to be a member of the over-the-road bargaining unit of Local 299. According to Hill, he and other Black truck drivers knew they were not welcome in the local. "You could never get in (Local 299)," Hill told the committee flatly. "You could walk into the office, but then you would just walk away, because they wouldn't talk to you."[84] Although Hill could drop off his cargo at Teamster terminals, he was barred from picking up freight for return runs to Youngstown because he was not a member of Local 299. Hill was thus forced to take the truck back to Youngstown empty and get in the car and drive home to Detroit, which cut his earnings in half. Within a year, poverty wages had forced Hill into debt. He sold his car and his house in a vain effort to fill the gap in his budget, but he eventually left Detroit in anger to start a new life and new career in Los Angeles.

Kennedy lost control of the hearing as Hill delivered his comments. During Hill's testimony, Sen. Barry Goldwater asked the obvious question of whether or not Local 299 was still segregated eight years after the events that Hill described. Kennedy interjected, seeming flustered and unprepared to engage the conversation about racism that he had helped start. "I have no information on that one way or the other," Kennedy stuttered in response to Goldwater's question, a surprising response given that Kennedy had assembled tens of thousands of pages of damaging evidence against the Detroit Teamsters. Hill, however, was very clear about how racism worked in the late 1950s, arguing that blanket segregation had given way to token membership for a few Black workers. "I think they would try to take a percentage to override the matter now," Hill told Goldwater. "It's funny, when highlights are on certain things (such as racism), they try to take a certain percentage of Negroes to make everyone feel that, 'I am a loyal citizen of this country.'"[85] Goldwater appeared compelled, asking Hill about what else he knew about segregation in the labor movement. "Do you, as a Negro, know of any other unions where segregation is practiced?" Goldwater asked awkwardly, seeming naïve. "Sure, quite a few," Hill responded before delivering a long list of unions from most sectors of the economy. Kennedy interrupted Hill. "The Sheet Metal Workers?" he barked, referencing the union whose leaders he had spent several weeks questioning and had apparently not asked about segregation. At the end of the exchange, Goldwater turned to Kennedy and ordered him to find out whether or not Ross was correct about segregation and tokenist racism in Local 299.[86]

Hill was indeed correct, and the damaging information he contributed exposed both a deep injustice within the Teamsters and the McClellan Committee's fundamental lack of the knowledge and the will to address that injustice. In the wake of Hill's hastily arranged appearance, Kennedy's deputies probed the racial makeup of Local 299 and discovered that there were 645 Black members at 1959's outset, about 5 percent of the local's roster.[87] All those truckers, however, held lower-paid city driving positions, and none held the top-wage, over-the-road jobs that Hill had tried to obtain. Two weeks later, Kennedy used Hill's allegations to grill Jimmy Hoffa during his third appearance in front of the McClellan Committee. Hoffa quickly turned the accusation of racism back on the committee, needling the senators for their hypocrisy. In front of the television cameras, Hoffa urged the senators to vote for the antidiscrimination plank of the new labor legislation that was coming before Congress.[88] Despite Barry Goldwater's impassioned words that "segregation being practiced in a union in any place in this country" would be "one of the most atrocious things that this committee has brought out,"[89] Hoffa was well aware that as avowed segregationists, Sens. McClellan and Ervin would oppose any labor bill that included antidiscrimination language. Defending segregation had been the primary focus of McClellan's and Ervin's careers in the Senate, and Hoffa understood that maintaining Jim Crow required corruption and violence far worse than anything the Teamsters had been accused of: a racist two-tier wage system, rigged elections, vigilante violence in Black people's homes and workplaces, and the murderous system of lynching. Hoffa's effort to change the subject was racist in and of itself, as the focus on McClellan's and Ervin's efforts to scuttle antilynching bills and block school desegregation allowed Hoffa to duck any accountability for the racism to which his members were subjected. But Kennedy's and the senators' ineptitude, and their apparent lack of understanding that Jim Crow union shops and Jim Crow management tactics were widespread in both the North and the South, left them helpless in response to Hoffa's rope-a-dope strategy.

Kennedy interrupted Hoffa to pull the hearings back toward the McClellan Committee's conventional focus. With a non sequitur, he turned to a familiar interrogation tactic: a rapid-fire recitation of the Irish, Jewish, and Italian surnames of Hoffa associates and their alleged criminal activities. "Herman Hendricks, arrested 100 times, convicted of possession of marihuana [sic] cigarettes," Kennedy began as he moved the conversation away from the racial dynamics of Local 299 and toward illicit actors Hoffa continued to associate with. He continued, "Harry Gross, convicted of extortion. Mike Singer took his girlfriend on union funds to Hawaii. Sandy O'Brien, receiving $14,000 in commissions. Ted Cozza. Bernie Adelstein."[90] The brief apparition of a new, dissident political practice for the late 1950s, in which an activist Black worker flew to Washington, confronted his union, and upended a Senate committee's performance for its suburban audience, vanished as quickly as it appeared. In the place of Hill, and in the place of further consideration of Black people's role in the Teamsters metropolis, came more questions about the bodily comportment of Jewish and Catholic eastern and southern European trade unionists. After Hoffa left the witness stand, and regardless of Goldwater's emphatic pronouncement that segregation would be the most atrocious thing the investigation revealed, the McClellan Committee held no further hearings on Ross Hill's case and would never again raise the issue of segregation in the Teamsters or in any other union.

Conclusion: The Teamsters Metropolis as Cultural Dissent

The sixty-five years that have passed since the McClellan Committee wrapped up its work have helped crystalize two conclusions to be drawn from the hearings. First, the proceedings swayed public opinion against both the International Brotherhood of Teamsters and the labor movement as a whole, which made it much more difficult for every union to recruit new members. During their televised comments, the senators defined union corruption not solely in terms of crimes such as embezzlement or extortion, but as a corruption of the natural social order of the United

States in which workers had gained undeserved power over the economy. McClellan Committee member Barry Goldwater, for example, quoted the famous conservative economist F. A. Hayek when he told the public that "the whole basis of our free society is gravely threatened by the powers arrogated by unions."[91] The committee's rhetorical focus on union power proved effective. A Gallup poll taken during the McClellan Committee's third year of operation in 1959, for example, ranked "labor union problems" as the eighth most important issue facing the United States, as urgent as the space race, national defense, and education.[92]

As the unsettling details in witness testimony turned a widening swath of the senators' constituents against the labor movement, Congress passed legislation that placed strict new fetters on union organizing. In September of 1959, President Dwight Eisenhower signed the Landrum-Griffin Act, which amended the landmark Wagner Act of 1935, the foundation of US labor law. The revision banned activists from using picket lines to pressure employers to recognize unions and tightened the already onerous restrictions on secondary boycotts, which made it illegal to target a company's customers as part of a larger bid to organize.[93] With Landrum-Griffin's passage, the pickets that George Connolly/Cohen sent out to organize liquor stores and barrel makers in Minneapolis became illegal. While fear of underworld infiltration of Hoffa-aligned Teamster locals convinced some elected officials to support Landrum-Griffin, Bobby Kennedy was particularly insistent that it was the Teamsters' nefarious impact on American metropolitan areas, and not organized crime itself, that justified the reforms. "It is not the gangster himself who is of concern," Kennedy told his audience in a 1961 speech at the University of Georgia Law School. "It is what he is doing to our cities, our communities, our moral fiber."[94]

To the Kennedy brothers' credit, they worked tirelessly with Senator Irving Ives to water down the bill's most draconian, antiunion components, which John McClellan and probusiness groups such as the Chamber of Commerce had inserted during the drafting process.[95] Nevertheless, three years of stories about George Conolly/Cohen's dynamiting, James Caggiano's body hurled out the window of the Lazarus Building, and Rocco Pranno/Martel terrorizing a man to the point of suicide gave probusiness activists and antiunion policymakers vast new political capital to countermobilize against the labor movement. The now infamous National Right to Work Committee, for example, was founded in 1955 and used Kennedy's revelations about nefarious Teamster endeavors to advance its campaign to make it more difficult for workers to organize in all sectors of the economy. The Landrum-Griffin Act's ban on organizational picketing and secondary boycotts is an early, significant example of that committee's political success.[96] Therefore, while historians are right to argue that the neoliberal programs of the 1970s and 1980s, such as deregulation, privatization, and financialization exacerbated the labor movement's steepening decline, the McClellan Committee's antiunion cultural discourse of the 1950s—one that framed the labor movement as reactionary, bloated, corrupt, and contrary to ordinary workers' self-interest—helped make those later, regressive reforms politically palatable.

The second conclusion to be drawn from the McClellan Committee's revelations is that the Teamsters union helped produce a working-class metropolitan world that rejected the bourgeois culture of the 1950s. Union leaders often touted the labor movement as an agent of heteronormalization and embourgeoisement, a means to turn itinerant working men into middle-class husbands who would provide for dependent wives and children.[97] Decades of bargaining for the family wage underscore this notion's validity. A more recent generation of scholars, however, ask us to question what lay below the varnished surface of this world. Steven Vider, for example, pushes us to think of the conventional domesticity at the center of 1950s culture not as an ideology, but as performativity. People cited and reiterated cultural scripts—the husband breadwinner, the dependent wife, the monogamous spouse, the depoliticized consumer—that journalists, policymakers, intellectuals, and employers invoked when they wrote and spoke about the world.[98] While people played these roles in a way that often convinced their families, their neighbors, and themselves, historians have shown that they sometimes lived private lives that ran counter to the script, having same-sex relationships, engaging in polyamory,[99] breaking gender norms, and adopting radical politics.[100]

While Robert Kennedy wanted to repress these and scores of other deviations from the script, the McClellan Committee hearings instead illuminated them. For three years, the cul-de-sac ranch homes and strip-mall restaurants of the suburbs, as well as the laundries, bakeries, hotels, and restaurants of the central city, were exposed as places where working people built personal and professional relationships that transgressed bourgeois aesthetics and broke the law. Rather than a means to shore up 1950s middle-class culture, the Teamsters metropolis vividly appeared during the proceedings as a place to disrupt that culture.

Rather than hide these disruptions, Teamster activists often embraced them. That unruliness and flamboyance was particularly blatant in a new part of the Teamsters metropolis that Jimmy Hoffa and his associates built for the union's members in the 1950s: the oceanfront hotels of Miami

Beach. Beginning a mere month after Hoffa was elected general president of the International Brotherhood of Teamsters, the union began to invest in a portfolio of tropical resorts where ordinary workers could enjoy a paid vacation or the comfortable retirement that came with a union pension. A landscape of pleasure, its luminous colors and bold design choices flouted middle-class restraint. This sunny respite from the performance of middle-class domesticity made Jimmy Hoffa immensely popular with many of his members. But it was also an object of cultural scorn that would drive a deepening wedge between Hoffa's Teamsters and a new 1960s generation that was younger, more highly educated, and more racially diverse. To the contentious politics on the beach of the Teamsters metropolis, the next chapter turns.

CHAPTER THREE

Invested in Pleasure
Resisting the Work Ethic
on Jimmy Hoffa's Miami Beach

Jimmy Hoffa celebrated in the dining room of the Fontainebleau Hotel on Miami Beach on the evening of Saturday, October 5, 1957. The previous afternoon, he had been inaugurated general president of the International Brotherhood of Teamsters, and he delivered a rousing acceptance speech to a crowd of rank-and-file workers in a nearby auditorium. With the formal recognition ceremony complete, Hoffa sat down to dinner with his closest kin, those whose ideas, emotional support, and activist solidarity had inspired his twenty-five-year career in the union. A photographer caught Hoffa's gleeful smile as he leaned toward his protégé Chuckie O'Brien, whose infant son bounced on O'Brien's lap. Hoffa's wife Josephine watched him pose, while Sylvia Pagano, Hoffa's longtime friend and business associate, looked straight at the camera and grinned. Strewn on the table amid martini glasses, dessert plates, and flower arrangements were piles of gift boxes, lids askew and tissue paper overflowing after Hoffa had clearly torn them open.[1]

The architecture of the Fontainebleau resonated with the photograph's joyful composition. Every guest made a grand entrance to the restaurant, as access required climbing three stairs and walking across a wide marble platform before descending three more stairs into the dining room. Pink spotlights—designed to accentuate patrons' suntans—illuminated the platform, allowing each guest to pose as if they were a model on a runway. Outside in the lobby, the design was decadent, featuring no fewer than twenty-seven colors in its palette and adorned with potted palms, Greek statuary, Roman busts, and ornate light fixtures that "dripped with jewels." Downstairs on the beach level, reclining chairs with views of the surf were arranged on two long S-shaped promenades. Strolling along the curve toward the pool, a person was always at the focal point of the design, which made one believe, if only for a moment, that they were the center of the universe.[2]

"Tropical opulence and glittering luxury" was the name for the Fontainebleau's aesthetic concept, which was the work of the famed architect Morris Lapidus. Born in Odessa, Ukraine, in 1902, Lapidus spent his childhood on Manhattan's Lower East Side among other eastern European Jewish immigrants. He was taken with the cinematic nature of city life, and Coney Island, vaudeville shows, and early cinema heavily influenced his style. "I imagined myself the set designer for a movie producer who wanted to create a hotel that would make a tremendous impression on viewers," Lapidus said of the Fontainebleau project in his memoir *Too Much Is Never Enough*, "so I designed a movie set."[3] Describing his work in superlatives as he often did, Lapidus recalled hiring Jules Gorlitz, "a man of exquisite taste," to coordinate decorating the Fontainebleau's lobby, which included, "a magnificent 19th century piano with marquetry and ormolu work, gilded cherubs, exquisite vases, and glowing crystal chandeliers."[4] Lapidus's hotels were an immediate success. The Fontainebleau sold out its first winter high season when it opened in December 1954, with rooms selling for $83 per night, the equivalent of $805 today.[5]

While he clearly relished his frequent stays at Fontainebleau, Jimmy Hoffa was no mere guest on Miami Beach. Hoffa was helping build the beachfront landscape that he and rank-and-file workers enjoyed. Beginning in the early 1950s, the Teamsters and other large unions won defined benefit pension plans for their members. New collective bargaining agreements required employers to set aside money to pay workers a monthly old age stipend that would augment Social Security. In addition to allowing workers to retire earlier, pensions aided workers by creating a pool of capital that unions could invest for their betterment. Jimmy Hoffa leveraged Miami Beach real estate as a centerpiece of the Teamsters' proworker investing strategy, using the pension fund to build oceanfront venues for activists to conduct union business, for workers to savor a paid vacation, and for retirees to spend their old age in the pleasures of the sun and surf. This investment in pleasure was part of a multipronged strategy to expand the union's footprint in the US South, the region with the lowest density since the failure of the Congress of Industrial Organizations' "Operation Dixie" campaign in the early 1940s. As the esteemed labor journalist Victor Riesel put it in 1961, Jimmy Hoffa was underwriting "the gayest of motels, strung across the South from Georgia to Louisiana, and from Savannah to Miami."[6] Hoffa coupled such gaiety with grassroots union organizing, launching a mass recruitment drive for public employees in South Florida, leading a strike among cannery workers to protest the harsh conditions in the citrus industry, and—just like they did in Cleveland, Allentown, and Brooklyn—signing up workers at small businesses across Miami's service sector.

This chapter delves into the Miami Beach landscapes at the core of Jimmy Hoffa's push to expand the Teamsters in the South. The Fontainebleau and dozens of other oceanfront hotels exemplified what Hoffa's cohort imagined luxury to be. Many of these activists began their careers amid the scarcity of the Great Depression and came from eastern and southern European Jewish and Catholic immigrant families that lacked the financial or cultural capital to understand the tastes, values, and customs of the US Protestant elite. Therefore, when they won unprecedented resources for working people through union activism, Hoffa and his associates made up their own version of the good life, building a flamboyant Miami Beach that simulated what wealth felt, tasted, and looked like to people who had grown up without it. Unrestrained, indulgent design elements defined their aesthetic: lavish, heavily adorned spaces, bright colors, loud patterns, dramatic flowing curves, and a built environment that encouraged people to eat, swim, dance, and socialize all night long. Unlike midcentury modernist styles that restrained people's bodies with sharp angles, hard surfaces, and a subdued palette, the Teamsters' Miami Beach indulged the body, stimulating desire and provoking pleasure through ornamentation, opulence, and excess. While the previous chapters described the Teamsters metropolis as a contiguous space that spanned the old central neighborhoods and new suburbs of the industrial cities of the North and East, this chapter demonstrates that to understand the cultural foundation of the Teamster movement requires a detailed analysis of the design and the style of its most indulgent component in the 1950s: the oceanfront of Miami Beach.

Jimmy Hoffa's investment in pleasure was rife with contradictions. When truck drivers, warehouse workers, bartenders, and uniform launderers from southern and eastern European immigrant families enjoyed the lush flowers, sweet flavors, and sultry erotics of Miami Beach, they often did so in proximity to, and with superiority over, the Black and Brown people whose images adorned the walls of hotels, and who cooked, cleaned, sang, and danced for tourists' enjoyment. Newly middle-class Jews and Catholics, for example, joyously cheered for

Aretha Franklin as she played antiracist anthems to sold-out crowds at the Fontainebleau in the early 1960s. As guests strolled to their hotel rooms at the end of the evening, Miami Beach's Jim Crow curfew forced Franklin to leave the barrier island by midnight.[7] And while Teamster real estate investments were a source of great enjoyment for some union members, Hoffa often channeled Florida financial deals through his associates in the Jewish and Sicilian underworlds. Those unruly alliances, when coupled with the unceasing surveillance of the Senate's McClellan Committee and from Attorney General Robert F. Kennedy, would eventually lead to an indictment, a conviction, and a thirteen-year prison sentence for Hoffa for bribery and fraud.

Debilitating though Miami Beach's constitutive contradictions would most certainly become to the Teamster leadership as the 1960s progressed, this chapter nevertheless proposes that Jimmy Hoffa's oceanfront strategy has a lesson to teach the labor movement. I argue that the Teamsters' investment in pleasure in Miami Beach contested the prowork ideology at the core of the Protestant work ethic, that which forces people to live to work rather than the reverse. As the political theorist Kathi Weeks has so persuasively argued, for the labor movement to be effective, it must challenge both the economic structures that exploit workers and the ideas that make work—and not bodily, emotional, or spiritual pleasures—the centerpiece of people's lives.[8] A vacation to Hoffa's Miami Beach contested those prowork ideas and incited new, sensuous desires that allowed rank-and-file Teamsters to imagine a world beyond work. This chapter explains why Jimmy Hoffa made those sensuous desires so central to his impassioned, unceasing—and deeply flawed—effort to build the Teamsters metropolis.

Coney Island in the Tropics: The Immigrant Industrial Metropolis Comes to Miami Beach

Morris Lapidus built the Fontainebleau for a broad swath of the US white middle class on a barrier island that had once been reserved for the Protestant elite. Because of its relatively remote location south of the Everglades, and because of its oppressively hot summer climate, Miami developed much later than most other US cities. The town was incorporated in 1896, when fewer than three hundred white settlers lived in the area. Most of the land was owned by Julia Tuttle, who was born Julia Sturtevant to an old-stock Dutch industrialist family from Cleveland. In 1898, Tuttle convinced Henry Flagler to extend his Florida East Coast Railway south to Miami from its existing terminal in Jacksonville. Flagler was a wealthy Presbyterian from New York who entered the railroad business after he, like the Sturtevants, made a fortune in Cleveland, in his case by founding the Standard Oil Company.[9] While Flagler's railroad augmented South Florida's transport infrastructure, it was also a tool to sell real estate. The plot of land where the Fontainebleau would later stand, for example, became a famous encampment for industrialists' families after Harvey Firestone, the rubber magnate from Columbiana, Ohio, developed it in 1924. By the end of the decade, Lindsey Hopkins of Coca-Cola, J.C. Penney, the Maytags, and the Vanderbilts had all built mansions on the Firestone property.[10] With the completion of these expansive private homes, Miami Beach had become a remote, opulent hideaway for the wealthiest Protestant families who had prospered amid the industrialization of the US Midwest in the second half of the nineteenth century.

New technology and a booming economy made Miami Beach more accessible to a wider, more ethnically diverse swath of the US middle class after World War II. Before the war, most of Miami Beach's hotels were extravagant, catering to a small cohort of wealthy Protestant guests, and following the Standard Practice Manual for Hotel Operation, which explicitly discouraged sales to Jews and other "undesirables."[11] But by the end of the 1940s, as the widespread use of air conditioning made even modest hotels comfortable on steamy afternoons, and as bigger, faster, and safer airliners made South Florida far more accessible to tourists from the Northeast and Midwest, the region's small Protestant elite struggled to meet the breakneck tourist demand. To fill the void, a new contingent of eastern European Jewish entrepreneurs who had benefited from New Deal housing, labor, tax, and welfare policy moved to Miami to work in the hospitality business, and they welcomed the large cohort of eastern and southern European immigrants who had been excluded during Miami Beach's formative years.

Ben Novack was one of these early entrepreneurs. The son of Russian Jewish immigrants to New York, Novack began his career managing hotels in the "Borscht Belt" of the Catskill Mountains, where Depression-era eastern European Jews who could afford a vacation often spent their leisure time. He moved to Miami in 1940, hoping to harness the growing South Florida travel market to enter the hotel development business. Novack's big breakthrough came in 1949, when he built the Sans Souci—"care free" in French—a large resort hotel on Miami Beach. During the early phases of the Sans Souci project, Novack traveled to New York on a business trip, where a mutual friend introduced him to Morris Lapidus. The two ended up working late into the evening in a Midtown Manhattan apartment on a concept for the new hotel.[12] That design made headlines for its glitz, with black marble tables, white leather couches, and gold beams that held shiny, globe-shaped cages with real birds whose song filled the lobby. "When the San Souci was opened in 1949," Lapidus recalled in his memoir, "guards were kept at the entrance to make sure that only the guests could get in, and to keep out the hordes of lookers who flocked to the hotel, attracted by the bright colors and light."[13] In collaboration with Lapidus, Novack had begun to define a new Miami Beach aesthetic, one that retained the opulence that defined Miami's early Protestant elite period but made it available to a far wider swath of visitors. It was now open to those who were white enough to comply with Florida's strict Jim Crow system but whose family roots lay in the shtetls of the Russian Pale, in the peasant villages of Ukraine, and in Sicily and Calabria rather than on the Mayflower.

Out of a new immigrant's journey came the design principles that guided Morris Lapidus's concept for Miami Beach. After arriving in the United States at eight months old in the summer of 1903, Lapidus spent his childhood in a Yiddish-speaking world, first on Manhattan's Lower East Side and then in Brooklyn's Williamsburg neighborhood. He thus learned how to be an American not from his elders but from popular culture in urban space. Unable to speak English as a young child, it was sight, sound, color, taste, and texture—and not language—that shaped Lapidus's understanding of the city and of American culture. Lapidus recalled being enthralled with Luna Park, the amusement carnival on Coney Island. "Luna Park was an earthly paradise for me, with flowers and trees and fairytale castles with pastel hues and all the colors of the rainbow . . . a street called the Bowery promised wonders, freaks of nature, dancing girls, mysteries, and laughter."[14] For a young Lapidus, the urban landscape conveyed meaning by arousing feelings: the pleasure of color, the wonderment of a fairy-tale castle, the allure of a dancing girl, and the suspense of a mystery. Lapidus remembered the particularly vivid sensations that came with watching Buffalo Bill's Wild West Show, a vaudeville performance that captivated his fascination with what he imagined the American West to be. "Naked Indians rode in on wild horses, swinging their tomahawks," Lapidus recalled seeing from the Coney Island audience. "Just when it seems like all was lost, Buffalo Bill kills all of the Indians and the settlers are saved, and the great Buffalo Bill, hero of the story and legend, rode toward the grandstand."[15]

As he told the story of a Yiddish-speaking Jewish boy being hailed into US citizenship amid a staged genocide of Indigenous people, Morris Lapidus describes what appears to be a contradiction. On the one hand,

Lapidus frames Coney Island as a venue for unruly sexuality, one where recently arrived immigrants from southern and eastern Europe openly claimed physical and sexual pleasures: the delight of bright colors, the smell of foods from around the world, and the gaze at the body of a dancing girl. Older-stock Protestant elites stigmatized such transgressions, which fueled nativist calls for what became the Johnson-Reed quota limitations of 1924. But on the other hand, Morris Lapidus also described the euphoric sensations of white racial fraternity and white supremacy, as he joined the crowd in gleeful cheers as Buffalo Bill slaughtered white settlers' racially marked adversaries in front of the grandstand's massive audience.

The staging of naked, hypersexual Indigenous bodies reconciled the apparent contradiction between inclusion and exclusion that Lapidus narrated. As historian Gail Bederman argues in her influential work *Manliness and Civilization*, while we might assume that the Protestant ethic prescribes only restrained bodily comportment, proximity to racially marked others has long allowed white men to forgo such restraints. Bederman shows that *The Winning of the West*, President Theodore Roosevelt's multivolume origin story for the United States, features a heroic, manly white American race that wins a series of violent battles against inferior, "savage" Indians.[16] Deploying racist tropes such as the "Indian rapist" and "Indian pillager" that portray the Indigenous body as wildly unrestrained, Roosevelt allows his white protagonists to temporarily forgo the physical self-control that would ordinarily define their whiteness in order to vanquish their racial adversary. Similarly, during the mass immigration wave that brought Morris Lapidus to the United States, Roosevelt espoused a vigorous pronatalism that staked the future of the nation on white men's virility. Roosevelt argued that abandoning sexual self-discipline was necessary for older-stock white Protestants to outpopulate newer Jewish and Catholic arrivals.[17] Therefore, while Lapidus's account of social inclusion amid sexual transgression might seem confounding when told from the perspective of an eastern European Jewish boy during the xenophobic upsurge of the 1910s, Lapidus's decision to juxtapose himself against naked, tomahawk-swinging "Indians" helps assuage that tension. By foregrounding an Indigenous body imagined to be far less restrained than a near-white Catholic or Jewish immigrant could ever be, Buffalo Bill's Wild West Show allowed Morris Lapidus new leeway to transgress bourgeois standards for bodily comportment while joining—at least tentatively—the body politic of the United States.

As an increasingly stable whiteness delivered new immigrants a widening latitude for bodily indulgence, Morris Lapidus launched a career that took full advantage of that privilege. By the end of the 1910s, he had become an actor in the Greenwich Village underground theater scene, joining the salons of the Bohemian "moderns" who embraced political radicalism, free love, and indulgent, romanticist aesthetics.[18] Lapidus won an architecture scholarship to Columbia University in the mid-1920s, where he intended to acquire the skills necessary for a career as a theater scenic designer.[19] On an early assignment as a student architect, Lapidus traveled to Chicago, where he stayed at the Palmer House, a dazzling, 1,600-room hotel originally built amid Gilded Age decadence in 1875. The Palmer House sparked Lapidus's affinity for what he called "refinement and luxury."[20] After returning from Chicago, Lapidus decorated his Flatbush, Brooklyn, apartment in a bold, Italianate Renaissance style that celebrated the sumptuous aesthetics of Medici-era Florence. Morris Lapidus never became a scene designer, although he did recall doing the makeup for a spur-of-the-moment cabaret on a ship from New York to Buenos Aires with the infamous urban planner Robert Moses just after he finished the Sans Souci in 1950.[21] Instead, he built an architecture career that theatricalized the landscape to satiate the corporeal desires of a wide consumer audience.

Morris Lapidus Designs an "Exotic Fairyland"

When he arrived in Miami Beach to begin his collaboration with Ben Novack in 1949, Lapidus used his fascination with pleasure and opulence to transform the Miami Beach hotel industry. Lapidus explicitly argued that hotel design should resist the Protestant ethic, that it should create a sensuousness that allowed a guest to escape the discipline of work. "What a resort hotel sold," Lapidus argued about the Sans Souci project, "was a feeling of relaxed luxury and a freedom from the everyday humdrum existence that the guests were trying to escape. In short, the merchandise for sale was fun and rest and a good time physically and emotionally."[22] Contrasting the Sans Souci with the "humdrum" of the midcentury workday, Lapidus framed work as something that restrains the body in both physical and emotional terms. A resort hotel, thus, should be work's antithesis, a joyful space of relaxation, freedom, and escape that incites pleasure through guests' interaction with the built environment. The formula was an instant success. With the Sans Souci booked solid, developers recruited Lapidus to design the Algiers in 1951, the Fontainebleau in 1954, the Eden Roc in 1955, and the Americana in 1956, among many other projects.

To encourage the sensations of fun and escape, Lapidus built his hotels around what he called "showcases," which would transform a person from a humdrum subject of the midcentury bureaucracy into the star of their own movie. The most well-known of these showcases was the "Lapidus landing."[23] The west stairway from the lobby of the Fontainebleau down to the valet station on Collins Avenue, for example, was broken in half, interrupted by a wide marble platform that encouraged a guest to stop and pose for passersby as if they were the most famous person in Miami Beach. In addition to installing a Lapidus landing outside the Fontainebleau's dining room and thus requiring every guest to make a grand entrance, Lapidus built "stairways to nowhere" in both the Fontainebleau and the Eden Roc.[24] Ascending from the lobby floor, the stairway had no destination, as there were no bathrooms, no conference facilities, and no guest suites to which it led. Instead, the entire point of the stairway was for guests to ascend, turn around, walk down, and pose for the camera on the Lapidus landing before cinematically alighting into the lobby's bejeweled crowd. Lapidus also used curves as showcases. According to Lapidus, "perfect" spaces are unpleasant. Like the human body that has no straight lines, people naturally meander and flow through landscapes. Curves, Lapidus argued, are "anti-spaces" that always put the viewer at the center of an evolving perspective, making a guest the constant star of their own private showcase.[25]

Over the showcases, Lapidus layered images of the tropics—plants, animals, and dark-skinned people—to accentuate the unrestrained style of his work. The Americana, for example, featured a giant, multistory terrarium with full-sized palm trees and live monkeys that entertained guests at the Carioca Room, the lobby bar built to resemble a sidewalk café on Rio de Janeiro's Copacabana Beach.[26] Similarly, Lapidus designed the Fontainebleau's lobby bar around brilliantly floral tropical carpet and what he described as "African" masks.[27] Far more excessive was the Fontainebleau's coffee shop, which Lapidus designed to evoke "the elegance of old Vienna at the height of the Strauss waltz era with Dresden figurines, rococo arches, gas lit crystal chandeliers, elegance, and old-world luxury."[28] Under each of the Viennese rococo arches, however, was a curvaceous, dark-skinned woman wearing a hat wildly decorated with birds and carrying armfuls of fruit and flowers for the guests she presumably aimed to welcome.[29] With these exorbitant designs, Morris Lapidus built hotels out of the fantasies of an immigrant Jewish boy on Coney Island, deploying vaudevillian theatrics to accentuate the cinematic nature of a walk through the city or a trip to the beach. But in many instances, Lapidus juxtaposed old-stock Protestants and newer Jews and Catholics who frolicked in the joy of food, drink, and dance against images of even-less-restrained, even-more-indulgent dark-skinned bodies. Those colonial images continually reminded guests that despite their physical dalliances, and regardless of their differences in ethnicity and national origin, they all shared the normalizing privilege of American whiteness.

Morris Lapidus was not alone among architects from eastern European Jewish immigrant families who built heavily-adorned, sensuous luxury hotels for white tourists on Miami Beach in the 1950s. In February of 1958, for example, Norman Giller's Carillon opened at Fifty-Seventh and Collins, fifteen blocks north of the Fontainebleau and the Eden Roc. The expansive resort included a widely patronized nightclub that Lou Walters, the father of the famous journalist Barbara Walters, managed during its most successful years. While Giller occasionally chided Lapidus for what he called the garish pastiche of styles that defined his hotels, his aesthetic principle—which he termed "ultra-modern luxury"—was nevertheless quite similar to Lapidus's.[30] At the Diplomat hotel, Giller adopted a bold white, gold, and aqua palette and filled the lobby with brilliant crystal and aluminum chandeliers that he rushed out of Cuba on the eve of the revolution. And like Lapidus, Giller used racialized colonial imagery to sell Miami's desirability to white middle-class tourists. For the Diplomat's restaurant, Giller chose the name "The Calcutta Room," projecting the exotic sultriness of the British imperial encounter with—and domination of—colonial India.[31]

Wholeheartedly embracing unrestrained design, Lapidus's cohort of designers and developers transgressed highbrow aesthetics as they built a beachfront paradise. At developer Ben Novack's behest, for example, Morris Lapidus used the oxymoron "modern French provincial" to describe the style of the Fontainebleau. Novack had once driven by the Chateau de Fontainebleau while on vacation outside Paris. Inspired by its ornamentation, Novack assigned Lapidus the task—theoretically impossible—of mashing up the palace's tenth-century style with the midcentury modernism in vogue a millennium later, a project that Lapidus embraced.[32] Similarly, Lapidus once claimed that when he asked Henry Mufson, the prominent Jewish developer who partnered with Lapidus on the Eden Roc project, whether he favored a baroque design scheme, Mufson responded, "I don't care if its baroque or Brooklyn, just get me plenty of glamor and make sure it screams luxury."[33] Lapidus himself was more than willing to flout highbrow norms. When designing the Eden Roc's ballroom, Lapidus decided that he wanted to decorate the forward wall with twenty-one large knockoffs of European artistic masterpieces, including a Mona Lisa replica. He found a vendor in Paris willing to make the copies at an afford-able price. French authorities, however, curtailed the international traf-fic of reproduced artworks without proper authorization. To get around the restriction, Lapidus recruited a friend who was a pilot for Pan Am to smuggle the copied artworks back from his Paris layovers, as customs officials rarely inspected the luggage of flight crews during this era.[34] The plan worked. Lapidus mounted the fakes in gilded frames, and called the space the Mona Lisa Room.

While they clearly transgressed bourgeois taste standards, the flam-boyant resort hotels of 1950s Miami Beach had a more ambiguous rela-tionship to the wider history of cultural transgression. In one sense, by describing his design as an "exotic fairyland," Morris Lapidus—perhaps unconsciously—referenced the openly queer sensibility of an earlier era of South Florida design. By the mid-1920s, Miami's remote opulence made the city attractive to Protestant elites who were unable or unwilling to align themselves with the strictures of US heteropatriarchy. As historian Julio Capó argues, lavish architecture and bedazzled interior design that referenced the colonial encounter with the tropics were a marker of elite sexual counterculture in Miami. James Deering, who had made a fortune in the agricultural equipment business in Chicago, left the Midwest for Miami in 1916, where he built a lush Italianate palazzo called Vizcaya. Deering hired Paul Chalfin, who identified as gay and lived openly with his male partner in downtown Miami, to create the concept for the man-sion's interior. Vizcaya soon became a destination for other wealthy, unat-tached white men who, as the press frequently observed, were building a bachelor society on Biscayne Bay.[35] Similarly, Cleveland multimillion-aire and Mayflower descendent Alvin Freeman moved to Miami in 1923 and joined Deering and Chalfin's bachelor society. In 1930, Freeman built Casa Casaurina on the south end of Miami Beach, which he outfitted in an ultra-adorned Mediterranean revival style that he described as a "mod-ern adaptation of the Alcázar de Colón." Freeman decorated the mansion with art objects procured on trips to Cuba and Haiti that he thought rep-resented the aesthetic of the colonial Caribbean.[36] Casa Casaurina would later become infamous as Gianni Versace's mansion, symbolizing both the hedonism of 1990s elite gay culture on South Beach and the tragedy of serial killer Andrew Cunanan's obsession with Versace and other wealthy gay men. Therefore, and as Capó argues, while the name "fairyland" did not explicitly refer to gender or sexual transgression, the openly queer, excessively decorated Vizcaya and Casa Casaurina meant that some people would have recognized the term as such by the time Lapidus used it to describe his own, wildly ornamented tropical designs.

Conversely, the new resort hotels tightly constrained white guests' interaction with the racially transgressive dimension of what Lapidus called an "exotic fairyland." Prior to the opening of the Sans Souci, and as a result of nineteenth-century urban planning, sexual indulgence in Miami had often required crossing boundaries of race and class. Like many elite white women of the early Progressive Era, landowner Julia Tuttle was a strict segregationist and temperance advocate, and she wrote covenants into the titles to her properties that banned the possession and sale of alcohol and required that "colored people (be) confined to certain localities."[37] Bars and taverns, thus, were kept out of central Miami and pushed north into Lemon City and Coconut Grove, where poor African Americans and Black Bahamians were forced to live. Because of Tuttle's restrictions, wealthy white Miamians would have to cross the color line to be able to drink, to dance, and to cavort in the evening breeze. According to Julio Capó, white Miamians welcomed—and eroticized—these class- and race-based restrictions, as "a sexual underground flourished in ethnic and racialized spaces just beyond the city limits . . . (to which) white middle- and upper-class Miamians were frequent visitors and craved access."[38] And as historian Chad Heap argues about the practice of "slumming" among moneyed white tourists, policing these spaces only enhanced their appeal, as evading the authorities added to the erotic allure of breaking taboos.[39]

After 1950, however, Miami Beach resort hotels restricted tourists' corporeal indulgences to private space on the white-only side of Jim Crow Miami Beach. The structural gigantism and diverse product offerings of the Fontainebleau, the Eden Roc, the Carillon, and other new properties cordoned tourists into a self-contained world. Inside the buildings were retail concourses where guests could shop for clothes, art, home furnishings, and souvenirs when they took a break from the sunny beach. And for nightlife, every hotel had cafes, restaurants, cocktail lounges, dance clubs, and pool terraces where guests could party without ever leaving the hotel. Business outside the resort hotels thus cratered in the 1950s, including the underground taverns and nightclubs that had signified Miami's allure in previous decades. By the early 1950s, the Latin Quarter, Copa City, the Five O'Clock Club, and Ciro's, all of which had been edgy, coveted places during World War II, had all closed down.[40] Therefore, even as Ben Novack, Henry Mufson, and other eastern European Jewish developers were selling an "exotic fairyland" that teased white consumers with ideas about sexual and racial difference, those consumers would do so in expensive, exclusive bars and hotels where managers and the police strictly enforced Jim Crow segregation. Both Julia Tuttle and Ben Novack's framework for sexual transgression rested on overtly racist population management by the state, corporate interests, and wealthy individuals. But with the Fontainebleau becoming the centerpiece of the Miami Beach imaginary, white pleasure seekers from the Teamsters metropolis would inevitably pursue physical, emotional, spiritual, and sexual pleasure with people of their own race.

As an increasingly stable whiteness allowed Miami's new guests both to benefit from and to be oblivious to the violence of South Florida's segregated society, nonelite, non-Protestant white people jumped at the chance to access luxury that had once been reserved for the wealthy. Millions of eastern and southern European Jews and Catholics began to take advantage of the oceanfront leisure that a union wage and paid vacation benefits provided for the first time. Jimmy Hoffa understood this, and he leveraged Miami Beach as a mechanism to support his wider effort to make the International Brotherhood of Teamsters the largest and most powerful union in the United States. By the time he toasted his inauguration in the Fontainebleau's sumptuous dining room with Josephine Hoffa, Chuckie O'Brien, and Sylvia Pagano, Hoffa had begun to funnel Teamster capital toward a rapid expansion of South Florida's "exotic fairyland."

Teetotaling Jimmy Hoffa's FUNderful Paradise

Jimmy Hoffa's interest in Miami Beach real estate intensified as he began to understand the power of what was, beyond a doubt, the most lucrative economic resource that labor activists had ever won for workers: the defined benefit pension plan. In January 1955, contract negotiators secured for the first time pensions for members of the International Brotherhood of Teamsters.[41] With a red-hot economy and a young, rapidly expanding workforce, Hoffa knew that the union's pension funds would accumulate more money than they paid out, as companies would contribute retirement money for workers in their twenties and thirties who would wait decades to retire and claim that money. Hoffa recognized that he could invest the surplus cash to provide new amenities for union members, including access to the South Florida oceanfront that he and other leaders frequented. Miami Beach had become a primary venue for Teamster business during the years of Dave Beck's presidency. In February 1953, for example, Hoffa flew John Dioguardi to Miami to help the higher-up in

New York's Lucchese family start a Teamsters local, a favor that would help Hoffa expand his sphere of influence among underworld figures and labor activists in the Northeast.[42] But while Hoffa, Dioguardi, and other top officials could afford to do business in hotels such as the Sans Souci and the Fontainebleau, rooms that started at the equivalent of $500 per night were off limits to ordinary truck drivers, produce distributors, laundry workers, and barkeeps. After negotiators won retirement benefits, however, Hoffa began to direct money from the pension funds to finance a second tier of still-luxurious beachfront properties that would deliver pleasures to ordinary union members.

Jimmy Hoffa's interest in the South Florida oceanfront stemmed from what he believed was the most important strategic goal for trade unionists: building worker power through centralized collective bargaining. Activists, Hoffa insisted, should form regional umbrella organizations to negotiate a single contract that would give all workers in each craft the power of speaking with one voice: one contract for truck drivers, one for warehouse workers, one for freight loaders, and so forth. Umbrella organizations within the Teamsters unit did not originate with Jimmy Hoffa. In 1934, a young Dave Beck helped solidify the Washington State Area Wide Agreement, which provided a statewide framework for trucking wages and working conditions.[43] Three years later, Beck founded the Western Conference of Teamsters, which helped coordinate the bargaining agenda in a vast region that spanned from Montana to California. As historian Donald Garnel has argued, these centralized umbrella organizations allowed Beck to redouble the union's commitment to mass organizing in the service and transportation sectors and to consolidate his power within the union by pooling money in an organization over which he had sole control.[44]

Adapting Beck's model to the Midwest, Hoffa helped launch an organizing drive among "over-the-road" truckers, drivers who hauled goods between metropolitan areas and whose worldviews and social networks tended to be less insular than those who worked at businesses in a single city or neighborhood. Hoffa developed this plan in tandem with Farrell Dobbs, the militant Trotskyist Teamster leader who helped orchestrate the 1934 Minneapolis general strike and who founded an umbrella organization for midwestern over-the-road truckers called Central States Drivers Council (CSDC) in 1937.[45] The next year, Teamster higher-ups reallocated some of Hoffa's work hours to assist Dobbs in Minneapolis, where he would recruit over-the-road drivers and lobby Teamster locals to support the CSDC.[46] Dobbs's and Hoffa's plan worked, and by the time Hoffa became negotiating chair for the CSDC in 1940, forty-six Teamster locals in eleven midwestern states had signed on to support centralized bargaining.[47]

Soon after Hoffa began directing negotiations for the CSDC, and amid the economic disruption of World War II, unions in other industries secured the first pension benefits for their members. Although wartime wage controls blocked companies from granting hourly pay hikes, federal regulations said nothing about other methods of contributing to workers' well-being. Recognizing the loophole, union activists in the garment industry settled a 1944 labor dispute by convincing management to set aside capital in a fund earmarked to pay a fixed amount—which they called a "defined benefit"—to retired workers every month. Labor leaders in other industries soon adopted the garment workers' strategy. In 1946, for example, United Mine Workers (UMW) president John L. Lewis settled a nationwide strike by accepting a ten-cents-on-the-dollar contribution to a union-controlled pension fund. The initial benefit would provide $100 per month to every miner with twenty or more years of seniority and who was at least sixty-two years old, which equates today to $1,450 per month.[48] By 1950, seven million US workers enjoyed defined benefit pensions plans.[49]

The string of union victories energized Hoffa, who realized that pensions could supercharge the campaign for centralized bargaining. As Hoffa's power grew within the Teamsters, he and his allies assigned the task of pension bargaining not to small, parochial union locals, but instead to regional umbrella groups such as the CSDC. The move lent new credibility to large-scale bargaining, as the regional groups delivered tangible resources that allowed workers to retire earlier and to be comfortable while doing so.[50] The tangibility of those resources was a direct result of Hoffa's refusal to let Wall Street banks invest workers' retirement in the stock and bond markets, which many large corporations did with employee pensions in the 1950s. As young activists, Hoffa's cohort of union leaders had witnessed the 1933 banking crisis destroy families' businesses and savings and were thus deeply skeptical of both banks and money managers.[51] Hoffa took a particularly pessimistic view of the macroeconomy, insisting that the long boom of the 1950s would end in another market crash.[52] Therefore, he insisted that the regional umbrella organizations invest pension funds in concrete assets that were valuable because of their immediate utility and not because of their long-term speculative potential.

Florida beachfront real estate quickly became the most important of these concrete assets. In January 1955, the Central States Drivers Council became the first Teamster regional organization to successfully negotiate a defined benefit pension plan for workers. The accord required trucking companies to place $1 million per month—the equivalent of $116 million per year in today's money—into a financial account called the Central States Pension Fund (CSPF).[53] Firmly in control of the CSPF's finances and hoping to reap robust returns in a profitable growth industry, Hoffa began to make construction loans to sunbelt hotels, apartment towers, retirement communities, and shopping malls. He believed that oceanfront vacation and retirement infrastructure would be particularly appealing to the Teamster rank-and-file. Out of economic necessity, many Teamsters had dropped out of high school or junior high school to work full-time in jobs that were dangerous, dirty, exhausting, and boring. The new CSPF investments would allow those workers a privilege they had never previously imagined: leaving the cold midwestern winter for a relaxing stay on a brightly colored, lavishly adorned tropical landscape. After making his first Miami Beach investment in late 1957, Hoffa rapidly accelerated the sunbelt strategy. Whereas the average corporate pension fund placed about half of its assets in stocks and bonds and only 3 percent in real estate in the mid-1950s, Hoffa invested 69 percent of the CSPF in real estate during the fund's first five years of existence, 40 percent of which was in Florida. For the 1963 CSPF budget year, a full 60 percent of invested funds would go to hotel projects.[54]

Hoffa's first investment in Miami Beach—the renovation of the Castaways Motel—exemplifies the playful, splashy new built environment that he financed for workers. The Castaways opened on the barrier island's far north end at 163rd Street and Collins Avenue in the early 1950s. Marketers called properties like it "resort motels," as they featured pools in the middle and rooms around the outside and were aimed at budget-oriented but still middle-class tourists who saved money by driving rather than flying to vacation destinations. Resort motels were not opulent like the Fontainebleau. They kept operating costs in check by forgoing doormen and bellboys and used straightforward tag lines such as "luxury without extravagance" that put at ease lower-middle-class guests who may not have felt comfortable around the glitz of properties such as Lapidus's.[55] Amid exponential growth in the Miami Beach hotel industry, and as union contract victories broadened the middle class, local real estate investors saw an opportunity to expand resort motels that had been conceived for an earlier, smaller South Florida tourist economy. By the mid-1950s, Joe Hart, a local developer who had become a friend of Jimmy Hoffa's, was raising funds to enlarge the Castaways.[56] Sensing an opportunity both to increase the CSPF's return on investment and to provide affordable hotel rooms to vacationing Teamsters, Hoffa got in on the deal and disbursed the first installment of a $1.25 million loan from the CSPF to Hart on May 29, 1957.[57]

Dramatic the makeover most certainly was. Hart and Hoffa's project took the architect Charles Foster McKirahan's original design for the Castaways and expanded it to include 540 rooms, five pools, and multiple bars and restaurants.[58] Although McKirahan was from Tulsa, he served in Hawaii, Guam, and Japan during World War II. Perhaps because of his experience in the Pacific, the vast majority of his work included colorful "oriental modern" and "neo-Polynesian" styles.[59] During the renovation, Hart's team exaggerated those references, rebuilding the hotel around the theme of a sunken galleon in the South Pacific, where patrons would party while "stranded" on the motel's ten-acre property. To access the lobby of a venue that billed itself "the most FUNderful resort motel," guests entered through a large, faux-pagoda gate. After passing through a lobby adorned with round turquoise leather couches, a floating staircase, tropical plants, and "Chinese" dragon designs, visitors would proceed to the high-dive-equipped "fairyland pool," and then to the guest rooms in one of eight two-story concourses with steeply angled, coral-colored rooflines. Dinner was served in an expansive, wildly adorned restaurant built to resemble a Shinto temple. For cocktails, patrons could stop at the Ginza Bar, which included hot pink furniture, lush purple carpet, dark wood, and water features. Downstairs was the Wreck Bar, which claimed to be the Cast-aways' "FUNderbar." To make drinkers feel like they were underwater in a shipwreck, guests peered out through portholes below the waterline of the fairyland pool. In an "authentic buccaneer atmosphere," maracas and tambourines were strewn on the tables so visitors could sing and dance in improvised performances as they drank and watched fellow vacationers swim by the portholes. After all the imbibing, guests could rejuvenate at the health club, where they rode stationary bikes, lifted free weights, and got massages from tanned, shirtless men with bulging, oiled muscles.[60]

While it amplified the culture of a union already infamous for indulgence and excess, the FUNderful paradise was—at first glance—a deeply ironic investment for Jimmy Hoffa. By all public accounts, Hoffa was a strict ascetic, a workaholic teetotaler who staunchly avoided most pleasures. In an era when union leaders and business executives marked their power by wearing designer ties and suede shoes and riding in chauffeured Cadillacs, Hoffa drove his own car, hailed his own cabs, and carried his own bags.[61] Hoffa never smoked or drank and was sufficiently critical of alcohol that most of his subordinates refused to drink in his presence. While the Teamsters' building in Washington was built to the opulent specs of Hoffa's predecessor Dave Beck, Hoffa's office was austere. He shared it with his ally Bert Brennan and decorated it only with photos of his children, a mounted game fish, and a Rembrandt print that was a gift from an Ohio Teamsters local.[62]

Hoffa pointedly rejected businessmen's and union leaders' crass participation in public and commercial sexual culture, a culture that was omnipresent in Miami Beach resort hotels. While groping women's bodies, making sexist jokes, and cavorting in strip bars were established norms for white men in positions of power in the 1950s, Hoffa was unwilling to take part in those traditions. He refused to go to nightclubs or to any venue where erotic material was pedaled. According to labor economists Estelle and Ralph James, who shadowed Hoffa for a year in the early 1960s, Hoffa stormed out of a show in New York's Latin Quarter in 1955 with his fourteen-year-old son James, angry that an explicit scene would corrupt his son's morals. When friends threw Hoffa a forty-ninth birthday party at the San Francisco burlesque club Bimbo's in 1962, his wife Josephine sat in front of Hoffa, purposely blocking his view in advance of a racy strip-tease by the famed performer Lili St. Cyr.[63] Hoffa was particularly critical of any employer who, as women's liberationists would later say, objectified women's bodies. "If I had a hotel union," Hoffa told a *Saturday Evening Post* reporter after observing a shift change where the manager required women to promenade for guests in revealing uniforms, "the first thing I would do is stop them from parading people like cattle." The reporter also claimed that Hoffa intervened to stop a Las Vegas nightclub from forcing women hat check workers to wear pushup bras.[64]

Jimmy Hoffa's temperance flummoxed the middle-class press, which struggled to square the Teamsters' often decadent culture with what they called the "prudery" of an "oddly moral man."[65] Hoffa's upbringing, however, makes his asceticism—and his egalitarian ideas about gender—less confounding. In his 1970 autobiography, Hoffa situated the genesis of the labor movement, and his decision to become a union leader, in the plight of working women like his mother. Viola Riddle was a strict, deeply devout member of the Eastern Congregationalist Church of Brazil, Indiana. Although she had been raised middle-class, she faced economic devastation when her young husband Jack Hoffa died in 1920. Lacking access to social safety net protections in the era before the New Deal, Viola Riddle Hoffa scrambled to cobble together informal and service work, running a laundry business out of her home, cooking in a restaurant on Brazil's Main Street, and doing domestic work for wealthy local families while raising seven-year-old Jimmy and his two small siblings.[66] In a chapter titled

"Viola Riddle Hoffa, Breadwinner," Hoffa argues that her "life as a mother has been the personification of the class struggle born of the Industrial Revolution. As a member of the labor movement, I am an extension of that struggle."[67]

As an emerging Teamster leader, Hoffa worked closely with women who, as Hoffa had said of his mother, stood out for their "independence, resourcefulness, and steadfastness."[68] Hoffa's protégé Chuckie O'Brien, for example, recalled standing on the roof of Detroit's Wolverine Hotel one afternoon in 1945, arm-to-arm with Hoffa and waitresses' union president Myra Wolfgang, lobbing eggs at customers who were crossing Wolfgang's members' picket line to have lunch at the White Tower restaurant across the street.[69] Wolfgang spent her life linking trade unionism to the women's movement, practicing what historian Dorothy Sue Cobble calls "labor feminism."[70] And by the end of the 1950s, Hoffa was regularly consulting his longtime associate Sylvia Pagano for financial guidance on many of the union's most lucrative investments, including some in Miami Beach.[71] Thus while the press chided Hoffa's public restraint as either a prudish, anachronistic quirk or a thin, cynical veil over his own moral turpitude, his outspoken rejection of men's public culture, from overt sexism to crass consumption, likely stemmed from Viola Riddle Hoffa, Myra Wolfgang, Sylvia Pagano, and other working women who taught Hoffa what it meant to be a labor activist.

Boozy cocktails, sun-kissed cleavage, and all-night dancing were never Jimmy Hoffa's idea of a good time. I propose, however, that the ascetic Hoffa built an indulgent oceanfront because he believed that ordinary people's comfort and pleasure were necessary foundations of the movement for workplace justice. As Kathi Weeks argues in *The Problem with Work*, to mount a challenge to the Protestant ethic, activists—and rank-and-file workers—must be able to build a rewarding life outside of work. Weeks shows that in *The German Ideology*, Marx and Engels describe the work process not just as one that produces objects and subjects, but as a "matter of creative activity, of doing and making." Marx and Engels called these laboring practices "living sensuous activity" and argued that such sensuous activity gives workers the capacity "not only to make commodities but to remake the world."[72] By framing sensuousness as something that builds new political capacities in workers, Marx and Engels push us to consider that sensuousness is a relevant category to labor activism. While the category of sensuousness elevates the corporeal over other ways of being, it does so by foregrounding physical gratification, including in sexual contexts. I thus take Weeks, Marx, and Engels to mean that to remake the world in such a way that upends work's discipline, workers must engage in living sensuous activity that produces physical gratification—in sexual and other contexts—that is far more pleasurable than work. Therefore, while it is tempting to reduce the Teamsters' Miami Beach investments to an example of the union's transactional embrace of 1950s mass consumption, I instead argue that Hoffa understood that a beautiful landscape of physical pleasure would make workers happy and would inspire them to remake the world on their own terms.

Investing in Pleasure as the Teamsters' Strategy for the South

The organizing power of workers' happiness was one prong of a wider Teamster mobilization strategy centered in Miami Beach. Union leaders understood that for the labor movement to build on the watershed advances made since the 1930s, it would have to continue to grow. Because of the widespread adoption of automation that reduced the demand for labor in the manufacturing sector, growth had become more difficult by the end of the 1950s, and once-unstoppable unions such as the United Automobile Workers had begun to shrink.[73] To arrest that trend, Jimmy Hoffa and other activists saw that they would have to tap the largest source of low-wage, nonunion employees in the United States: workers who lived in the South. The Teamsters had a strategic advantage in this realm, as the over-the-road trucker movement that Farrell Dobbs and Jimmy Hoffa had helped build in the 1930s had given the union a strong presence among transport workers in scores of southern cities where people had rebuffed the labor movement's other advances.[74] For the southern organizing to enjoy wider success, however, Hoffa would have to lead the Teamsters into the sectors of the southern economy home to millions of Black, Brown, and white marginal workers: small-scale manufacturing, service, and retail, the very industries where activists had built the Teamsters metropolis in the North. Miami was an ideal place to launch this effort, as thousands of Teamsters—many of whom were enthusiastic union supporters who would spread labor's message—vacationed in the region every winter, and thousands more were permanently relocating to Florida as they retired.

Soon after his inauguration as general president, Hoffa and his allies launched new, grassroots union projects across the South, efforts that were focused in South Florida. At a February 1958 Teamsters' Executive Board meeting that took place amid the grand reopening ceremony at the Castaways Motel, Hoffa ordered the members of all 891 Teamster locals in the United States to boycott the products of the Florida Citrus

Canners corporation. Citrus processing was among the most physically draining, low-wage work in Florida, and 850 Teamsters had walked out on strike on January 17 to demand basic union protections: seniority-based pay and promotions, an 8.5-cent hourly raise, and two paid holidays each year.[75] While they worked to settle the cannery strike, Teamster activists launched a campaign to organize all municipal employees in the Miami metropolitan area,[76] pushing the union into a public sector that, in conjunction with increasingly militant civil rights and feminist movements, would soon become the most important growth area for the labor movement in the 1960s and 1970s.[77] Hoffa also announced a new foray into the airline industry, mobilizing stock clerks at Pan American and flight engineers at Eastern, carriers that both had large operations at Miami International Airport. These and other organizing efforts led to growing Teamster membership rolls in South Florida.[78] While the union had a meager 350 Miami-based members in 1956, for example, that number had grown to 5,000 by the middle of 1959.[79]

The resort hotels of Miami Beach provided an operational base for Hoffa's southern organizing campaign. Various Teamster entities, from political action committees to regional umbrella organizations to the Executive Board, would hold multiple conferences on the oceanfront each year. Leaders would invite and pay for thousands of rank-and-file activists— liquor delivery drivers from Tacoma, warehouse workers from Kansas City, waste haulers from Dayton, city truckers from Nashville—to fly down to Miami, where they would design campaign strategy and build bonds of friendship and solidarity as the waves crashed on the shore. Hoffa would use the cinematic backdrop of ordinary workers cavorting on a landscape built for movie stars to project the union's success and to publicize the latest organizing project in the South and beyond. During an Executive Board meeting at Morris Lapidus's splashy Eden Roc Hotel in February 1959, for example, Hoffa announced a vast new commitment to organizing seventy thousand sales clerks at Sears Roebuck stores.[80] The following summer, Hoffa held a news conference at the Castaways Motel during a national meeting of DRIVE, the Teamster political action committee that called itself the Democratic Republican Independent Voter Education project. In front of the microphones and with the Fairyland pool and the Wreck Bar in the background, Hoffa announced that while the Teamsters had focused on grassroots union organizing in South Florida, they would now enter the political realm, endorsing candidates for public office based on their support for trade union causes.[81] In February 1961 Hoffa was back at the Eden Roc, delivering news of a three-million-dollar Teamster investment in the Miami North General Hospital, which would serve the growing number of vacationers and retirees on the barrier islands' more affordable north end.[82] And perhaps most joyous was Hoffa's re-election in July 1961, during which Hoffa's wife Josephine led a conga-line of pro-Hoffa rank-and-file activists who danced their way from the glitzy Deauville where the Hoffas were staying to Norman Giller's award-winning and bedazzled Carillon Hotel.[83]

Despite the vast resources of the Teamsters union that by the end of the 1950s, had 1.6 million members, organizing in Florida was slower going than it was in Michigan or Ohio or Pennsylvania. To propel the new campaigns, Hoffa continued to invest in pleasure in an effort to build public support for the union. During a sunny Christmas week luncheon at the Orlando Country Club in 1960, Hoffa announced that the Teamsters would spend $40 million per year in real estate in the US South as part of the campaign to expand the union.[84] Most of those deals were in Florida; for example, $3.3 million went to the renovation of the Everglades Hotel in 1958. Although moneyed tourists had coveted the downtown Miami property when it opened in 1925, it had fallen on hard times after decades of underinvestment.[85] The Teamsters funded a transformation of the hotel that included a giant, terraced pool deck built to resemble a steamship that was ringed with the flags of the world and with cabanas in all the colors of the rainbow.[86] On top of the hotel was another pool that borrowed a page from the Castaways' playbook. When patrons finished their swim, they could descend a half-flight of stairs and pull up a stool to the bar, where they would enjoy snacks and cocktails while fellow guests swam by the bar's windows, which were set just below the pool's waterline.

Among other Teamster investments was the Montmartre Hotel, six blocks south of the Fontainebleau at Forty-Seventh and Collins Avenue on Miami Beach.[87] "If you dream of Paris, and like the sun, fun, and frolic, then you'll love the Montmartre!" promised a postcard that touted the hotel's 1959 opening. Mashing up images of Salvador Dali and Pablo Picasso's transgressive Paris neighborhood with Scandinavian modern furniture, cherub lamps, and minimalist, aluminum chandeliers, the Montmartre echoed the pastiche of Morris Lapidus's flagship resorts but was available at a far lower price. Rooms averaged $18 per night—or the equivalent of $160 today—during its early years after its Teamsters-funded renovation.[88] The Montmartre was the work of the architect Melvin Grossman, who worked regularly on building projects for Hoffa, including the Centurion Tower at Caesar's Palace in Las Vegas that the Central States Pension Fund financed in 1966.[89]

The Teamsters also invested in vacation homes and retirement apartments at multiple price points. Three million dollars, for example, went to Morris Lapidus's Crystal House in 1961, a luxury apartment tower complex six blocks north of the Fontainebleau on Miami Beach. Lapidus accommodated the developer's appreciation of Mies van der Rohe's sleek, minimalist modernism by incorporating more straight lines than in his other projects. Nevertheless, he found a way to work in rococo arches over the carport, loud, contrasting marble patterns on the walls, and Da Vinci knockoff statuary for the lobby.[90] Hoffa funded two middle-of-the-market projects in 1958, allocating $2.17 million to the Blair House apartments on Bay Harbor Island just west of Miami Beach, and $1 million to the Belle Towers on the causeway between South Beach and downtown Miami.[91] On the low end were retirement homes for low-income seniors. In February 1960, Hoffa signed off on a $1 million pension fund loan to the Catholic Diocese of South Florida, money the bishop would use to complete beachfront apartments for ailing parishioners.[92]

While Miami Beach real estate was far more central to the Teamsters' financial and political strategy than it was for most unions, other labor leaders also invested in the Florida oceanfront to build a pleasurable respite for their members outside the workplace. Particularly ambitious was the President Madison Hotel, an American renaissance-style, three-story, 205-room hotel that had been built on central Miami Beach in 1939. In July 1960, Four Freedoms Hotels bought the President Madison. A joint venture between the United Automobile Workers, the American Radio Association, the National Maritime Union, and several other unions, Four Freedoms planned to buy properties across the Sun Belt and operate them as not-for-profit housing for retired workers. Although Four Freedoms pitched the President Madison to an older, more frugal crowd, they nevertheless used design idioms that echoed the opulence of Morris Lapidus during the hotel's redevelopment.[93] Guests lay in aqua blue lounge chairs on a wide, sweeping, two-story oceanfront promenade, where they could either face west and watch guests swim in a pool lined with palm trees and lemon-yellow umbrellas, or they could turn around and face east to see the mesmerizing surf crash on the sandy beach.[94] Four Freedoms Hotels ran the poolside bar and the sundry shop in the lobby on a not-for-profit basis to help retirees stretch their monthly union pension payments. Residents paid $125 per month—the equivalent of $1,090 today—for an apartment with an ocean view. While prices were a fraction of those at the President Madison's towering, opulent neighbors, Four Freedoms Hotels purposely charged nearly twice as much as Miami Beach's dingy, low-end senior housing complexes. They did so on purpose, aiming to demonstrate "how much better off a retired union man is than a non-union man. . . . He can afford to pay more, and we, as a union project, give him more."[95]

Typical of the President Madison's residents were Dorothy and Morris Sorrin. Both were visibly tan on sunny morning as they returned from the beach to be interviewed by a reporter for the *Miami News*. The couple moved into their oceanfront room in December 1960, just after Morris retired from a forty-three-year career in New York's garment district. Like many other first- and second-generation eastern European Jewish immigrants, Sorrin's job came with membership in the garment workers' union, which made him eligible to live in the President Madison. The Sorrins raved about their new home, with Dorothy calling it "a wonderful place for people who need sun." At the top of their list of praises was the food. Breakfast was leisurely, running from eight to eleven each morning. Lunch was a sandwich spread set out from one to three, and while dinner was cafeteria style from five to seven, each night came with two entrée choices, and the Sorrins never felt rushed through the line. For workers whose childhoods had been marred by food insecurity, the unlimited, all-inclusive meal plan was a pleasure. "You can eat as many sandwiches as you want for lunch," Morris gleefully told the reporter. "You can drink as many cups a tea as you want, and no one watches you!" The Sorrins reported enjoying watching their neighbor, a retired ship's engineer who came to the United States from Glasgow in 1907, work on his oil paintings next to the beach each afternoon, and they raved about the work of Buddy Byrne, the hotel's cabana director, who managed the beach equipment and the shuffleboard games.[96] While the Sorrins and their neighbors undoubtedly bore the scars of traumatic migration, of economic scarcity, and of decades of physical toil, union activists designed the President Madison—and the scores of other hotels that the labor movement financed—to entitle those aging, laboring bodies to pleasures once reserved for a privileged few.

"Uninspired Superschlock": Tanking the Teamsters' Investment in Pleasure

Union-financed projects on the Florida oceanfront were wildly popular, becoming part of the social fabric of Miami Beach and of the labor movement. Rooms at the President Madison, for example, were so coveted that by 1962 the hotel's owners had arranged Federal Housing Administration funding for a new fourteen-story tower where hundreds more retirees could enjoy a respite in the sun.[97] The Castaways sold out most nights with visitors from out of state,[98] and local groups—from the Miami Beach symphony who performed for dinner guests[99] to the Jewish service organization B'nai B'rith[100]—made regular use of the hotel's facilities. But despite patrons' enjoyment of these flamboyant resorts, the Teamsters' new foray into southern organizing faced strong headwinds from its outset. External adversaries and internal contradictions undermined both the economic value and political effectiveness of Jimmy Hoffa's investment in pleasure.

Most vocal among the Teamsters' external opponents was Miami's press. While low union density had blocked the labor movement from mounting an effective challenge to the open shop, Jim Crow status quo that shaped most journalists' work, the national political context of the late 1950s amplified the local media's hostility. The Teamsters made their first Miami Beach real estate investment in mid-1957, which coincided with Jimmy Hoffa's initial appearance in front of the U.S. Senate's McClellan Committee investigation of trade union corruption. As historian David Witwer has argued, the committee's chief counsel, Robert F. Kennedy, worked to restrain the power of the labor movement by turning public opinion against unions, framing Teamster activists as racketeers and thugs, and often alerting the press in advance of salacious, damaging testimony.[101] Miami's two major newspapers—the *Miami Herald* and an evening paper called the *Miami News*—took full advantage of Kennedy's sleuthing, coupling coverage of the McClellan Committee's televised revelations with its own beat reporting to launch broadside attacks against the Teamsters. Sometimes articles repeated the details of the McClellan Committee's findings. The *Miami News*, for example, reran the committee's claim that Hoffa's Detroit associate Henry Lower had swindled union members in a real estate Ponzi scheme near Boynton Beach, a scheme that Lower marketed as "Sun Valley."[102] The paper also repeated on multiple occasions Massachusetts senator and McClellan Committee member John F. Kennedy's infamous assertion that Jimmy Hoffa posed a "grave threat to the United States."[103]

Far more common, however, was a generalized, jaundiced framing of the International Brotherhood of Teamsters as a foreign, illegitimate, and corrupt threat to South Florida's social and economic norms. In January 1959, for example, the *Miami News* ran a breathless headline in towering, bold font that read "Hoffa Moving in on Miami." The article announced that the Teamsters were buying up property in the "town's heart" and questioned the integrity of those purchases.[104] Both major newspapers printed stories describing the Teamsters' southern organizing effort as an "invasion,"[105] with the *Miami News* claiming that "America's sundrenched, paradise-playground has problems: hurricanes, heat, insects, and Teamsters."[106] Neither paper ever referred to Hoffa with his formal title of general president. Instead, they used pejoratives that undermined his legitimacy, calling him in various instances, "a stubby Teamsters mogul,"[107] a "stubby boss,"[108] and a "squat union boss"[109] who ran a "scandal tainted union" full of "hoodlums and racketeers."[110] When recounting a Teamsters' political action committee meeting, the *Miami Herald* claimed without evidence that politicians would "run for cover" from an endorsement from a Teamster "boss" that would be a "kiss of death."[111]

Jimmy Hoffa's bold unscrupulousness delivered some validity to the anti-Teamsters media campaign that one could otherwise dismiss as biased and overwrought. Solid historical evidence shows that since the mid-1940s, and like a host of other union leaders across the service, retail, and light manufacturing sectors, Hoffa had built the Teamsters metropolis in part through alliances with local small business owners. Some of those entrepreneurs were aligned with the Italian and Jewish underworlds, and some engaged in extortion, fraud, money laundering, and other practices that skirted the law. It appears that Hoffa used those same tactics as he expanded Teamster infrastructure in Miami. Hoffa, for example, leveraged the Miami Beach connections of Ben Dranow, a businessman from Minneapolis who sometimes went by Buck Dranow or Joe Gorman or Ben Grossman or Ben Hobbs or Alec Morris.[112] Dranow came into Hoffa's sphere of influence in the mid-1950s, when Teamster activists were trying to augment the union's presence in the retail industry in the Midwest. After a years-long labor dispute at the John W. Thomas Department Store on Eighth Street and Nicollet Avenue in downtown Minneapolis, Hoffa loaned Dranow $1 million from the Central States Pension Fund to purchase the store as part of what may have been a wider plan to bringing Thomas's store clerks into the Teamsters. That effort sometimes used violent tactics, and Dranow fled Minneapolis for a period in 1956 after a close associate dynamited the car and the home of an opposing union activist.[113]

Shortly thereafter, Dranow seems to have temporarily relocated to Miami, where he began to work as a conduit between Hoffa, the Teamster pension funds, and high-profile South Florida building projects such as the construction of the North Miami Beach Hospital and the renovation of the Everglades Hotel. These were legitimate projects, ones that treated patients, hosted union conferences, and welcomed rank-and-file workers seeking oceanfront pleasures, and they provided a healthy return on investment to the CSPF. There is also strong evidence that Hoffa, Dranow, and other operatives took large, fraudulent commissions on pension fund

dollars that did not belong to them.[114] Therefore, while the Miami newspapers were undoubtedly inflammatory—the *Miami Herald* nastily called
Dranow a "tubby five-foot-five two-hundred-pounder with receding gray
hair" in 1962[115]—Hoffa's apparent willingness to self-deal and to flout the
law lent significant credibility to his adversaries' otherwise ruthless campaign against the Teamsters' organizing.

A far more significant barrier to the strategic success of the Teamsters
in South Florida was the deep racial inequity that Miami Beach pleasure
seeking produced. The Teamsters union often spoke in incrementalist
terms about antiracist activism, with a 1964 brochure announcing the
union's commitment to "Civil Rights without the hoopla." But by the late
1950s, Jimmy Hoffa was offering more assertive support for civil rights
struggles, publicly speaking out against segregated AFL locals in the
South, dedicating funds to organizing Black service workers in Memphis
and other big southern cities, and promoting Harold Gibbons—a white
activist who led an aggressive, integrated, antiracist union movement in
conjunction with the local branch of the NAACP in Saint Louis—to be
among his most trusted lieutenants.[116] The culture of the Teamsters' investment in pleasure on Miami Beach, however, undermined those pursuits.
When white rank-and-file Teamsters claimed a space for the "living sensuous activity" that Marx and Engels thought was so important to social
change, they did so in Jim Crow, segregated resorts while juxtaposed
against Black and Brown people who were imagined to be excessively and
irrevocably sensuous. Indeed, as eastern and southern European Jewish
and Catholic workers forwent restraint, they frolicked adjacent to Black
and Brown people whose sensuousness—the penchant to sing, dance, cel-
ebrate, and arouse—was a historical marker of racial inferiority, proof to
white people that Black and Brown people were controlled by the irratio-
nal senses of the body and not by the mind.[117]

This racist juxtaposition was explicit in the marketing materials for
the Castaways Motel, the Teamsters' most successful investment in the
early 1960s. After the Teamster-funded renovation, the Castaways circulated postcards that touted the pleasures of dance at the bar adjacent to
the Fairyland pool. The cards featured four black musicians in flowered,
open-collared shirts and fedoras playing drums, bass, guitar, and maracas. Pale-skinned, sun-kissed white women in flowered bikinis and white
men in tight, high-waisted swim shorts danced in front of the band, flailing
their arms in showy moves that appear to amuse other white onlookers.[118]
The Castaways clearly gave its guests new license to be sensuous—and
indeed sexual—subjects, forgoing the daily grind of work to dance amid

the curves of breasts and buttocks, to peer at swimmers' nether regions as they passed by the portholes downstairs at the Wreck Bar, and to spend the day eating, drinking, swimming, and gazing at the alluring sites. But as the postcards alluded to white people's physical pleasure and sexual self-indulgence, they relegated Black people to the background as entertainers, which reminds the postcard's viewers of the Castaways' investment in Miami Beach's strict, state-mandated white supremacist order. Through the embodied practice of sensuality at the Castaways, white rank-and-file Teamsters resisted the work ethic by, if only temporarily, living in a world without work. Black people, however, were reduced to sensuous servility in the process, singing, playing, dancing, cooking, and cleaning for white people's pleasure and denied workplace protections from the state or from a union.

While Jim Crow culture undermined the strategic and moral value of the Teamsters' Miami Beach projects, the wider cultural transformation that began in the 1960s helped tank the value of its assets. Hotels like the Castaways offered unprecedented pleasures to a cohort that had grown up amid scarcity: people who had been born in the first two decades of the twentieth century, whose families had come to the United States from Sicily, Ukraine, Poland, Hungary, and Russia, and who had suffered through the anti-immigrant fervor of the 1920s and the Great Depression. "The people who came down here to vacation came to this country as poor immigrants," Irma Rosenblatt recalled about Miami Beach after visiting frequently in the 1950s. "They didn't know anything about class. This was class."[119] By 1960, however, three decades of New Deal policy had delivered new privileges to second- and third-generation eastern and southern European immigrants. That privilege—and the changing tastes of younger people from these same immigrant families—would make Miami Beach's gaudiness a far less desirable commodity in the 1960s than it had been during its debut a decade earlier.

This generational cultural schism initiated a downturn in Miami Beach real estate values at the outset of the 1960s. A younger, more highly educated group of critics began to malign Miami Beach as a vestigial remnant of an older immigrant culture that was too vulgar, too garish, and too flamboyant. Despite the initial popularity of the Fontainebleau and the Eden Roc with guests, the northeastern cultural establishment denigrated Morris Lapidus's hotels from the moment they opened. Reviews called his work "rank commercialism," "hearty vulgarity," "boarding house baroque," and "appealing to the great mass of people who don't know the difference between architecture and Coney Island."[120] *Art in America* dismissed the Fontainebleau as "hedonism's vacuum in a materialist culture." After eviscerating Miami Beach as the "final dumping ground for throwaway architecture," *Architectural Forum* shunned Morris Lapidus, never discussing his hotels again. *Progressive Architecture* and *Architectural Record* followed suit, rendering the Fontainebleau and similar properties unspeakable.[121]

Although snide critiques of a Jewish architect's excess were predictable from the northeastern Protestant intellectual elite, younger Jewish thinkers also condemned Lapidus's work. The *New York Times* architectural critic Ada Louise Huxtable, for example, called Lapidus "the high priest of high kitsch" and panned the Fontainebleau as "uninspired superschlock," choosing a Yiddish insult to propel her invective. "I have never felt more joyless than in Miami amidst all that joy," Huxtable complained. "I was depressed in direct ratio of esthetic illiteracy and hokey pretensions to the shoddiness of the execution. I got a terrible case of the Fontainebleaus."[122] A generation Lapidus's junior, Huxtable clearly recognized that in Miami Beach, immigrant Jews and Catholics had claimed a space for unrestrained comportment and bodily self-indulgence. But rather than imagining that sensuousness as part of the wider struggle for workplace justice, as Karl Marx might have, both Huxtable and her Protestant colleagues dismissed it as evidence of the crass materialism of older, poorer, less refined immigrants.

Structural changes exacerbated the critics' scorn in undermining the Miami Beach boom. On October 26, 1958, Pan American World Airways inaugurated jet airline service in the United States, cutting travel time on major routes in half. With jetliners making trips to Europe, California, and the Caribbean far more convenient for wealthy travelers, real estate market forecasts predicated on Miami's unparalleled accessibility for the northeastern elite proved far too optimistic. Declining high-end tourism forced beachfront property managers to drop prices and to sell budget-oriented package deals, which compromised Miami's allure as a glitzy place to gaze at famous people. By the early 1960s, for example, beachfront hotels were pitching self-consciously middlebrow social events to retirees and to midwestern families: staff-led Conga lines, free rhumba lessons, Polaroid cameras for the kids, and beachfront square dances with "authentic Ozark callers."[123] Hotels began to offer the "American plan," which lumped three daily meals into the room charge. Larger restaurant volumes led hotels to skimp on quality to control food costs, which made such properties less desirable to wealthier tourists who had the money to go elsewhere. As a result, Miami Beach was increasingly likely to serve the older, lower-middle-class, second-generation immigrant clientele that both *Architectural Forum* and Ada Louise Huxtable stigmatized in their barbs against Morris Lapidus. By the mid-1960s, the average patron at Miami Beach's second-tier hotels was fifty-eight years old, and 90 percent of customers were Jewish.[124] In an era when a strong labor movement had given millions of Jews and Catholics access to a homogenized American whiteness, Miami Beach came to represent an older, overadorned, ethnically inflected white culture that both elite tastemakers and union members' own middle-class children had come to disdain.

Cultural derision and the cut-throat jet age tourist market sent Miami Beach into a decades-long downward spiral. Miami Beach's hotel of the year contest, which Morris Lapidus won multiple times in the 1950s, came to an abrupt halt after the 1959 high season. A year later, 10 percent of the barrier island's hotels were in bankruptcy as occupancy rates and prices plummeted.[125] By 1965, the Teamsters' Blair House and Executive Apartments were insolvent, which left the Central States Pension Fund on the hook for at least $10 million.[126] The trend only worsened as the years went by, when the downturn spread to Miami Beach's most prestigious properties. Facing personal bankruptcy as demand for rooms at top-tier properties cratered after 1965, Ben Novack sold the Fontainebleau at a fire-sale price to a group of investors in 1977 who covered the bold black, pink, and white ceramic floor with beige carpet and who tore out the Lapidus landing and the "stairway to nowhere" to make room for an escalator to the second floor. By 1983, Novack's personal finances were so dire that he was forced to auction off a warehouse full of decorations from the Fontainebleau, unwillingly parting with personal treasures from the hotel: a photomontage of himself with Ann-Margret in the lobby, a Cuban cigar box he had personally received from Batista, and monogrammed Fontainebleau swizzle sticks and silverware from the 1950s.[127]

The diversity of the Teamsters' giant pension investment portfolio shielded the union from the worst financial fallout of the Miami Beach downturn. And while the union continued to invest in pleasure in the emerging market of Las Vegas in the mid-1960s, Hoffa's dealings in South Florida played a central role in the intensifying legal crisis that he and his allies faced. On August 18, 1964, a Chicago jury convicted Teamsters general president Jimmy Hoffa, Teamsters loan consultant Ben Dranow, building contractor Calvin Kovens, and real estate developer Saul Hyman for fraudulently investing $20 million of worker pension money in real estate in Florida, Louisiana, and Alabama, among other states, and of diverting $1 million for their own use.[128] Though he appealed the ruling, and while another conviction—for jury tampering during a trial in Chattanooga—would wind up sending Hoffa to prison in 1967, the hostile media cacophony and the drain on Hoffa's time undoubtedly hobbled the union's organizing efforts, and Hoffa's plan to build the Teamsters metropolis across the South never came to full fruition. Therefore, while Miami Beach remained popular with many union members despite the searing scorn of a younger middle class, it was clear by the middle of the 1960s that Jimmy Hoffa's investment in pleasure had failed as a long-term organizing strategy.

Conclusion: Miami Beach Freedom Dreams

As white tastemakers soured on Miami Beach's flamboyance, the *Chicago Defender*—one of the premier Black newspapers in the United States—ran a story on the President Madison Hotel in its March 18, 1961, national edition. Readers learned that unions representing two million workers had funded the renovation of the President Madison and of similar hotels, and that the labor movement's long-standing commitment to a safe, affordable, dignified retirement for all workers had come to fruition in the project. They read the names of the union leaders who had conceived the oceanfront retirement concept, and they learned that President Kennedy's "New Frontier" social programs had inspired them.[129] The *Chicago Defender* and its audience were, of course, all too aware that because of the Jim Crow laws, and even though their union dues had helped build the President Madison, Black union members were banned from staying at the hotel and from meandering along its promenade after midnight. But the paper ran the story anyway. While neutral in tone, the piece was subtly jarring, as it described the fruits of the struggle for workplace justice that were categorically denied to most of its readers. For the *Chicago Defender*, Miami Beach was not a tired testament to passé notions of luxury, but an incitement to political action aimed at contesting the stark inequalities that defined the labor market, the union movement, and the popular culture of the mid-twentieth century United States.

Framing Miami Beach in terms of both workplace justice and racist exclusion, the *Chicago Defender* identified the most important lessons from Jimmy Hoffa's investment in pleasure in Miami Beach. The first involves the labor movement as an antiwork political practice. While historians have often—rightfully in many cases—claimed that the Teamsters represented the apex of depoliticized business unionism of the mid-twentieth century, Miami Beach shows that Teamster activists had built a deep-rooted cultural movement in the 1950s. Robust new Teamster contracts allowed rank-and-file union members to work less, shortening the work year with more weeks of paid vacation, and shortening the work life with a pension program that allowed workers to retire earlier. Teamster victories also made life more pleasurable. After the union won pension benefits, companies took care of saving for retirement, which allowed workers to spend more of their paychecks on themselves and their loved ones. And by subsidizing sunny Miami afternoons under palm fronds that blew in the wind, Jimmy Hoffa's Teamsters union incited pleasure, opening a space for living sensuous activity that rejuvenated the body rather than exhausting it. The *Chicago Defender* clearly recognized this and let their Black readership—who had been bitterly exploited with too much work and not enough pleasure—know all about it even if Jim Crow rendered those pleasures off-limits.

In Black workers' knowledge of forbidden pleasures lay the second lesson of Jimmy Hoffa's Miami Beach. Bodily indulgence on Miami Beach in the 1950s reinforced rather than contested second- and third-generation eastern and southern European immigrants' status as middle-class American white people. Most of the truckers from Chicago, bakers from Indianapolis, beer delivery workers from Akron, and laundry drivers from Buffalo had grown up poor, and many could barely afford a vacation at the Castaways Motel even with their union job. But they all crossed Jim Crow's threshold to get there, and once they unpacked their bags they were adjacent to yet superior to Black and Brown bodies on the walls, in the statuary, on the stage, and in the kitchen. Therefore, even if those Teamsters broke sexual boundaries in the fog of too many Mai Tais in the shipwreck of the Castaways, they did so in a place that put them squarely within a newly concrete identity: the middle-class white American tourist. For these Teamsters, a Miami Beach vacation, and the unrestrained comportment and sexual indulgence it may have included, elevated—in W. E. B. DuBois's famous words—whiteness's public and psychological wage. Reaping the wages of whiteness, rank-and-file workers drove back up north to the Teamsters metropolis as more secure members of the white middle-class even as they often disdained bourgeois culture.

At the intersection between these two lessons lay the International Brotherhood of Teamsters' challenge for the 1960s. As white union members claimed a bold, visible space to indulge their desires on Miami Beach, workers of color saw those freedoms and demanded access to them. Seeing Morris Lapidus's splashy oceanfront in *Life* magazine,[130] reading about racially restricted union hotels in the *Chicago Defender*, and witnessing racial hierarchy in the neighborhoods, workplaces, and union locals of the Teamsters metropolis, Black and Brown workers countermobilized, demanding the material benefits that Jewish, Italian, and eastern European workers had won through the Teamsters union. With those demands, union activists of color argued that Black and Brown people would have to transform themselves from objects of desire—in racist paintings and statuary or while singing and dancing for white guests in Morris Lapidus's hotels—into subjects of desire who harnessed the freedom to dream for a world beyond work. Those freedom dreams, and the challenge they presented for Jimmy Hoffa, are the subject of the next chapter of *Teamsters Metropolis*.

CHAPTER FOUR

What Are We Paying Dues For?
Young Workers of Color Confront the Teamsters Metropolis

In 1967, four young, working-class Black women from Portsmouth, Virginia, recorded a song that projected the joyfully insurgent culture of the mid-twentieth-century US city. While their album's liner notes list only first names—Carlise, Loris, Peaches, and Peggy—the group called themselves the Idets. The tune begins with a catchy blues guitar riff over a growling bass. A scratchiness pervades the recording, making it sound more like a live performance in a smoky nightclub than a professional studio cut. When the lead vocal kicks in, harmonizing backup singers follow, revealing the song's Motown influence. "How much is that doggie in the window? The one with the waggily tail?" a young, sultry-sounding voice asks while three other voices wail "Waggily tail! Waggily tail!" Listeners would immediately recognize the lyrics, as the song was a cover of Patti Page's 1952 pop hit "Doggie in the Window."[1] Page's version pointed to women's growing physical and economic mobility in the 1950s, telling a story about a girl who takes a trip to California and buys a dog to keep her sweetheart company in her absence. Yet despite the liberated subject matter, Page's conventionally feminine voice, her smooth white skin, a halo of blond hair, round cheeks, an innocent smile, and the story of a conventional romance place the original recording squarely within the boundary of middle-class white American heterosexuality.

The Idets' "Doggie in the Window" transgressed those boundaries. The song emerged from the cultural underground, from the hardscrabble blocks of the city where Jimmy Hoffa was organizing a Teamsters metropolis. They cut the song in a storefront recording studio in Norfolk called Shiptown Records, which had opened in the heart of the city's historically Black business and cultural district in the early 1950s. Noah Biggs, Shiptown's founder, had originally come to Norfolk during the Great Depression seeking work as a longshoreman. He instead found comrades among Norfolk's "bookies, hustlers, and boardinghouse ramblers," people not unlike those who were building the Teamsters union in the warehouses, taverns, bakeries, and industrial lofts of Norfolk and scores of other cities. The driving force behind Biggs's enterprise was his business and romantic partner Ida Sands, who kept the books, negotiated contracts, managed the copyrights, directed rehearsals, and made her own music. Sands had grown up in Portsmouth with Carlise, Loris, Peaches, and Peggy, and that connection delivered both the band's name and a record deal with Shiptown.[2]

Ida Sands and the Idets produced a bold new song with the cover of "Doggie in the Window." Whereas white heterosexual romance is the backdrop for the Patti Page version, the Idets' truncated lyrics drop the reference to a sweetheart and instead tell a story about young Black women's conspicuous consumption. The vocalist sings to her audience about passing the "doggie" while window shopping, falling in love with its adorable image, deciding afterward to make a purchase, and scouring the want ads to find the dog and cut a deal. With a sensuous singing style and libidinous instrumentation absent in the original version, the song equates Black women's purchasing power with autonomous individualism and personal pleasure. By portraying young Black women as subjects of desire, the Idets reference the style of an older generation of Black blues women, singers whose work the music historian Daphne Duval Harrison has described as "more assertive, sexy, sexually aware, independent, realistic, complex, and alive" than music that had come before it.[3] The song also indexes the aspirations of a younger cohort of Black women, those stemming from the second Great Migration and from the growing list of civil rights movement victories. By 1960, consumerism was becoming a means to express those aspirations. As art historian Kristina Wilson argues, consumption had begun to allow Black people "to show and to fantasize about how Black upper middle-class life was possible," as consumer products and spaces were becoming "vehicles for bodily comfort and confident sociability."[4] Falling in love with the "doggie in the window," affording the purchase price, and singing this story to a dancing crowd in a sexy, Motown-inflected style, Carlise, Loris, Peaches, and Peggy brimmed with the new confidence that Wilson describes.

That confidence would present a challenge to Jimmy Hoffa. Ambitious young Black people like Noah Biggs, Ida Sands, and the Idets symbolized an ever-growing swath of the workforce in the industrial metropolis of the 1950s, which represented a demographic shift from earlier periods in the Teamsters' history. During the union's first rapid expansion in the 1930s, second-generation Catholic and Jewish immigrants from eastern and southern Europe performed most of the marginal work in the service, light manufacturing, and transportation sectors where the Teamsters organized. From that Great Depression generation came the union's 1950s leadership: Dave Beck, Bert Brennan, Harold Gibbons, and Jimmy Hoffa, among others. But after the Johnson-Reed Act curtailed most immigration in 1924, the flow of immigrants from Russia, Hungry, Ukraine, Calabria, and Sicily slowed. In place of the earlier wave came a new cohort of migrants fleeing poverty, hunger, segregation, colonial dispossession, and racist violence: Black people from the Jim Crow South and Black and Brown people from the Caribbean, Mexico, and Central America. As Carlese, Loris, Peaches, and Peggy's singing shows, many of these 1950s arrivals had similar aspirations to the eastern and southern Europeans who had come before them, and they would undoubtedly see the International Brotherhood of Teamsters as a means to satisfy those desires.

The problem for Jimmy Hoffa was that an overtly racist labor market, education system, and federal housing policy would systematically deny these young migrants' dreams. As the previous chapters of this book have shown, eastern and southern European Jewish and Catholic immigrants had used the union to win unprecedented mobility through time and space in the industrial metropolis. They conducted union business in the posh downtown hotels built during the nineteenth century's gilded age. They ate, drank, worked, and organized in the old Irish, Italian, and Jewish neighborhoods where their parents and grandparents first lived when they immigrated in the early decades of the twentieth century. And with the family wage that their unions had begun to provide, they indulged in mass consumption and heterosexual domesticity in brand-new, comfortable, affordable midcentury modern homes in the suburbs. In contrast to that mobility, people of African, Caribbean, and Latin American origin lived tightly constricted lives in the 1950s industrial city. Locked out of the suburbs by the racist lending practices of the Federal Housing Administration and private banks, new arrivals were forced to reside in a few crowded central city neighborhoods where absentee landlords charged exorbitant rents. While many of their white counterparts sent their kids to brand-new suburban campuses, Black and Brown children were forced into segregated schools where sewage overflowed from open air latrines, where rats ran wild through cafeterias, and where teachers gave lessons in freezing cold classrooms without heat or textbooks.[5]

Rather than forge new solidarities to contest employers' and policy-makers' racism, some members of Jimmy Hoffa's cohort began to exploit it. To build the unions that delivered metropolitan mobility, the eastern and southern European immigrant generation had used licit organizing tactics, canvassing workers' homes to sign people up, supporting strikes with food, money, and bodies, and banding together to fight off violence from strikebreakers and the police. But they also used illicit ones and made assault, vandalism, extortion, and embezzlement a regular part of their work in the movement. There is strong historical evidence that by the late 1940s, some of these older activists—and especially ones affiliated with the Jewish and Sicilian underworlds—had turned to a new underhanded tactic. They signed collusive union contracts with eastern and southern European small business owners that forced Black and Brown workers to pay union dues while earning minimum wage, receiving no benefits, and working mandatory overtime without any pay. While racist contracts did not originate with Jimmy Hoffa, and though they persisted in other industries for years after the Teamsters disbanded them,[6] Hoffa harnessed these practices. In New York, Detroit, and other cities, Teamster locals that sold racist, collusive contracts provided Hoffa with money, with political connections, and with muscle, all of which helped him win the union's presidency in 1957.

Instrumental though these resources were for Jimmy Hoffa, they weakened the Teamsters strategically, compromising the union's ability to build a broad-based workers movement after 1960. For the union to continue to grow at the breakneck pace that had made it into the largest and most powerful union of the 1950s, Hoffa would have had to harness the ambitions of the next generation of young working people just like he had leveraged the desires of the eastern and southern European immigrants who had come before them. These young Black and Brown people's hopes—their yearning for pleasure, comfort, and satisfaction that the Idets described in their cover of "Doggie in the Window"—gave rise to a new, openly antiracist movement within the Teamsters, a movement that is the subject of this chapter. But instead of embracing those younger activists' desires, in at least some cases Hoffa's cohort undermined their movement by becoming the accomplices of older, eastern and southern European entrepreneurs who cashed in on northern cities' Jim Crow labor market. Absent solidarity with the new generation, the Teamsters' once-unstoppable expansion withered at the outset of a new decade, which compromised its ability to seize the revolutionary potential of the new social movements of the 1960s.

Illicit Unionism as a Gateway to the Suburban Middle Class

Young Black and Brown workers would first encounter the Teamsters union as it brought stability and order to the undercapitalized, European immigrant family businesses where the migrants found their first jobs upon arriving in the city in the 1950s. As chapter 1 demonstrates, Jimmy Hoffa accomplished this task by circumventing the strictures of US labor law and in some instances by condoning nefarious organizing techniques. The strategy worked, and it brought unprecedented upward mobility to hundreds of thousands of new members of the Teamsters union in the decades after the Great Depression. Most of these workers had grown up on the margin of the industrial metropolis of the 1920s and 1930s, living in cramped apartments without proper plumbing and ventilation, speaking Russian, Yiddish, Italian, or Polish far more often than English, facing xenophobic bigotry from the white Protestant political hierarchy, and joining militant anarchist and socialist movements to fight that xenophobia and elitism. But after the Teamsters' many wins, these same workers forged comfortable new lives in the immediate postwar era, buying plush suburban homes with a private bedroom for every child, proving their fitness for citizenship by embracing mass consumption and speaking fluent English, and adopting the mainstream, culturally conservative politics of the US middle class. Teamster militancy, in other words, helped make eastern and southern European immigrants into ethnically unmarked suburban white people.

Marshall Miller's journey through the industrial metropolis illustrates the personal transformation that union power enabled. Born to an eastern European Jewish immigrant family in Brooklyn in 1912, Miller lived on the road during the Great Depression, working as a grassroots labor organizer in the shipbuilding industry. He landed in Detroit at the outset of World War II, where he took a series of short-term activist gigs. After he moved back to New York in the late 1940s, Miller's social status increased appreciably. He became an organizer for the Upholsterer's International Union, started a labor-management consulting firm, and secured work as an adviser to the New York state government in Albany on labor and industrial conditions. By 1956, Miller and his wife lived with their three children in a spacious home in Lawrence, New York, a quiet community in suburban Long Island.[7]

Labor activism delivered similar upward mobility to Samuel Zakman, Marshall Miller's associate in New York's service-sector labor movement. Like Miller, Zakman had left the central city for the suburbs in the mid-1950s, when he bought a home in Levittown, Long Island. Three blocks from the baseball field at Wisdom Lane Middle School, and a short drive from the shopping malls along Wantagh Parkway, the 1,300-square-foot, 3-bedroom, 2-bathroom Cape Cod bungalow was an archetypical home in the archetypical community of postwar suburbia.[8] The federal government and private capital worked together to provide and to maintain the privileges of middle-class whiteness, heterosexuality, and domesticity for Samuel Zakman and his neighbors. Developer William Levitt strictly regulated the comportment of residents' homes and bodies, mandating a set lawn-mowing schedule each week, outlining the color and composition of the flower gardens, preventing the drying of laundry outdoors on Sundays and holidays, and banning large or loud social gatherings.[9] If a resident purchased a home with a Federal Housing Administration mortgage, as most owners did, the state tacked on more restrictions, banning stables, pig pens, and other land uses that had marked the ethnic and class marginality of residents' elders.[10] Like the FHA had done in previous decades, Levitt racially restricted all of his developments. Although he was a third-generation German Jewish immigrant, Levitt excluded newer, poorer eastern European Jews from Strassmore-at-Manhasset, his first suburban project in the 1940s. And while Samuel Zakman and other Jews were welcome in Levittown by the 1950s, Black people were not. Levitt held sales events in Levittown's restaurants that refused to serve Black patrons, and he waged a long-term, bitter, and ultimately unsuccessful legal campaign to keep Levittown segregated in the late 1950s.[11]

Levittown's leafy homogeneity was a vast departure from the tumultuous world of Samuel Zakman's youth. Born in Russia in 1913, Zakman emigrated to the United States in 1920. Three years later, his father passed away unexpectedly, which left his mother, brother, and sister in financial crisis. Zakman quit school and worked full-time to support his family from the time he was ten years old. At the outset of the Great Depression, when Zakman was a teenager, he began to make leftist and labor activism a central component of his hustle through a vastly unstable metropolitan economy. He helped beauticians and drugstore clerks in his neighborhood unionize, and he joined the Communist Youth League with most of his friends along Wilkins Avenue in the Bronx in 1937. Radicalized by the Communist Party's culture, Zakman joined the Lincoln Brigade in September 1937, leaving New York for Madrid to join other leftists fighting Francisco Franco's fascist regime. Zakman returned to New York in December 1938 and worked a string of odd jobs, fixing machinery for the Tip-Top Bread Company, working the assembly line for Mack Truck, and becoming a full-time activist in 1942 when he took a job organizing for Mickey Finn, a friend from the Communist Party who ran a local chapter of the United Automobile Workers.[12]

Not long after he began working for Finn, and as war raged across his ancestors' home in Europe, Samuel Zakman's politics began to shift rightward. Perhaps because he had felt betrayed by the 1939 Molotov-Ribbentrop nonaggression pact between the Soviet Union and Nazi Germany, perhaps because his increasingly stable middle-class and white identities were no longer congruent with radicalism, or perhaps because of both of these historical trajectories, Zakman broke with the left in 1945. He denounced the Communist Party and quit his job organizing for fellow-traveler Mickey Finn.[13] Like Zakman, Marshall Miller also took a sharp right turn in the mid-1940s, abandoning his work with the left-leaning CIO, and running for State Senate in Michigan under the slogan, "The Only Candidate Openly Fighting the Communists."[14]

Miller and Zakman's stinging, public rebuke of the left would transform their relationship to trade unionism. In Zakman's case, he adopted a new, entrepreneurial approach to organizing. While he still worked for Mickey Finn, Zakman had come to believe that thousands of attendants at the city's gasoline filling stations were ripe for organizing. Instead of recruiting the attendants to join an already-established union like Finn's, Zakman decided to go independent, and he began looking for a union that would issue a "charter"—a piece of paper that authorized the creation of a new local chapter—for an organization that Zakman could run on his own. He planned to fill the new local union with gas station attendants and to live off the revenue that would come from the dues they paid. Sometime in 1950, Zakman went to a meeting at the Hampshire House, a posh, art deco hotel with a view of the nature sanctuary and the pond on the south end of Central Park. Over an indulgent luncheon, a group of labor operatives connected Zakman to John Dioguardi, a higher-up in the Lucchese underworld family who was running an effort to organize New York's thirty thousand taxi drivers. It appears that Dioguardi hoped to skim money off of the dues that the drivers would pay if the campaign was successful, to share that cash with his associates in La Cosa Nostra, and to expand the system of labor profiteering to other industries.[15]

To scale up his operation, Dioguardi sought charters for new locals from relatively inactive unions associated with the American Federation of

Labor: the Allied Industrial Workers, the Retail Clerks, the Jewelry Workers, and a small splinter group of the Auto Workers called the UAW-AFL.[16] Dioguardi planned to hire organizers to sign up workers for the locals and to share the members' dues with the Sicilian underworld. It seems that Samuel Zakman became one of those organizers. In April 1951, the UAW-AFL charted Local 102 in New York City. Zakman was the new union's president and John Dioguardi was its business manager. As part of the agreement that launched Local 102, Dioguardi agreed to cover Zakman's salary until he could recruit enough members to pay his own wage.[17]

Once he assumed Local 102's presidency, Samuel Zakman embraced activist tactics that, while outside the boundaries of middle-class physical comportment, provided middle-class social mobility for himself and for others from Jewish and Italian immigrant families. In July 1952, for example, Zakman and his associate Nicholas Leone walked into the executive office of Mercury Service Systems, a messenger company based in midtown Manhattan. They announced that they intended to organize the firm's employees. Rather than lobbying rank-and-file workers to join the union as labor law required, Zakman and Leone went directly to the firm's proprietor and demanded an $8,000 payment for their services.[18] In exchange for the money, Mercury's owner would receive a union contract that would allow the company to pay its employees minimum wage and that would provide no benefits or grievance process for those on the front lines. Mercury would pay dues to Zakman's local on behalf of the workers, most of who would not even know they were in a union. Because Zakman's union helped companies lock in rock-bottom labor costs, many proprietors embraced Zakman's tactic and paid the fees he demanded. For those who didn't, violence would follow. In December 1952, for example, Zakman and Nicholas Leone called the owners of all eighteen messenger firms in midtown Manhattan into a meeting, where Zakman ordered them to sign contracts with his union and where Leone barked, "Either you sign or I will fracture each one of you individually."[19] Zakman in turn used the money to pay for physical and economic mobility. While he lived in a working-class section of Jamaica, Queens, when he became president of Local 102, the proceeds soon funded his move outward and upward to Levittown.

Samuel Zakman was by no means alone in buying metropolitan mobility through unruly tactics. Sometime in 1954, for example, Max Chester—who also sometimes identified as Immanuel Kessler—appeared at Paul Claude's business and insisted that his employees join a union called Retail Clerks Local 405. Claude lived in a modest neighborhood in Flushing,

Queens, and owned a small machine shop in Green Point, Brooklyn, with fifteen employees. Chester/Kessler ordered Claude to pay $2,000 in cash for a minimum-wage contract for the workers. After Claude refused and demanded that Chester/Kessler leave the property, picketers who were not Claude's employees surrounded the machine shop, shaming Claude for "union busting" in a heavily unionized, prolabor Brooklyn neighborhood. After Chester/Kessler threatened Claude's children, Claude acquiesced to the threats, and eventually paid the retail clerks' union $1,400 for the contract. It is unclear if Claude took advantage of the rock-bottom wages that the contract allowed. While he clearly spent significant time and money fighting off Chester/Kessler's unwanted incursion, Claude nevertheless could have used the contract to lower his labor costs and to fund his own move outward and upward to New York City's suburbs.[20]

Marginal Workers in the Constrained Metropolis

Lucrative though they were for union operatives and second-generation European immigrant entrepreneurs, John Dioguardi and Samuel Zakman's contracts were gravely adverse for those who worked under them. During a decade when the economic gains and membership rolls of the labor movement broke records in the United States, collusive contracts began to lock a new, younger cohort of workers out of the "American standard" of living that many union members had come to expect in the 1950s: a family wage, paid vacation, health insurance, and an old-age pension.[21] Union organizing in the service, retail, and light manufacturing trades had been riddled with racial and gender inequity since those industries boomed at the twentieth century's outset. To further their effort to bring order and stability to undercapitalized sectors of the economy, many service-sector activists mobilized around their identities as men who were light-skinned enough to claim the full privileges of American citizenship. Therefore, while they demanded better pay, shorter hours, and safer working conditions, these unionists also sought to prevent white women and workers of color from joining their ranks.[22] Larger employers exploited working men's racism amid conflict on the job and often hired Black migrants fleeing the Jim Crow South as replacements during strikes and lockouts. Rather than condemning managers' duplicity, service-sector activists regularly blamed trafficked workers themselves, and publicly conflated rising corporate power, racial inclusivity, and the permanent subordination of all "workers,"[23] a word that in this case referred to white men who worked in the service and light manufacturing sectors of the economy.

To some extent, the International Brotherhood of Teamsters diverged from this racist pattern. Teaming work had long been stigmatized, as it kept teamsters away from home for long stretches of time, paid little, and was physically exhausting. Therefore, although the overwhelming majority of teamsters were men, the work delivered few of the material or ideological privileges of American manhood. Because of the wider racism of the US labor market, many Black people joined the trade out of necessity. In 1900, 13 percent of teamsters were Black, and by 1912 one-seventh of the members of the International Brotherhood of Teamsters were Black.[24] As labor historian David Witwer argues, while the Teamsters often chartered segregated locals in the South and rarely advocated for racial equality in explicit terms during the union's early years, "a diverse workforce checked the worst racist predilections of the white Teamster leadership."[25]

The racist past of service-sector unionism became newly contentious in the 1940s and 1950s because of the demographic transformation of the industrial metropolises of the North and East. The dual violences of industrial agriculture and white terrorism drove Black sharecroppers northward out of the Jim Crow South, and as a result, the Black populations of cities expanded rapidly after World War II.[26] While Detroit was 8 percent Black in 1930, that number had nearly quadrupled to 29 percent by 1960.[27] Similarly, while New York City was only 2 percent Black in 1900, it was 15 percent Black in 1960.[28] And as the sugar industry pushed Puerto Rican farmers off their land and into low-wage industrial jobs, many people left for the US mainland in search of a more sustainable livelihood. Nearly half a million Puerto Ricans boarded *la guagua aérea*—the flying bus—to New York City in the 1950s, more than twice the number who migrated in any decade before or since.[29] With the 1924 Johnson-Reed immigration restrictions continuing to deny entry to most poor, rural southern and eastern Europeans, and with racially restricted New Deal housing and labor policies lifting many second- and third-generation eastern and southern European immigrants out of poverty, Black and Brown migrants were filling the dirtiest and most dangerous jobs in the cities of the 1950s. But because of the collusive contract system, and because of service-sector unionism's racist past, the labor movement was in many cases a far less effective tool for these new marginal workers than it had been for the Jewish and Catholic migrants who had come before them.

Bertha Nunez's journey through New York City's labor market in the mid-1950s reveals the daunting consequences of the racist contract system. In 1953, when she was twenty-three years old, Nunez arrived in New York City from Honduras. She approached a labor contractor to find a job, which most migrants from the Caribbean and Central America were forced to do in the 1950s. She paid the contractor $12—the equivalent of $117 today—for a job at an electric appliance factory called Century Product Works, a job she started in March 1955. According to Nunez, most of the 150 workers in the shop were Puerto Rican, and only about 5 percent spoke English. Not long after she began her job, two operatives for a union that John Dioguardi had recently chartered called the Allied Industrial Workers Local 250 walked into Century Product Works's executive office and announced plans to organize rank-and-file workers. They negotiated with the proprietor for a few hours, after which the factory foreman called Nunez and all the employees into a meeting. Nunez recalled that Dioguardi's representatives promised pay and benefit improvements before passing out union cards, ordering everyone to sign, and indicating that anyone who refused to sign would be fired on the spot. The contract did deliver a $2 raise to $38 per week, but the raise was meaningless given that all workers were about to be bumped to $40 because of an increase in the federal minimum wage. Although the government and not the union would mandate that raise, Nunez and her colleagues were required to pay the $20 union initiation fee and the monthly dues of $4. Despite asking to see it, Nunez never saw a copy of the contract, and she never received any of the health benefits that her white neighbors were winning through their union activism.[30]

Rather than an anomaly or the work of a few rogue actors, Bertha Nunez's wages and working conditions reflected a remarkably consistent pattern of racist inequality in the metropolitan labor economy. Like Nunez, Mario Montalvo also worked in a factory with a collusive union contract. Montalvo's employer, a ball-point pen manufacturer on Broadway in Manhattan called the Miro Pen Company, employed 160 people, 55 percent of whom according to Montalvo were Black, and 45 percent of whom were Puerto Rican. One afternoon in the mid-1950s, James Iscola, an organizer for the same union that Bertha Nunez was forced to join, arrived at Miro Pen for a meeting with the owner. Shortly thereafter, he walked out on the shop floor and forced every rank-and-file worker to sign a union card and to pay the union's initiation fee. Other than three paid holidays, Montalvo's coworkers received no benefits, made minimum wage, and never saw the contract they presumably worked under.[31]

For every Bertha Nunez or Mario Montalvo, there were thousands more concurring accounts. Carmen Rosas and Mary Aviles, two young Puerto Rican women, commuted from their homes in the South Bronx to the Pearl Curtain Company in midtown Manhattan. To secure their jobs, they were required to join a union under the leadership of Marshall Miller, the labor consultant and anticommunist political entrepreneur from Long Island described above. A contract with Miller's union allowed Pearl Curtain to pay the federal minimum wage while extending no employment benefits. But whereas the minimum wage was $40 for a forty-hour week, Pearl Curtain mandated that Rosas, Aviles, and all their colleagues work fifty-seven hours per week, a clear violation of overtime laws and the minimum wage.[32] Similar standards were enforced on the members of Stanley Seglin's union, which signed collusive deals with laundromat owners in Brooklyn. Like Rosas and Aviles, the laundromat attendants earned $40 for fifty-seven hours on the job each week.[33] Jerome Fine imposed the exact same standards on the twenty-five Black and Puerto Rican workers at Seal Tight Quilting Company, a small shop that he owned on Manhattan Avenue in Brooklyn.[34]

Harsh working conditions accompanied the sweatshop wages. While the massive postwar factories that dotted the fringe of the metropolitan area hired tens of thousands of workers, the collusive contract system centered on small industrial lofts[35] and service businesses in the central city, most of which employed fewer than two hundred people. Whereas large corporations ran the suburban factories, most downtown shops were owned by a single proprietor or family, two-thirds of whom were eastern European Jews in New York in the 1950s.[36] For example, the Pearl Curtain Company's factory occupied an upper floor of a seventeen-story building on West Thirty-Sixth Street in Manhattan's garment district. The famed architects George and Edward Blum (see chapter 2) designed the ornate, Gothic-Deco skyscraper in 1926,[37] and Pearl Curtain rented its loft space twelve years later in 1938. Dozens of small businesses leased similar industrial lofts that month alone, with U-Glow Fabrics making sportswear, Valentine and Company making varnish, Hollywood, Inc. making linens, and Brilliant Fabrics making bulk textiles, among many others.[38] Progressive-era reforms that came in the wake of the 1911 Triangle Shirtwaist fire required newer industrial lofts like Pearl Curtain's to be far safer than their nineteenth-century counterparts, mandating basic fire suppression and banning the most egregiously risky practices such as locking emergency exits from the outside. Nevertheless, the work remained exhausting and dangerous. Carmen Rosas, Mary Aviles, and other workers were expected to arrive for their shift with partially completed products that they had begun to manufacture at home, work that they often performed without pay during the night after tending to family responsibilities.[39] While winter temperatures often dipped below freezing, and though the temperature soared to one hundred degrees Fahrenheit on some July afternoons, managers rarely paid for heating, air conditioning, or electric fans to ventilate industrial lofts, which made work shifts far more physically taxing.

Grim working conditions—and the racist union contracts that enabled them—were by no means limited to New York City in the 1950s. Dubious deals between unions and proprietors were common in marginal workplaces in other industrial cities. For example, Gus Richardson lived in a single room with his wife and three children at the Century Hotel on Vernor Avenue in Detroit. Like scores of other Black workers in the motor city, Richardson washed cars for a living.[40] Richardson started a job at Tony's Five Minute Auto Wash in 1953 that paid $30 per week. In the spring of 1955, two representatives from Teamsters Local 985 walked into the car wash and told the employees to join the union. Richardson and his peers knew that Bill Bufalino, a close associate of Detroit's Meli family, controlled Local 985 and was skimming dues money for himself and for the Sicilian underworld.[41] Recognizing the union as an adversary and not as an ally, Richardson's colleagues rebuffed Bufalino's operatives. The following day, three carloads of picketers—none of whom worked at Tony's Five Minute Auto Wash—arrived on the premises. Richardson was furious and confronted the pickets as they tried to block cars from entering. "I am looking right at you, and I see you," Richardson shouted at one of the operatives. "You walk on that sidewalk and leave those cars alone!" Richardson recounted that the man "told me that I was one of those things—a curse word," perhaps calling Richardson a scab or perhaps hurling a racial slur. Despite their protests, Richardson and his coworkers were forced into the union, after which their wage decreased $5 per week to $25.[42] Since the racist standard of a segregated labor market set the workweek at seventy hours for Black car wash workers regardless of union status—a flagrant violation of purportedly progressive midcentury labor laws—Richardson took home a mere thirty-five cents an hour before taxes. While being a card-carrying, dues-paying member of the International Brotherhood of Teamsters, Richardson earned less than half of the federal minimum wage and made less with six years of seniority than he did on his first day on the job. While Local 985 provided vast economic mobility for the Italians who employed him and who ran his union, it trapped Gus Richardson's family in poverty.

As Bertha Nunez, Mario Montalvo, Gus Richardson, and scores of other rank-and-file workers were forced into collusive contracts, experts in the academic, media, and policymaking apparatuses gave cover to the shop owners and union operatives who exploited them. Black and Brown migrants to the industrial metropolis were disproportionately poor, the experts insisted, not because of an economic problem, but because of a cultural—and sexual—one. Sex had long carried disproportionate weight in explaining Black and Brown marginal workers' poverty. In Puerto Ricans' case, after sugar companies turned the island into a monocrop economy in the first decades of the twentieth century, many subsistence farmers were pushed into low-wage sweatshop work in the textile industry. But according to Carmen Teresa Whalen and other historians, rather than recommending land reform or protecting the right to organize, the experts on the US mainland who made policy for Puerto Rico claimed that the islands were "overpopulated." To solve the problem of what they imagined to be an overly sexual population that procreated prodigiously, policymakers designed a system of contract labor emigration, which uprooted Puerto Ricans from their island lives and sent them to the mainland to stave off overpopulation.[43]

Once Puerto Rican migrants arrived on the mainland and joined their Black neighbors in sweatshop and service labor, experts used similar sexual arguments to explain their poverty. Black and Brown workers were poor, the professors, reporters, senators, and representatives argued, not because of a problem with work that stemmed from collusive contracts or managerial exploitation or industrial agriculture, but because of a problem with migrants' work ethic. Rather than embrace personal responsibility, economic independence, and hard work, the experts argued, Black and Brown people decadently indulged their bodies' physical desires and chose welfare over work to make ends meet. In part because of the collusive contract system, Black and Brown workers were indeed more likely to access welfare benefits than white workers in the 1950s. Labor activists estimated that about 35,000 of New York City's 125,000 Spanish-speaking employees worked under collusive contracts in the mid-1950s and that up to 90 percent of unionized Black and Puerto Rican employees worked under the sham deals.[44] Thus half of Puerto Ricans, and a similarly large subset of Black workers, used food and housing aid to supplement their incomes. But as historian Laura Briggs has argued, in both popular cultural representations such as *West Side Story*, and in social scientists' peer-reviewed work, welfare "dependency" was imagined to be the consequence of Puerto Rican hypersexuality, the marker of a moral and physiological problem in which overly fertile, sexually insatiable migrants from the island made physical pleasure—rather than the discipline of work—the center of their lives on the mainland. And as is evident in New York senator Daniel Patrick Moynihan's infamous 1965 report that insulted Black families as matriarchal "tangles of pathology," influential policymakers imagined welfare use as both proof of and the cause of Black women's immoral refusal of the ethics that are the bedrock of American culture: independence, deferred gratification, monogamy, and domesticity.[45]

With sexualized racism defining the middle-class public debate about migrants from the Caribbean and the Jim Crow South, Jewish and Italian shop owners avoided public scrutiny as they exploited the new arrivals to the metropolis. Prior to World War II, and as ethnic studies scholar Eithne Luibhéid has shown, families such as John Dioguardi's and Samuel Zakman's had been subjected to sexualized xenophobia that relied on tropes similar to the anti-Black and anti–Puerto Rican discourses of the 1950s. They bore insults about Jewish men's bookish effeminacy, about Irish women's overprocreation, and about Italian men's unscrupulous sexual ambitions.[46] But after union contracts and federal labor and housing policy delivered a family wage and suburban domesticity to Dioguardi and Zakman's generation, they were shielded from those cultural attacks. With new anti-Black and anti–Puerto Rican sexual scorn heaped on the workers they took advantage of, Dioguardi, Zakman, and dozens of other operatives found wide new leeway to expand the collusive contract system without—at least for a time—significant pushback from law enforcement, from public officials, or from the wider labor movement.

Jimmy Hoffa's "Paper Locals":
Building the Teamsters Metropolis with Racist Contracts

While John Dioguardi, Samuel Zakman, Marshall Miller, and dozens of other union officials capitalized on the racist contracts they sold to small shop owners, Jimmy Hoffa took an ever-greater interest in the central city neighborhoods where they were operating. The ever-ambitious Hoffa was frustrated, believing that despite unprecedented success at recruiting new members, the Teamsters' disparate bargaining strategy was failing to deliver the material improvements that should have accompanied the union's growth. For Hoffa, this was especially evident in New York City's trucking industry, where the workforce was overwhelmingly Irish and Italian. Teamster contracts had made truck driving relatively high-wage work by the mid-1950s, with truckers on long-distance routes averaging $100 per week, the equivalent of an annual salary today of $51,000.[47] Nevertheless, Hoffa insisted that scattershot negotiations were diluting truckers' economic power. The region's drivers were broken into twelve different locals, each of which administered multiple contracts with different pay rates.[48] If one local scored a contractual advance, trucking companies would close down terminals in the neighborhoods that the improved contract covered and reopen in different locations where wages were lower, which diminished negotiators' leverage and attenuated drivers' job security. Hoffa contended that to stop companies from taking advantage of disparate contracts, all the locals in the metropolitan area should band together and bargain for the same pay and benefits for every trucker regardless of the neighborhood where their employer was based.[49]

Particularly informative of Jimmy Hoffa's commitment to centralized collective bargaining was the headline-making New York City trucking strike of 1954. On October 16, all twenty-four thousand Teamster truck drivers in the region walked off the job. Parking their trucks and hoisting their picket signs, truckers left grocery stores without food, department stores without merchandise, hotels without linens, bars without beer, and factories without raw materials. From a distance, the strike was an extraordinary demonstration of the union's power. A mere twenty-four hours after the walkout began, and after Teamster president Dave Beck threatened to expand the shutdown to the Midwest and the Southeast if trucking companies failed to continue negotiating in New York, management began to capitulate.[50] New York's three largest grocery chains, for example, agreed to meet all the Teamsters' demands if truckers resumed food deliveries.[51] Four days later, the remaining employers succumbed to strikers' pressure, and all drivers returned to work on the union's terms.[52]

Below the surface of the short, effective strike, however, was a deep chasm between the activists that led the movement. Afraid of the disruption that a citywide trucking strike would cause, Mayor Wagner called Teamster leaders and trucking management representatives into mediation, compelling them to hash out an agreement that would prevent a strike. Although they were unsuccessful in averting the walkout, they drafted a plan that most of the participants believed would stabilize the industry over the longer term. While trucking companies would provide a twenty-five-cent-per-hour pay hike for all truckers in the metropolitan area, they agreed to give an extra bump to lower-paid drivers in Westchester County and in northern New Jersey. Pay parity, most committee members hoped, would discourage trucking companies from relocating terminals in search of lower wages, a phenomenon that had inflamed drivers' anger and caused strikes in the past. As Mayor Wagner's mediation panel moved toward compromise, Jimmy Hoffa—who was a vocal participant in the talks and a strong proponent of the agreement—prepared to achieve the wage standardization he insisted was crucial to the union's success.[53]

Shortly before the group inked the deal, however, Thomas Hickey balked. Hickey was the chairperson of the union's delegation to Mayor Wagner's mediation and had driven trucks since he was a teenage boy in 1919. As he rose through the ranks of the Teamsters, Hickey remained fiercely loyal to the front-line truckers from his Flatbush, Brooklyn, neighborhood whom he had worked with for decades.[54] Neighborhood-based union activism had delivered unprecedented social and economic mobility to Hickey's generation of mostly Irish truckers, which made him wary of a new system where workers would bargain at the metropolitan—rather than the local—scale. In particular, Hickey was adamantly opposed to a settlement that would deliver extra pay to faraway drivers from the suburbs while denying a similar bump to his Irish comrades from Brooklyn. Hickey thus stonewalled, threatening to derail the entire process to stop the wage parity proposal.[55]

Jimmy Hoffa was furious, irate that Hickey would favor his own local agenda over a compromise that would make bargaining simpler and more effective for all truckers in New York. To thwart Hickey's intransigence, Hoffa led an effort that ousted Hickey from his position as chair of the union's negotiating committee and replaced him with Hoffa loyalist John O'Rourke. Despite Hoffa's intervention, talks collapsed after Hickey convinced allies who remained at the table to abandon the mediation. Though the strike was an undeniable success, and while trucking companies paid the full twenty-five-cent raise despite the failure of the mediation, Hickey's departure scuttled Hoffa's metropolitan wage standardization plan.[56] From that defeat, Jimmy Hoffa learned a clear lesson. To achieve his goals, he would need to build a network of associates who were committed to neutralizing what Hoffa saw as the self-interested, neighborhood-based provincialism of leaders like Thomas Hickey.

John Dioguardi would soon become particularly important among those associates. Although racist contracts were a core of Dioguardi's labor dealings in the mid-1950s, he was also involved in legitimate organizing and had invested $200,000 in a campaign to help New York's cab drivers unionize. Jimmy Hoffa undoubtedly knew about Dioguardi's connection to the Lucchese underworld operation and of the violent tactics he used to establish himself as a labor operative in New York's garment industry in the 1930s. Regardless of that infamy, Hoffa thought that Dioguardi was a skilled organizer, and he was impressed with the progress Dioguardi had made on the taxi industry campaign.[57] Hoffa believed, however, that cabbies belonged in the Teamsters and not in Dioguardi's unions, and he thus made an overture to Dioguardi. He would bring Dioguardi into the Teamsters, supercharging Dioguardi's organizing with the money and muscle of a much larger labor organization. To do so, Hoffa would persuade Teamster president Dave Beck to issue charters that would turn the unions Dioguardi controlled—such as Samuel Zakman's UAW-AFL Local 102—into Teamsters locals. As was typical when Hoffa wanted to demonstrate respect and admiration for another organizer, Hoffa flew Dioguardi down to Miami Beach for a working vacation at an oceanside resort in February 1953, where he introduced Dioguardi to Dave Beck and laid out his plan to acquire Dioguardi's operation. Beck, however, rebuffed Hoffa, worried that Dioguardi's widely publicized underworld ties would subject the Teamsters to the federal government's intensifying antiracketeering dragnet.[58]

After the collapse of his wage stabilization plan during the 1954 truckers strike, Hoffa circled back to John Dioguardi. Hoffa had come to believe that to implement standardized collective bargaining in New York and other metropolitan areas, he needed to take control of the Teamsters' regional governing bodies. According to the union's organizational structure, these bodies—each of which is called a "joint council"—coordinate the strategy of all the locals in each major city, setting bargaining goals, linking organizing campaigns, and building alliances with other unions. Much to Hoffa's chagrin, however, New York's joint council was under the control of Martin Lacey, another older, Irish American Teamster who favored decentralized control grounded in neighborhood-scale relationships. To prevent Lacey's parochialism from continuing to set the bargaining agenda in New York, Hoffa hoped to oust Lacey from the joint council's leadership when he was up for re-election and to replace him with John O'Rourke, who had been Hoffa's ally on Mayor Wagner's panel.[59] The problem for Hoffa was that both Lacey and O'Rourke were widely popular with rank-and-file Teamsters. Since every local would cast an equally weighted vote in the election, O'Rourke would need to garner the support of the majority of the locals in the New York metropolitan area. By Hoffa's own estimate, however, O'Rourke was slightly behind Lacey in that contest.

To tilt the electoral odds in O'Rourke's favor, Hoffa resurrected the plan he had first pitched to Teamster president Dave Beck in Miami Beach. He urged Beck to issue charters that would bring John Dioguardi's seven union locals into the Teamsters. Since all seven of the locals would be based in the New York metropolitan area, they would each receive a vote in the upcoming joint council election. If John Dioguardi gave all his votes to O'Rourke—which he presumably would given his close relationship to Hoffa—he could flip a narrow Lacey victory into a narrow O'Rourke victory. Martin Lacey and his allies were enraged at Hoffa's intervention, insisting that since Dioguardi had recruited many of his members through nefarious tactics, his "unions" were nothing more than lists of names on paper. These sham organizations, which some activists called "paper locals," were not unique to the Teamsters. Sicilian underworld operatives had, for example, used paper locals to take control of the union for New York's dock workers in the 1940s.[60] Despite activists' long-standing efforts to ban paper locals, it seems that Hoffa prevailed on Dave Beck and other prominent Teamster leaders that the Dioguardi deal was necessary to bring centralized bargaining to New York. On November 8, 1955, and unbeknownst to the existing leadership of New York's joint council, Dave Beck issued charters for all seven locals, which formally incorporated John Dioguardi into the Teamster hierarchy.[61] On February 14, 1956, with the support of the Dioguardi locals and despite what Martin Lacey called a "big hullabaloo" from activists opposed to Hoffa's intervention, John O'Rourke defeated Martin Lacey to become the new president of New York's joint council.[62]

Jimmy Hoffa's instrumental relationship with John Dioguardi exemplifies the Teamsters' wider approach to the issue of race in the 1950s, an approach that was transactional, opaque, and immensely disparate. Rigorous historical research on the topic remains elusive, both because the Teamster leadership rarely spoke explicitly about race until the 1960s, and because the Black-white racial binary has shaped most academic work on race in the Teamsters, which underrepresents the thousands of Asian American cannery workers in California and Mexican American truckers in Texas who had joined the union in the 1950s.[63] Perhaps most important about the available relevant information is that in both the trucking industry and in warehousing, light manufacturing, services, and retail, most Teamsters worked for small businesses, almost all of which were white-owned. Most of these firms were too small and too undercapitalized to hire trained personnel managers and instead relied on family members to perform administrative functions. They rarely developed written hiring standards or posted job advertisements and instead relied on kinship and social ties to recruit new workers, practices which overwhelmingly excluded Black and Brown applicants.[64] Adding to the racial barriers were the insular, defensive, local ethnic networks that controlled employers and Teamsters locals in many metropolitan areas and that made hiring off-limits to Black and Brown migrants to the city: the Irish in Boston and Brooklyn, Italians in northern New Jersey, and Poles in Chicago, among others.[65] And while Teamster organizers recruited tens of thousands of workers of color from low-wage, sweatshop work, white rank-and-file truckers fiercely defended coveted, lucrative, long-haul driver positions and threw out Teamster leaders who supported efforts to desegregate the trucking industry.[66] Therefore, while the Teamsters represented 20 percent of all Black union members in the United States by the mid-1960s, 95 percent of the highest paid workers in the union were white.[67]

Teamster leaders were just as uneven in their approach to race as the small businesses where they recruited their members. The union's decentralized, parochial structure gave local leaders wide latitude for discriminatory practices. Jimmy Hoffa began to change that as part of his uncompromising bid for uniformity in the Teamsters, banning segregated locals just months after he was elected general president and publicly ordering all affiliates to follow the union's stated commitment to equal treatment. During his first year in office, Hoffa donated $25,000 from the Teamsters' treasury—the equivalent of $263,000 today—to Martin Luther King's campaign against the Jim Crow laws. Some locals revolted, and both Hoffa and Harold Gibbons traveled to these locations to personally lobby rank-and-file workers to support the civil rights movement. Regardless of those overtures, however, Hoffa failed to bring uniformity to the Teamsters' racial policy.[68] While Black and Brown workers often leveraged Teamster membership to make meaningful wage gains in the service and light manufacturing sectors, and while many locals in these industries had taken explicitly antiracist, leftist activist stances by the late 1960s, Hoffa was never able to open a meaningful number of long-haul truck driver positions to Black or Brown workers, and thus the union's most desirable jobs remained largely segregated until deregulation destroyed those positions in the 1980s.[69]

Through the Teamsters' uneven, transactional approach to race, conditions deteriorated for many Black and Brown workers in the 1950s. Jimmy Hoffa's willingness to work with John Dioguardi would have two immensely negative consequences for Black and Brown workers who were trapped in the paper locals that Hoffa had instrumentalized. First, Dioguardi's alliance with the Teamsters provided an injection of capital and a sheen of legitimacy that made exploitive contracts far more difficult to contest. When the dozen Black and Puerto Rican car wash workers at Boulevard Auto Wash were forced into a collusive contract in the early 1950s, for example, they were pushed into a small, underfunded union called UAW-AFL Local 224.[70] And though that organization was the domain of John Dioguardi, who was often abusive and violent, his sphere of influence was limited to New York's Sicilian and Jewish underworlds. But after the Hoffa-Dioguardi alliance transferred those workers into the Teamsters without their consent, they became members of the largest union in the United States, one that had hundreds of millions of dollars in its pension funds and that was widely respected by the million workers it had lifted out of poverty. As the owners of trucking companies, grocery chains, and department stores learned during the 1954 truckers strike, that union could be a formidable adversary, which was a daunting prospect for workers in paper locals that administered racist contracts.

Second and more importantly, collusive contracts' sweatshop wages meant that despite being union members, Black and Brown Teamsters were disproportionately likely to be welfare recipients,[71] which exacerbated narratives among the media, policymakers, and academics that blamed culture and sex—and not economics and history—for racial inequality. With its workers in a Teamster paper local, for example, Boulevard Auto Wash was able to violate minimum wage and overtime laws and pay $40 for a fifty-seven-hour workweek. That poverty wage forced Boulevard Auto Wash's workers to live in complex households that policymakers scorned: in crowded, single-room apartments where spouses, children, friends, and distant relatives pooled resources—including food stamps and government cash assistance—to meet their daily needs. But at the same time as it pushed workers of color out of the nuclear family and into poverty, a Teamsters paper local allowed Boulevard Auto Wash's owner Murray Garren to live a solidly middle-class life. He used the profits that were a direct result of a sweatshop-wage contract to buy a spacious three-bedroom house where he lived with his wife and children in the Long Island bedroom community of Rockville Center.[72] That suburban single-family home, and the family wage that paid for it, were proof to journalists and academics that Garren, unlike his Black and Brown employees, fully aligned with the bedrock values that defined the U.S. middle class: the husband breadwinner, the dependent wife, monogamous domesticity, and personal responsibility. Thus a racist contract arranged by a Hoffa-aligned Teamster paper local helped both to naturalize the white privilege that richly rewarded Murray Garren, John Dioguardi, and Jimmy Hoffa, and to justify the poverty, the racism, and the sexism to which workers of color were subjected.

The New Labor Activist Movement against Racist Contracts

When they arrived in the industrial metropolis, young people whose families had worked in the cotton fields of Mississippi, in the lumber mills of small-town Alabama, in the sweatshops of Kingston and Aguadilla, and on the factory farms of Mexico, Guatemala, and El Salvador had their own vision for the future, a vision that transcended the racist tropes in which academics, policymakers, John Dioguardi, and Murray Garren trafficked. Although poverty, violence, and exploitation are inevitable features of these migrants' stories, a new generation of scholars is challenging historical narratives that present such racist practices as natural and self-evident. Instead, and as Adam Green writes so compellingly in the book *Selling the Race*, we only know about the details of these struggles because of the cultural infrastructure that people of color built, infrastructure that broadcast both the beauty and the tragedy of migrants' journey to the city: record companies like Noah Biggs's and Ida Sands's Shiptown that made songs about Black joy and Black pain; magazines like *Ebony* and *Jet* that allowed Black people to fantasize about suburban comfort and that documented the horrors of lynching; Black and Spanish-language newspapers that advertised venues where new arrivals in the city could work, worship, eat, dance, and sing; and, by the end of the 1950s, Spanish language-television shows made by and for people of Latin American and Caribbean origin.[73] Green argues that this raft of midcentury cultural production was just as often about pleasure and leisure as it was about labor, activism, and uplift, the categories that often appear in conventional accounts of Black and Brown people's history.[74] Writers, artists, and journalists framed material resources not just as tools to meet young migrants' needs, but also as a means to provide physical comfort, emotional satisfaction, and a sense of community.[75]

Striving for material pleasure and physical comfort would also propel the struggle for economic justice and against the most exploitive, racist work. While an openly segregated labor market met the new migrants in all northern cities, many arrivals began to refuse to perform work that had been a historical marker of servility. In Chicago, for example, 38 percent of Black women did domestic work in 1940. That percentage dropped appreciably to 13 percent by 1960.[76] To escape the most oppressive work and to share in the consumer abundance that defined US society in the 1950s, the new cohort of service-sector workers understood that they would have to leverage the resources of the labor movement. That commitment to trade unionism touched off a stinging new conflict between the new migrants and the older Teamster operatives and immigrant entrepreneurs who sold racist contracts for profit.

Noteworthy among the upstart activists was Annie May Anderson, who worked grueling ten-hour shifts spraying the salt and grime off the sleek fins and wide chrome grills of Buicks, DeSotos, and Studebakers at a car wash in suburban Detroit. Anderson had joined the industry in 1954, taking a nonunion position at Steam Auto Wash. Not long after she started, an organizer from Teamsters Local 985, Detroit's service-sector local that Hoffa associate and underworld operative Bill Bufalino controlled, walked into the wash's business office and convinced the proprietor to place its all-Black workforce in the union. Front-line employee pay fell by a third when the deal took effect, and after Local 985 agents rebuffed Anderson's demands to restore her original wage and to provide a copy of her union contract, she quit her job in protest. Over the coming years, conditions in Detroit's car wash industry worsened as Local 985's racist labor agreements became more prevalent. By the end of 1958, and absent other work opportunities in a segregated labor market, Anderson was making just forty-two cents per hour under a collusive contract at Dukes Five Minute Auto Wash, which was less than half the federal minimum wage. She worked seventy hours per week, with no days off except for when the wash was closed due to inclement weather. But for each of those days, her employer docked Anderson's weekly pay by $4.25.[77]

Despite this turmoil, Annie May Anderson remained staunchly committed to building a middle-class lifestyle for herself, her husband, and her fifteen-year-old daughter. Anderson and her family rented a modest but comfortable prewar bungalow in Detroit's East Village neighborhood.[78] The CIO union jobs inside the nearby Mack Truck and Chrysler Kercheval factories helped Anderson's friends and neighbors in Detroit earn the highest average wage for Black workers in any US city in the 1950s.[79] Perhaps because of the gains she saw other migrants from the Jim Crow South making, Anderson believed that a Black woman could be a breadwinner and could provide the same privileges for her family that had defined white people's journey into the middle class. Fashion was particularly important to Anderson, who spoke of the brand-new skirt, sweater, and pair of shoes she planned to purchase for her daughter to make a good impression on the first day of her sophomore year in high school. Domestic work and segregated manual labor were, conversely, not in Anderson's plan for her daughter's future. Instead, she put a small amount of money aside every week to pay for a college degree that she hoped would deliver the upward mobility that eastern and southern European immigrants had achieved in the previous generation.[80]

These ambitions for family stability and material prosperity compelled Annie May Anderson to act politically. During a shift on a freezing afternoon in December 1958, Anderson spotted Bill Shaw, a business agent for Teamsters Local 985, walking from his car into the office of Dukes Five Minute Auto Wash. She hung up her spray wand, charged across the parking lot, and confronted him. "Shaw, you come out here and go straight to the office. You never talk to us!" she recalled yelling. "You don't tell us anything! We don't have nobody to complain to! Nobody to protect us! We don't have a steward! What I want to know is, what are we paying dues for?"

"To protect your job!" Shaw barked, pushing past Anderson and then ignoring her.

By the time a lull in the traffic allowed Anderson to step away from spraying, buffing, and shining, Shaw had left the premises. Refusing to accept his blatant disregard, however, Anderson took up the issue with car wash supervisor Bill Stradder. Anderson implored Stradder to stop deducting the sixty cents from her weekly paycheck that covered her union dues. "Bill, you know I have a daughter to take care of and that sixty cents a week would mean a lot more to me in my pocket than to Shaw in his pocket," she argued. Insisting that the money provided nothing in return, Anderson threatened to walk off the job if Stradder continued to collect the dues. Stradder clearly understood that Anderson was unwavering, and he thus accommodated her demand in an effort to defuse the confrontation. He promised to restore the sixty cents in weekly pay and offered to cover Anderson's union dues on her behalf. But Anderson was unmoved by the workaround. She maintained that no one—not Dukes Five Minute Auto Wash, not Bill Stradder, and certainly not she—should give that money to a Teamsters local that sold racist contracts.[81]

While Anderson soon quit her job at Dukes just like she had quit her job at Steam Auto Wash, she began to take collective action against the collusive contract system. Suspicious that her supervisor had continued to pay her union dues despite his claim to the contrary, Anderson took the bus to the Teamsters' office on Jefferson Avenue to investigate. She befriended the records clerk, most likely another young, working-class woman, who informed her that her dues had indeed been paid in full, most likely because her supervisor was afraid of financial or physical retribution from Bill Bufalino's lieutenants at Local 985. Frustrated but undaunted, Anderson began making connections with other Black workers who shared her determination, including Gus Richardson, the Black car wash worker described above who was fighting the collusive contract system in his Detroit workplace.[82] By the outset of 1959, she had joined a growing group of activists who had begun to involve policymakers, law enforcement, and civil rights leaders in their campaign against Local 985.

The movement was also taking off in New York City. Puerto Rican activists led much of that grassroots labor activist effort, in part because the racial geography and institutional history of New York's city government had denied island arrivals access to conventional forms of political representation. As a consequence of residential segregation, most Puerto Ricans lived in a single City Council district in the 1950s, one that spanned the Upper East Side, East Harlem, and the South Bronx. During the immediate postwar years, Vito Marcantonio had held the seat for that district. Fluent in English, Italian, Spanish, and Yiddish, Marcantonio had come of age in the CIO and in the Italian American left, and he saw the neighborhood as a place to build cross-racial alliances between the older Jews and Italians whose families had come to the area in the first two decades of the twentieth century and newer Black and Puerto Rican people who began to arrive after the war.[83]

With Sen. Joseph McCarthy's rise to power, however, and with the purge of radicals from the labor movement and from government, Marcantonio was red-baited out of office in 1950. In his place came John Merli. The son of Italian immigrants who traveled in steerage from Sicily, Merli was born in East Harlem in 1904 and had spent his whole life living in the same small apartment when he was elected to the City Council. Although he shared roots similar to Marcantonio's, Merli saw the neighborhood not as a place for solidarity but rather as a venue for upward mobility. Merli strongly identified with other first- and second-generation Italian Americans who had transitioned from tenement residents into the owners of tenements where Puerto Ricans lived. Although he understood that Italian landlords often subjected Puerto Rican migrants to squalid living conditions, he believed that with hard work, Puerto Ricans would lift themselves out of poverty and into the middle class, which would make Puerto Ricans the landlords for the next generation of arrivals.[84] Absent from Merli's teleological account of neighborhood history, however, were the structural forces—the FHA's refusal to insure integrated housing development, the segregated lending and labor markets, and the racially inequitable unions like John Dioguardi's paper locals—that thrust Italians upward and Puerto Ricans downward in the mid-twentieth century. Locked into a district with a councilman who favored their landlords' needs over their own and who saw natural evolution rather than structural intervention as the primary means to ameliorate poverty, the vast majority of the four hundred thousand Puerto Ricans who arrived in New York in the 1950s had no formal mechanism to advocate for their political interests.

Without an official political channel, the growing wave of Puerto Rican activists turned to grassroots labor organizing and cultural production.

Particularly illustrative of this strategy was José Lumen Roman, a beat reporter for the Spanish-language daily newspaper *El Diario de Nueva York*. As he covered the restaurants, churches, and street corners of East Harlem, Roman was inundated with disturbing accounts of sweatshop wages, exhaustingly long hours, and deadly workplace accidents in small service businesses' industrial shops that employed Puerto Rican workers and where employees' unions did nothing to challenge such abuses. As historian Linda Delgado has argued, many young Puerto Rican migrants were already familiar with workplace activism when they arrived on the mainland, as they came from families and neighborhoods on the island where people participated in the Socialist Party, joined the anarcho-syndicalist Tobacco Workers Union, or shut down the ports in militant dockworkers' strikes.[85] They thus expected their unions to protect their health, safety, and economic well-being, and recognized that it was unethical and illegal for union operatives to withhold representation. Therefore, as word spread of José Lumen Roman's interest in documenting factory owners' and union leaders' malfeasance, rank-and-file activists organized their colleagues to submit additional testimony.

José Lumen Roman soon broadcast the stories he collected on television. In addition to writing for *El Diario*, Roman also hosted a locally broadcast network television talk show called *What Is Your Problem?* The show was controversial among Puerto Rican New Yorkers, since it took a frank look at addiction, violence, joblessness, housing insecurity, and racism, difficult issues that some worried would reflect negatively on a population struggling to gain a foothold in the city. Roman, however, saw painful public conversations as a means to galvanize Puerto Ricans.[86] Most illustrative of Roman's strategy was a November 1956 episode of the show in which Ana Cordero and Nereida Rosas confronted Marshall Miller, the labor operative described above who financed his suburban Long Island lifestyle by selling racist contracts for John Dioguardi. Like thousands of other young Puerto Rican women workers, Cordero and Rosas took the subway every day from their homes in East Harlem and the South Bronx to one of many of small factories, where they stitched garments, sewed curtains, made lampshades, forged plastic products, and assembled electronic equipment. Cordero and Rosas alleged that their union was a sham and forced them to pay dues while earning minimum wage, receiving no benefits, and working unpaid overtime. Dismissing the women's claims, Miller insisted that the union brought valuable material resources to its members and pointed out to the audience that the glasses both women wore had been compliments of the union's health fund.

Miller clearly crossed a line with that assertion. Either Cordero or Rosas—the historical record does not distinguish which—interrupted Miller and shouted that she had bought the glasses for $12 with no help from the union. Without the health insurance that white union members expected in the 1950s, she was forced to spend a third of her weekly salary on a new pair, which further burdened a family that was already stretched thin. Tearing the glasses from her face, she launched them toward Miller. Like a foul ball hit toward an unsuspecting fan at Yankee Stadium, the flying spectacles rocketed through the air and struck Marshall Miller.[87]

Roman, Cordero, and Rosas backed up their dramatic broadcast work by building grassroots alliances on the other side of the camera. They reached out to the Association of Catholic Trade Unionists (ACTU), a volunteer labor advocacy organization of undergraduate and law students, many with ties to the Irish and Italian Catholic left. The ACTU had begun to offer grassroots, Spanish-language labor schools in Manhattan and the Bronx in 1953, where activists collected accounts of unions' inequitable treatment and briefed workers on the protections that labor law provided.[88] They soon accumulated six hundred narratives that identified a clear, remarkably consistent pattern.[89] Small manufacturing shops were buying contracts from fraudulent paper locals and using the contracts to lock workers into a fifty-seven-hour workweek that paid the federal minimum wage for the first forty hours and provided no compensation at all for the seventeen hours of overtime. Since federal labor law allows only one union at a time in a workplace, these collusive contracts blocked workers from forming new, legitimate unions, leaving them with as little representation in the labor movement as they had in city government.[90]

Energized amid the growing din in *El Diario* and on *What Is Your Problem?*, and through the deepening alliance with the ACTU, young workers of color began to use another activist tool: direct action. Although she was a generation younger than her supervisor at Century Product Works, and while she had been in the United States for less than two years after leaving her Honduras home, Bertha Nunez fought back against the exploitation she faced from her first days on the job. She attended one of the few meetings that her Dioguardi-controlled Teamsters paper local ever held, demanding to see a copy of the contract and joining her peers in shouting "Racketeers!" when Dioguardi's agents refused. She ordered the union officials to explain why they did nothing to improve the factory's deplorable working conditions. Despite New York's frigid winters, Nunez's workplace had no heat. When one of her colleagues found out she was pregnant, the young woman asked for time off work, fearing that the harsh, cold factory would harm her pregnancy. Management refused, and after the union failed to intervene, the woman contracted pneumonia and suffered a miscarriage. Angered by their colleagues' loss and furious when the factory announced it would terminate all of the workers after they finished making home appliances for the holiday rush, Nunez helped lead a strike to block the layoff in November 1955, a strike the workers won.[91]

Although localized direct action protests like Nunez's were successful, activists understood that they needed to scale up their mobilization in order to boost its impact. To coordinate that effort, they worked with José Lumen Roman and the ACTU to loop in Charles Fay, an avowedly leftist activist who was a longtime advocate for cross-racial labor coalitions and who was the president of International Union of Electricians Local 485.[92] In tandem with Fay, grassroots activists decided that in factories where employees had been forced into a paper local, workers would band together and approach the proprietor, demanding to leave the paper local, to scrap the racist contract, and to join Local 485. If management balked, employees would walk out on strike and picket the plant until the owner gave in. And rather than demanding to change unions on an isolated basis, organizers planned to act in unison across the metropolitan area.

Activists executed that plan in the summer of 1957. Bertha Nunez, for example, circulated a petition among her colleagues ordering her employer to end its relationship with Teamsters Local 362, a paper local that John Dioguardi controlled and that had been brought into the Teamsters as a result of the Hoffa-Dioguardi accord in November 1955. Well aware of Nunez's shop floor militancy, the proprietor acquiesced to the petition, apparently deciding that it would be simpler to accommodate Nunez than to risk another costly, embarrassing protest. He recognized IUE Local 485, and Century Product Works terminated its collusive contract with the Teamsters on June 24, 1957.[93] A similar sequence of events took place in Mario Montalvo's workplace. Montalvo had been fired from the Miro Pen Company in February of 1957 after he led a one-day strike against a Dioguardi-aligned paper local that he and his colleagues had been required to join. Workers marched in front of the plant with signs that read "This is a Racket Shop," and "Local 250 is Johnny Dio's Racket Local." Because he lacked financial and legal resources, Montalvo opted not to fight the termination and instead found a new job at Del Pen, another nearby ball-point pen factory. Soon thereafter, however, Dioguardi's representatives arrived at that plant, insisting that the owner force Montalvo and his new colleagues into the same paper local. Adamantly refusing to join, Montalvo led a work stoppage that ended when management rebuffed Dioguardi and recognized Local 485 as the sole representative for Del Pen's workforce.[94] And at the Radley Metzger Company, a plastics and textile manufacturer in the South Bronx, its seventy mostly Puerto Rican workers walked out on strike on August 21, 1957, barricading the loading docks and blocking the plant from shipping $10,000 worth of goods each day. Daunted at the lost sales, the plant's owner capitulated to the workers, recognized Local 485, and terminated his racist contract with a paper local that Lucchese family higher-up Anthony Corallo controlled.[95]

Although John Dioguardi, Marshall Miller, and scores of other operatives from Teamster-aligned paper locals were undoubtedly surprised and angered at young Black and Brown workers' insubordination, they had few tools to thwart their effort. Since a collusive contract could be construed as a bribe, an illicit payment to a union designed to subvert workers' rights under labor law, most employers were reticent to seek formal legal recourse to protect those contracts.[96] Without an above-board remedy, some companies tried to pay off rank-and-file activists to stop organizing. According to Bertha Nunez, her supervisor at Century Product Works called her on the telephone and offered a monthly cash payment if she agreed to recant her support for Local 485.[97] Similarly, the proprietor of the Del Pen company offered Mario Montalvo a one-time cash payment of $100—the equivalent today of $940—plus lifetime job security if Montalvo agreed to withdraw from the effort to join Local 485.[98] But because most rank-and-file activists were politically and morally committed to the antiracist labor movement they were building, bribes failed to neutralize the campaign.

Far more importantly, however, was that the most potent weapon of the Teamsters and of the Jewish and Sicilian underworlds—muscle—was a far less effective tool when applied against workers of color than it was when used against other Jews and Italians. Muscle had three targets when wielded by Teamster and underworld agents: capital, comfort, and the body (see chapter 2). Whether by throwing stink bombs into a warehouse, dissolving a pool table in acid, or burning down a car wash, operatives used muscle to destroy the capital that their opponents had invested in small businesses. When that failed, operatives deployed muscle to interrupt suburban comfort, terrorizing wives with death threats on the telephone at 3 a.m., blatantly and ominously trailing families as they returned to their cul-de-sacs, and beating adversaries on their front lawns with the neighbors watching. Black and Brown workers, however, had little access to capital or comfort, no family businesses to destroy or suburban tranquility to disturb. Even physical violence proved futile. Because of racial segregation, Jewish or Italian operatives were visibly conspicuous when they crossed the color line into Black or Puerto Rican or Central American blocks of the South Bronx or Harlem, places where activist workers were surrounded with friends, family, and neighbors who could help fight off an attack from unwelcome white intruders from outside the area.[99]

With Teamster and underworld operatives unable to inspire the fear necessary to subdue the dissident activists, the movement surged forward. Organizers added new tactics that brought visibility and institutional recognition. Most importantly, rank-and-file leaders Bertha Nunez and Mario Montalvo got on the docket to testify in front of the McClellan Committee in Washington, DC, in early August 1957. Their Black comrades Annie May Anderson and Gus Richardson from the Detroit car wash industry would soon join them. Like most trade unionists, Anderson, Montalvo, Nunez, and Richardson were deeply skeptical of Robert F. Kennedy's motives and were well aware that the committee's chair, Arkansas senator John McClellan, had been an unyielding advocate of the corrupt, violent effort to defend the Jim Crow system of white supremacy. The New York and Detroit activists repeatedly asserted in press interviews that broad, prolabor reforms such as raising the minimum wage would be a far more effective means to advocate for marginal workers than a seemingly relentless federal probe of Jimmy Hoffa's moral character. Nevertheless, they understood that Kennedy was feeding a stream of news stories about union corruption to his extensive list of press contacts, which in this case would generate exposure for the dissident movement in periodicals that had a wide, influential readership, such as the *New York Times*.[100] The media din would both pressure the political and labor establishment to take Black and Brown workers' cause more seriously and subject the middle-class factory owners who took advantage of racist contracts to public exposure and thus to shame.

Activists' media strategy worked. On August 3, 1957, photographs of twenty-seven-year-old Bertha Nunez and twenty-two-year-old John McNiff—a law student volunteer with the Association of Catholic Trade Unionists who was fresh out of Vassar College—appeared on the front page of the *New York Times*. Below their images, a long article relayed Nunez's graphic testimony about the sweatshop conditions in her workplace and described excerpts of worker testimonies that José Lumen Roman had collected and that McNiff read aloud for the television cameras at the hearings.[101] The following day, the *New York Times* ran another front-page story on the topic, in this case describing a new labor organization called the "Committee to Ease the Exploitation of Spanish Speaking Peoples." The accompanying photograph featured the well-known labor leaders who led that group: Harry Van Arsdale, the famed proponent of the thirty-hour workweek who had become the president of New York City's Central Labor Council, Morris Iushewitz, a leftist Jewish activist who had been the secretary-treasurer of the New York CIO, and Peter McGavin, an assistant to AFL-CIO president George Meany. The *Times* announced that the committee was deploying Spanish-speaking organizers, who would fan out across the small industrial shops in Manhattan, Brooklyn, Queens, and the Bronx to assist workers of color who were trapped in paper locals. In cases where factory owners refused to cut their ties with underhanded unions, the committee urged workers to walk out on strike and stay out until the proprietor agreed to negotiate with a legitimate union.[102]

Mayoral committees and middle-class press coverage provided no guarantee of substantive political change. What the string of advances did provide, however, was a sense of momentum for the dissident labor movement. Over the coming months and years, Black and Brown workers translated that momentum into a broad-based movement for fair, equitable access to the workplace, to the neighborhood, and to the metropolitan area. First and foremost, the string of victories against the paper locals touched off a new wave of union militancy. In January 1958, for example, employees in the lamp and lampshade production industry launched a citywide strike. The almost entirely Black and Puerto Rican workforce had organized with the International Brotherhood of Electrical Workers, which unlike the Teamster paper locals put the rank-and-file in charge of the bargaining agenda and the political strategy. Overwhelming solidarity led to a quick strike victory, which delivered the first-ever standardized contract that covered all 147 lamp factories in the metropolitan area. With a minimum wage of $50 per week, a $5 per week retroactive raise, and robust vacation and health benefits, grassroots organizers turned sweatshop work into a modest but stable career.[103]

Two months later, workers in New York's garment industry—about half of whom were Black and Puerto Rican women—staged a five-day walkout, the first apparel industry strike in New York since 1935. Prior to the strike, the leadership of the garment workers' union had been almost entirely Jewish, which reflected the makeup of the previous generation of textile workers. But as organizers prepared for the action, a new, younger generation of activists—Louise Delgado the most visible among them—took over key leadership positions. Their work, and Delgado's connection to organizers in Black and Puerto Rican communities beyond the workplace, helped deliver significant economic gains, including the first ever industry-wide minimum wage.[104] Victory in the garment strike soon inspired a grueling but ultimately successful three-year strike for recognition among laundry, food service, and janitorial workers in New York's public hospitals, virtually all of whom were Black or Latino. A final, positive resolution to that conflict in 1963[105] gave way to headline-making rent strikes and student walkouts in the spring of 1964, both of which benefited from alliances between Black and Puerto Rican labor activists.[106] In the wake of these advances, it was clear that on the same city blocks of Brooklyn and the Bronx—and of similar blocks in Pittsburgh, Detroit, Chicago, Kansas City, and scores of other industrial cities—where Jimmy Hoffa had orchestrated his rise to power in the International Brotherhood of Teamsters, an upsurge of antiracist activism was invigorating the labor movement as the 1960s approached.

Conclusion: Service Workers' Ambitions in a Changing Society

As young women like Annie May Anderson, Louise Delgado, and Bertha Nunez were staking a claim on the labor movement, Jimmy Hoffa had solidified his own rise to power through a similar activist project: organizing workers at small businesses in the service sector of the economy. He began that work as a young man in early-1930s Detroit, rallying his fellow warehouse workers at the Kroger grocery chain to strike for recognition of their Teamsters local. While the trucking industry always remained the focus of Hoffa's leadership, he used the power he consolidated as president of the regional body for midwestern truck drivers in the 1940s to direct ever more resources to service-sector organizing. Hoffa formalized that commitment at a beachfront resort on Miami Beach in February 1956, when he announced a mass organizing drive in the service, retail, and light manufacturing sectors, promising to recruit millions of bartenders, hairstylists, furniture builders, brewers, electronics assemblers, and millions of others on the periphery of the midcentury US manufacturing economy.[107] In part because of the popularity of the new project with rank-and-file Teamsters, Hoffa won his election to become the union's general president in 1957. What was also clear, however, was that despite the Teamsters' relatively diverse membership rolls, Hoffa's cohort of leaders proved less able and less willing to organize the next cohort of service workers—most of whom were Black or Brown women—with the same vigor as they had organized the previous generation. The question for labor historians, then, involves why Jimmy Hoffa failed to bridge these racial, gender, and generational gaps more effectively.

The answer, I argue, is because effective organizing requires a nuanced understanding of the full spectrum of workers' desires. Hoffa maintained his unflagging popularity with eastern and southern European immigrant activists like Marshall Miller and Samuel Zakman because he empathized with the contradictory contours of the life they wanted to live. Rather than trying to enforce middle-class restraint on Miller and Zakman, he allowed them to continue to use the tactics that defined their identity on the hard-scrabble streets of their youth: raising their voices, swinging their fists, coercing their adversaries, and collaborating with the Jewish and Italian underworlds. But Hoffa also understood that Miller and Zakman were not their parents, and that despite their abrasive, unrestrained style, their generation expected to live pleasurable middle-class lifestyles, those rooted in consumer abundance, leisure time, and a single-family home in a verdant neighborhood on the edge of the metropolis.

Regardless of any raise that Hoffa could have provided to Annie May Anderson and Bertha Nunez's cohort, they would never achieve the suburban comfort of Zakman's cohort, as Black and Brown families faced lawsuits, arrests, vandalism, and physical assault from the police, from elected officials, and from vigilante neighbors when they tried to move to the suburbs.[108] In part because of those exclusions, the new generation of migrants developed their own, complex vision for how they would live in the metropolis. That vision came into view in a low-budget storefront studio in Norfolk, where a group of young Black women sung, recorded, marketed, and distributed "Doggie in the Window" to project their aspirations with style, humor, and irony. While the nuances of those ambitions were undoubtedly lost on Jimmy Hoffa's generation, who lacked the tools and the will to fully understand them, those desires translated much more clearly to younger activists who had both fantasized about those middle-class pleasures and been denied them because of a racist housing, education, and employment system. By the middle of the 1960s, a new set of unions—those representing public employees, clerical workers, janitors, and hospital workers[109]—understood the translation, and Anderson and Nunez's cohort began to join those unions en masse as they built coalitions between organized labor and the new social movements.

While Jimmy Hoffa struggled to empathize with and to accommodate workers' new desires that materialized in the social movements of the 1960s, historical evidence shows that senior leadership of the International Brotherhood of Teamsters nevertheless violated conventional cultural norms just as blatantly as many younger migrants to the metropolis. While monogamous heterosexual marriage, the suburban single-family home, the husband breadwinner, and the dependent wife were ideals that distributed money and power to many rank-and-file Teamsters while denying them to Annie May Anderson, Bertha Nunez, and other working women, Jimmy Hoffa's network of comrades and kin refused to conform to those expectations. The next chapter of *Teamsters Metropolis* provides an intimate history of that nonconformity. Set inside the downtown Detroit apartment of Hoffa's business partner, financial adviser, and underworld liaison Sylvia Pagano, the chapter tells the story of a group of friends who blended entrepreneurship, activism, illicit dealings, friendship, intimacy, and sex. Their transgressions demonstrate that despite its often conservative worldview and paralyzing contradictions, the International Brotherhood of Teamsters remained a dissident rather than a dominant cultural institution during an era of intensifying social change.

CHAPTER FIVE

What If We Had Known about Sylvia Pagano?
An Intimate History of a Downtown Apartment
in the Age of Suburbia

Saturday, March 9, 1963. Sylvia Pagano's apartment is, as always, a bee-hive of activity. At 7:59 a.m. the phone rings for the first time that morning. Pagano's friend Margaret is on the line, sounding concerned at first. The previous week, Pagano had been hospitalized for surgery to remove a tumor that doctors had found during a routine medical examination. Pagano quickly puts Margaret at ease, however, promising that she has recovered and that she is all set to participate in the giant Teamsters rally planned for the next day. Twenty-five thousand truck drivers and their wives would assemble at Detroit's Cobo Hall arena to demonstrate the union's power and to mobilize for a standardized, national contract for all truckers. Frenetic as she often was, Pagano abruptly switches topics, telling Margaret about a conversation she planned to have with her stockbroker. Pagano was annoyed that some of her portfolio was "doing nothing." She hoped to sell off the underperforming stocks and transfer the money to shares of the Budd corporation, a maker of transit vehicles that Pagano thought was well-run and that she heard had just gotten access to a new, $25 million line of credit.

After a few more minutes of business talk, Pagano hangs up with Margaret and spends the rest of the morning making turnout calls to fellow Teamsters for Sunday's rally, promising that Jimmy Hoffa would be there to shake hands with activists from across the movement. She worked the phones from the living room of apartment 606C of the Alden Park Manor, where Pagano had lived for four years. The Alden Park was a stately place, situated in a picturesque bend of the Detroit River in the downtown Gold

Coast neighborhood. Built in 1923, the Alden Park's four eight-story red brick towers housed 352 apartments with wide, projecting bay windows under an ornate limestone roofline. A retail concourse spanned the first floor of the complex, which put groceries and liquor, dry cleaning, and a beauty salon in walking distance of every apartment.[1] Impressive though the Alden Park certainly remained, the building was somewhat of an anachronism in 1963, as most of Detroit's middle class—and most of Sylvia Pagano's associates in the Teamsters union and La Cosa Nostra—had left the high-density blocks of the central city for Detroit's leafy suburbs.

At 11:15 a.m. the doorbell rings. One of those suburbanites, Pagano's friend, lover, and business associate Anthony Giacalone, had driven from his sprawling, 4,500-square-foot home in Grosse Point Park to pay Pagano a visit. They flirt as he enters.

"I had a feeling you were coming," Pagano remarks. "Now sit down . . ."

". . . you motherfucker," Giacalone laughs as Pagano begins to model a mink coat that she recently purchased. As she poses in her attire, she references another mink coat that Giacalone was having made for her, a coat Pagano seemed to think would be even more elegant than the one she showed off.

Flirtation quickly gave way to the topic that occupied the majority of Pagano and Giacalone's time together: business. "All right, so I talked to Frank's Trucking, and I can get that account," Pagano interjects after apparently putting the mink coat aside. Giacalone and Pagano were in the process of forming a company that would sell advertising billboard space on the trailers of trucks that Teamsters drove. While Giacalone and several other underworld operatives were minority stakeholders in the business, Pagano's extensive connections to the trucking industry solidified through her friendship with Jimmy Hoffa gave her a 35 percent stake in the firm, a swath large enough to ensure final control over all operational decisions. She discusses the public policy context for the new company, strategizing about ways to obtain the necessary approval from the Interstate Commerce Commission, the government agency that regulated the trucking business prior to 1980. Giacalone presses her on the company's articles of incorporation, asking who she intends to designate as executive officers for legal reasons.

"Did you draw up the incorporation?" Giacalone asks.

"No, not yet. I told you—before they had to get the okay of the Interstate Commerce Commission," Pagano responds, seemingly annoyed that Giacalone's comprehension lags behind her rapid-fire analysis of the issues at hand.

"And who is in this corporation?" Giacalone inquires.

"There is Sharm in Mount Clemens—three people," Pagano continues, brainstorming aloud in partial thoughts.

"And who is the next man?"

"Cary," Pagano continues.

"And who is the next man?"

"Me," Pagano flatly finishes before returning to the topic of her mink coats. The conversation then fades, and Giacalone and Pagano spend the rest of the afternoon joking and laughing as they watch wrestling and the Saturday afternoon movie on television.[2]

During the late 1950s and 1960s, when she was "top man" in the trucking advertising company and several other businesses, an extensive trove of documents shows that Sylvia Pagano also worked as an investment consultant for Jimmy Hoffa, facilitating loans from the union's deep coffers to companies associated with the Sicilian and Jewish syndicates. But despite her significant influence over the financial affairs of both the International Brotherhood of Teamsters and the underworld, Pagano remained wholly invisible in public discourse for almost two decades until well after her death in 1970. Her absence is striking, given the unflagging scrutiny to which law enforcement, policymakers, and the mainstream press subjected the Teamsters during the years when Pagano was the most active in union business. In the twenty-five-thousand-page transcript that recorded all of the sworn testimony from the McClellan Committee investigation, for example, Pagano's name appears exactly one time. During remarks recorded on page 13,287, while probing Jimmy Hoffa about the allegedly nefarious affairs of a Detroit laundry workers union business agent, Chief Counsel Robert F. Kennedy noted that the business agent had been married to a woman named Sylvia. He never mentioned her again.[3] Similarly, although Pagano's son Chuckie O'Brien was living with Jimmy and Josephine Hoffa when the *Saturday Evening Post* ran a four-part series about Hoffa's home life, the magazine never referred to her.[4] And even though labor economists Ralph and Estelle James painted a detailed portrait of Hoffa's views on family, gender, sex, and culture after they shadowed Hoffa for a year in the mid-1960s, Sylvia Pagano's name is wholly absent from the book they published about his affairs.[5] In an age when scrutiny of the ties between Jimmy Hoffa and the underworld had become a national pastime for middle-class cultural commentators, it seems that no one knew about the person who was a linchpin between the two. As it grapples with the causes and consequences of this historical omission, this chapter springs from a question for those of us who study the labor movement's past: What if we had known about Sylvia Pagano?

Sylvia Pagano evaded scrutiny for two decades because she lived far outside the prescribed cultural context for middle-class white women in the mid-twentieth-century United States: the heterosexual nuclear family. To understand a social location that was illegible to the press, to legislators, to historians and other academics, and for a time to law enforcement, this chapter provides an intimate history of Pagano's home, apartment 606C at the Alden Park Manor. In rooms with a view of downtown Detroit, furnished with gleaming chandeliers and lush green wallpaper,[6] she and her friends transgressed the institution of conventional domesticity. They shared waged and unwaged productive and reproductive labor among men and women. They blurred the lines between public and private, between friendship, love, business, and family. They built evolving friendships that included love, sex, solidarity, and betrayal both within the institution of marriage and outside it. They mixed intimate ties with professional and political ones, building companies, building the Teamsters, and building the Italian and Jewish underworlds.

It is those unruly intimacies that the events inside of apartment 606C reveal. If we would have known about those events, known about Pagano, her kin, her activism, and her businesses, labor scholars and labor activists would revise the story we sometimes tell about the mid-twentieth century. That narrative frames Jimmy Hoffa's Teamsters as the paragon of conservative business unionism, an organization that helped turn restive workers who came of age in the Depression into a depoliticized Cold War middle-class forged in domesticity, mass consumption, and patriotism.[7] While there are significant truths in that story, and while it fits some Teamsters members and leaders well, the events inside apartment 606C push us to understand the mid-twentieth-century labor movement with far greater nuance. If we would have known about these events, we would have seen that the Teamsters union was built not of cultural consensus, but of cultural struggle. If we would have known about Sylvia Pagano, we would have seen that in at least some cases, the International Brotherhood of Teamsters was a site of passionate debate over the appropriate relationship between business, friendship, sex, and love, over the tense relationship between heterogeneous central city neighborhoods and comfortable suburban landscapes, and over whether the labor movement should be about middle-class aspiration or explicit cultural dissent. By the early 1960s, Sylvia Pagano's home had become a theater for that discontent.

Aligning the Teamsters and the Underworld

From the time she was a child, Sylvia Pagano's life took place at the confluence of immigrant labor, workplace organizing, and the Italian political and economic network that her friends called La Cosa Nostra. Pagano was born to an immigrant family in Kansas City on August 9, 1914. Her mother was Maggie Campo, the granddaughter of a Sicilian cheesemaker who had been a seamstress at Jewish entrepreneur Herbert Morris Wolfe's luxury dry goods store. Her father was Joseph Pagano, a Sicilian immigrant. Before Sylvia was born, and after a stint as a Prohibition-era bootlegger, Joseph Pagano worked his way up to foreman at a local factory in Kansas City. Together with her brothers Paul and Mario, Sylvia and her parents lived in a small apartment on East Fifth Street near downtown Kansas City, one that five decades later was demolished with thousands of others to make way for the interstate highway system.[8]

Like many working-class women from immigrant families, Sylvia Pagano married young by today's standards. Her walk home from high school each day took her past a gas station, where one of the attendants was a young man named Charles Lenton O'Brien. It appears that O'Brien had a hardscrabble upbringing in Saint Louis after his birth in 1910, having wound up in reform school in Booneville, Missouri, which he left to move to Kansas City in 1930. Perhaps to supplement the income he earned from a low-wage job, the young O'Brien became a bodyguard, driver, and fixer for Charlie Binaggio, a higher-up in the Kansas City Italian syndicate that locals sometimes called The Black Hand. Probably while O'Brien was working for Binaggio, he struck up a friendship and romance with Pagano. The two married while Pagano was a senior in high school in 1931, and had a child in November 1932, when Pagano was eighteen. They named the baby Charles Lenton O'Brien Junior, and called him Chuckie.[9]

Little is known about Pagano's affairs until her life changed drastically at the end of the 1930s. Likely because of turmoil in his work within La Cosa Nostra, Pagano's husband disappeared from Kansas City and would later die by suicide. The family never saw him again. As was typical during a crisis in the Italian community, underworld higher-ups helped craft a plan to protect Pagano's emotional and economic well-being. Because the economy was stronger in Depression-era Detroit that it was in Kansas City, they put her in touch with William Tocco, a founder of Detroit's syndicate who was a well-respected community leader.[10] Tocco owned a fruit and vegetable terminal that supplied produce to the region's grocery stores. According to Chuckie O'Brien, Sylvia sent him to live with relatives in Colorado when he was about eight years old. She moved to Detroit, took a job in Tocco's produce terminal, and worked to get her financial footing.[11]

Exactly how that happened remains a mystery. As is often the case for working-class women, the historical record leaves us a sketchy tale. On the one hand, it seems that Sylvia Pagano became a labor activist. Around

1940, Pagano met Bert Brennan, a close friend and comrade of Jimmy Hoffa's. Brennan and Hoffa were young, still in their twenties. But they had already developed a national reputation as skilled organizers. A couple of years earlier, when he was twenty-four years old, Hoffa was elected president of Teamsters Local 299. Although that union represented Detroit's truck drivers primarily, Hoffa wanted to organize everyone at every business where truckers picked up and dropped off goods. Produce warehouses like William Tocco's were central to that strategy. Either after he met her on the job at Tocco's,[12] or at the tavern owned by underworld higher-up Frank Coppola where Pagano bartended and where Brennan regularly socialized,[13] Brennan hired Sylvia Pagano to become what activists call a salt. Pagano would walk into a business, get a job, and then begin to talk covertly to her coworkers about organizing. It was Pagano's responsibility to convince her colleagues to vote in the Teamsters as the sole bargaining representative for their workplace. Pagano salted for the Teamsters in stints at the A&P and Kroger grocery chains, as well as in a local potato chip factory.[14] The organizing work was difficult. Friends remember that Pagano destroyed her hands while spending hours frying potatoes in boiling, salty oil, the literal salt leaving Pagano with permanent injuries from her job as a metaphorical salt.[15]

On the other hand, and maybe while she was doing dirty, exhausting work for the Teamsters, Pagano also lived a cosmopolitan life helping Anthony Giacalone run Detroit's numbers game, which was an important source of revenue for La Cosa Nostra after the repeal of Prohibition. Pagano kept an apartment in the storied Whittier Hotel in the early 1940s. The fifteen-story Italianate renaissance tower operated as an apartment hotel, where guests could check in for short stays or rent their units long-term while enjoying the guest services of a luxury hotel. Eleanor Roosevelt, Mae West, and Frank Sinatra had all lived or stayed there, and the underworld—especially a Jewish outfit called the Purple Gang that operated out of Cleveland during Prohibition—had made the Whittier its base of operations in Detroit.[16] It seems that in addition to living in one apartment that may or may not have functioned as a decoy for the police, Pagano maintained another unit, where she managed the money and paperwork for Giacalone's gambling ring. Pagano's son Chuckie later insisted that she kept all of her records on special paper that would dissolve in water. If the Detroit police or the FBI came knocking, down the toilet everything would go.[17]

Deepening connections to unions and to La Cosa Nostra—connections she built with chutzpah and grit—explain why Sylvia Pagano caught the attention of Jimmy Hoffa. Since the nineteenth century, physical violence had been the primary means employers used to dissuade workers from joining unions. By 1930, Detroit's Italian syndicate was perpetuating that violence, using antiunionism to get a foothold in a competitive urban economy. Underworld higher-up Santo Perrone coordinated this process. Born in Alcamo, Sicily, in 1895, Perrone came to the United States in 1915 and took a job at a small factory called Detroit Stove Works. After the 1924 immigration restriction, Perrone helped smuggle undocumented Sicilians across the US border at Windsor, Ontario, and connected them to employment once they finished crossing into Detroit. One of the jobs he gave undocumented Sicilians was to break strikes in stove making, scrap hauling, and other trades that were populated by small family firms. This package—a squadron of antagonists who would attack, maim, and kill union activists, ruin their strikes, and steal their jobs—was a product that Perrone sold to other businessmen, which elevated his stature in both the Detroit economy and the Detroit Sicilian syndicate.[18]

It now appears that Sylvia Pagano rose to prominence in the eyes of the Teamster leadership because she helped convince Santo Perrone to stop selling that product. According to some historians, Pagano did that convincing during a Teamster strike for recognition at the Detroit Lumber Company in May 1941. During that strike, Pagano's associate Anthony Giacalone had organized a violent gang of antiunion activists to attack the picket line. One of the assailants threw a brick, killing a young striker named Arthur Queasebarth.[19] Facing Giacalone's heavily armed, ruthless crews, and unable to turn to a police department that was weak, corrupt, and infamously antiunion, Jimmy Hoffa and other young Teamster leaders faced a stark choice. They could try to overpower La Cosa Nostra. But doing so would have resulted in a bloodbath that would have paralyzed ordinary workers with fear and destroyed the union's ability to organize the unorganized. Or they could reach out to the underworld, convince the Detroit family that its interests lay with, and not against, the largest and boldest union in Detroit, and cut a deal.

Many sources now agree that Sylvia Pagano helped Jimmy Hoffa and fellow activists take the second of those two options. Leveraging the legitimacy that she established while working for both Bert Brennan and Anthony Giacalone, Pagano helped arrange a meeting between Jimmy Hoffa and top officials in the Detroit family, probably Santo Perrone and Angelo Meli. No one knows exactly where or when this sit-down took place, but law enforcement, prominent labor historians, and Pagano's family firmly believe that it happened.[20] All that we know for sure is that by

the mid-1940s, the Detroit family had divested from its antiunion practices. Amid a marked decrease in picket line violence, Teamster organizing surged, which helped activists organize a hundred thousand workers
per year in the 1950s. It seems that Pagano's connection was pivotal to
Hoffa's long-standing goal to turn the industrial city into the Teamsters
metropolis.

Sylvia Pagano's connection to Hoffa ran deeper than their shared ties
to the Teamsters union. By the mid-1940s, Jimmy and Josephine Hoffa
were helping Pagano balance her responsibilities as a single mother with
the business endeavors that were her life's primary focus. Her son Chuckie
O'Brien remembered being sent out of state to live with relatives during
particularly frantic times in Pagano's work life, and he recalled walking
the picket line with waitresses' union president Myra Wolfgang and other
Detroit union activists while Pagano focused on her jobs.[21] With Pagano
busy making deals on many weekends, the Hoffas would take O'Brien and
their biological children Barbara and James to the family's cabin in Lake
Orion, Michigan. Some of O'Brien's fondest memories as a child involved
the weeks he spent each summer with the Hoffas at the lake. The relationship became so close that O'Brien began to understand Hoffa as a father
figure, and Hoffa often identified the boy as his "foster son."[22] Although it
is clear that Sylvia Pagano's connection to Jimmy Hoffa grew out of union
business, by 1950 she, Chuckie, and the Hoffas had built a family that
existed beyond blood relations, beyond a single household, and beyond
conventional domesticity.

The Wire: Revealing Sylvia Pagano's Metropolitan Lifestyle

Readers may notice an inconsistency in this telling of Sylvia Pagano's story.
If the premise of this chapter is that the public did not know about Pagano's pivotal role in the affairs of the International Brotherhood of Teamsters during the period when she was most active in the union, then how is
it possible to know specific details about her activities on a Saturday afternoon in March 1963? How do we know that Anthony Giacalone arrived
at her home at exactly 11:15? How do we know that she won a business
account with Frank's Trucking? How do we know that wrestling is what
she chose to watch on television?

These details exist because during the time they took place, the federal
government of the United States recorded every detail of Sylvia Pagano's
life. Between the spring of 1963 and the end of 1964, one of the most intrusive domestic surveillance programs in US history targeted Sylvia Pagano.

The FBI placed a microphone inside of Sylvia Pagano's living room in apartment 606C, recording all her most private dealings: business meetings with labor and underworld leaders, care that she gave to Josephine Hoffa during a mental health crisis, the long Sicilian lunches she cooked for her friends, and the romance she had with the men who loved her. FBI informants recorded all of her movements. Undercover agents tailed her car as she made mundane trips to the beauty salon and when she traveled to high-level meetings with the leadership of the Teamsters and with La Cosa Nostra. The FBI pressured airline reservation agents and hotel clerks to provide a constant stream of information about Pagano's movements. The massive trove of documents they collected paints a concrete picture of Sylvia Pagano as a powerbroker: a person who made a lot of money, who was unendingly busy, and who was at the center of Jimmy Hoffa's zealous effort to make the International Brotherhood of Teamsters the largest and powerful union in North America.

The ethical stakes of using the wiretap of apartment 606C to tell Pagano's story are immense. FBI surveillance was a tremendous invasion of Sylvia Pagano's privacy. It was unethical and illegal. The US Supreme Court ruled that bugging someone's home without a warrant violates the Fourth Amendment. Attorney General Robert F. Kennedy knew that and ordered the surveillance anyway. While Sylvia Pagano was caught up in the dragnet surrounding organized crime, Kennedy cast a much wider net. On October 10, 1963, for example, while his agents tailed Pagano every day, Kennedy approved the surveillance of Dr. Martin Luther King Jr. The FBI then leaked information from that probe, revealing extramarital affairs they claimed King was having and using information about his sexual transgressions to undermine King and to weaken the civil rights movement as a whole.[23] Given the deplorability of Robert F. Kennedy's actions, we must take great care when using the products of his grave violation of the compact between the state and the citizen.

I decided to use these materials because I believe that Sylvia Pagano would have approved of doing so. As labor historian David Witwer has argued, Robert F. Kennedy's Justice Department ran a sophisticated, comprehensive media campaign against the Teamsters during the years the wiretap took place, regularly leaking information that produced sensationalist stories in widely read publications from *Life* to *The Saturday Evening Post*.[24] Media outlets told a story about who Kennedy and his ghostwriter John Siegenthaler called "The Enemy Within," a morally bankrupt, culturally reactionary organization that stole from its members and undermined the economy.[25] In a script that Kennedy and his colleagues wrote entirely about white immigrant men's unrestrained comportment and aberrant values (see chapter 2), Pagano was an impossible subject, entirely elided from the story. The transcript from apartment 606C upends that narrative. As Harvard Law School professor Jack Goldsmith has argued, the transcript confirms and clarifies this far more dynamic story about the Teamsters, a tale in which Sylvia Pagano played a central role.[26] And perhaps more importantly, and as the words the microphone in her living room reveal, Pagano was a stinging critic of the professors, policymakers, lawyers, and police who painted an ugly portrait of the Teamsters while she was alive. I think Sylvia Pagano would have taken any chance she could get to toss out their expert ideas and prove them wrong.

The rhythm of daily life captured by the FBI's microphone provides a vivid account of Pagano's career as a businesswoman. She conducted a network of friends, vendors, and associates like a symphony. Pagano usually got up around 7 a.m. On went the record player or the radio, and on went the stove. Friends were often over for breakfast by 8:30. Two different domestic workers, one named Ruby and one named Marie, would—depending on the day—arrive at about the same time. For the duration of the FBI's surveillance, they literally never stopped vacuuming, giving Pagano what must have been the cleanest carpeting in all of Detroit.[27] While the vacuum whined in the background, Pagano worked the phones. July 16, 1963: Before she runs out to pick up some calves' liver she would serve for dinner, she calls a delivery boy to bring up a pack of Newport cigarettes, her brand of choice.[28] October 10, 1963: She calls Louie at the meat market, saying that she needs a roast to feed ten. Louie's service clearly irritated Pagano. "If you don't want to send the groceries up then you can forget about them," she complains.[29] American Airlines also gets her ire as well. She calls customer service, shocked that on a Teamster trip to Dallas they left her bag out in the rain, soaking all of her clothes.[30] She calls a furniture delivery company, confirming that a shipment made it Jimmy Hoffa's Washington DC apartment.[31] She calls Josephine Hoffa, telling her when to expect the drape cleaning service to arrive at their Lake Orion cabin.[32]

When she wrapped up managing what seems to have been a well-oiled domestic operation each morning, Pagano got to work on the jobs that paid those bills. During the time the FBI microphone recorded her affairs, Pagano ran several small- and medium-sized businesses with an unceasing hustle. June 13th, 1963: Pagano, Anthony Giacalone, and Chuckie O'Brien are in apartment 606C's living room debating buying the Henrose Hotel. Built on Cadillac Square in downtown Detroit in 1927, the Henrose was glamorous in its day, with ballrooms, restaurants decked out in palm trees, and luxurious suites at the top of the twenty-one-story red brick tower. But as Detroit's middle class was leaving the central city for the suburbs, the hotel had fallen on hard times. Pagano saw an opportunity, however, hoping to buy a gorgeous property on the cheap, renovate it, and operate at a profit. It is unclear if Pagano closed this particular deal. It is apparent, however, that Pagano was also building another company in the hospitality industry.[33] September 9, 1963: Pagano hashes out details for a janitorial business whose shares she had recently acquired. The firm had been struggling, but Pagano hoped to shore up its finances with new contracts at the Detroit Leland, the Sheraton Cadillac, the Statier, and other prominent convention hotels. Pagano figured that if her plan worked, she would take home at least $800—the equivalent of $7,200 today—every month.[34]

While evidence suggests that most of Pagano's businesses were in wholesaling, distribution, and hospitality, she was also involved in the finance and insurance sectors. She can be heard many times on the FBI microphone talking about stock trades. September 30th, 1963: Sylvia is in the kitchen, cooking lunch for Anthony Giacalone. Their conversation is interrupted by constant phone calls, all of which Pagano takes despite Giacalone's presence. After she hangs up with her daughter-in-law Mary Ann, Pagano tells Giacalone that she has made a deal to buy five hundred shares of the Polychrome Uranium Company for $1 per share, which she thinks is a stellar price.[35] November 27, 1963: Pagano works on forming an automobile leasing company with her friends and underworld associates Anthony and Danny Cimini. For a 25 percent stake in the firm, Pagano would broker a deal with Jimmy Hoffa to become the primary lessor for Teamster business agents' cars, an agreement that Pagano promised would undercut the union's current vendors and save Hoffa money. And while she was working on the auto finance transaction, Pagano was also getting certified to sell insurance.[36] February 27, 1964: FBI agents tail Pagano to the Living Room Lounge, a bar that her underworld friend Mike Polizzi owned. She sat down with several associates to discuss forming a corporation that would write life insurance policies for the employees of their businesses. Pagano's colleagues knew that she worked closely with Allan Dorfman, a higher-up in the Chicago outfit who managed the retirement fund for midwestern truckers called the Central States Pension Fund (CSPF). The group hoped to leverage Dorfman's industry connections to make their own inroads in the business in Detroit.[37]

The link to the Central States Pension Fund was—by far—the most important part of Sylvia Pagano's business portfolio, and it explains why she was such a powerbroker in Detroit. By 1963, Pagano regularly advised Jimmy Hoffa on how to invest the money in the CSPF. In the early 1950s, the International Brotherhood of Teamsters had won lucrative pension benefits for its members, policies that required employers to contribute the equivalent to 10 percent of a worker's income to a fund controlled by the union. Jimmy Hoffa came of age during the Great Depression and was deeply suspicious of a banking industry that he believed had destroyed the US economy in the 1930s and would soon destroy it again (see chapter 3). Refusing to financialize Teamsters' retirements, Hoffa aimed to invest the CSPF in assets he understood: in real estate and in the small- and medium-sized businesses of eastern and southern European Catholic and Jewish immigrants. Since the Italian and Jewish syndicates ran some of those businesses, and because underworld operatives were frequently denied loans from conventional banks, such firms often turned to illicit finance for access to capital. After 1960, Hoffa recognized that he could provide that capital in exchange for influence in the industries the Teamsters hoped to organize, aligning the interests of the union and the underworld as he had during his original professional dealings with Sylvia Pagano in the 1940s. In many cases, CSPF loans supported legitimate business projects and provided robust returns the union would pass on to members in the form of improved pension payments. But as historian David Witwer has demonstrated, while most unions and corporations used external financial administrators to manage their pension funds, Hoffa opted to run the fund himself with a small group of deferential allies. While that decision was rooted in Hoffa's scorn for elite bankers, it gave Hoffa unprecedented control over vast sums of capital. That control allowed Hoffa to consolidate power within the Teamsters and to make transactions that were extremely lucrative for Sylvia Pagano, for himself and Josephine Hoffa, and for many of their underworld friends and associates.[38]

The FBI microphone in apartment 606C recorded many details of Sylvia Pagano's connection to the CSPF. Some of her work involved appraising and endorsing investments for Hoffa. 6:30 p.m., June 13th, 1963: Pagano, Chuckie O'Brien, and Anthony Giacalone are sitting in the living room discussing business. Pagano tells the group that earlier in the afternoon, her associate Mike Polizzi had sent one of his errand boys to the Alden Park Manor. He drove into the basement and handed a letter to Sam, one of the building's maintenance men. Sam brought the letter up the service elevator to Pagano's apartment. The next afternoon she would hand deliver the document to Jimmy Hoffa and recommend that he approve a business loan of $190,000 that Polizzi requested in the letter. Other parts of the transcript record the money that Pagano made on such transactions.[39] 12:15 p.m., March 3, 1964: Pagano calls Anthony Giacalone at his office at the Home Juice Company, a beverage distributor he co-owned with his brother Vito and where the FBI had also wiretapped the phones. Pagano talks to Giacalone about an insurance investment that most likely drew funds from the CSPF. As was typical of such deals, the agreement came with a 10 percent commission. In this case, Jimmy and Josephine Hoffa split half the proceeds, the Giacalone brothers split 25 percent, and Pagano kept the remaining 25 percent for herself. On a single afternoon, she took home $15,000, the equivalent in today's money of $135,000. Still in other cases, underworld associates were heard asking Pagano to broker Teamster loans.[40] May 5, 1964: Anthony Giacalone and Pagano are discussing business in the living room of apartment 606C. He reminds her that the next time she sees Teamsters Local 985 president Bill Bufalino, Pagano should mention that George Rubin is a friend of hers. Rubin owned the Atlantic Towers Hotel on Collins Avenue in Miami Beach, and the FBI believed that Rubin sought a Teamster loan, perhaps to renovate the hotel.[41]

Even more telling than Pagano's own words were those of her male associates about her political stature and her logistical competence. June 3, 1963: Anthony Giacalone is at the office talking to his brother Vito in earshot of the FBI microphone. He explains to Vito that if their associates fail to treat Pagano with respect and to compensate her financially, she will "knock" their CSPF loan requests, scuttling the deals. "This guy . . . didn't want to come up with no more money (for Pagano) and she knocked the fucking loan and the guy didn't get no fucking loan." Giacalone continues, beginning to speak in Pagano's voice to make his point. "If they think they're going to get the loan without me, they're not going to come up with the money. Tell them not to fill (the application) out, because I'll knock it."[42] Giacalone clearly demonstrates that it was Sylvia Pagano—and not any man from the Teamsters or La Cosa Nostra—who had the ultimate influence over Hoffa's financial decisions. In other cases, men are heard admitting that their dealings depended on Pagano's sway. February 21, 1964: Anthony Zerilli is in Anthony Giacalone's office, and the two discuss a business trip to Palm Springs. In order to evade law enforcement surveillance, the two hoped to use the Teamsters' private plane rather than taking a commercial flight. Giacalone interjects that although Pagano is in Newark with Anthony Provenzano, a high-ranking official in New York's Genovese underworld family, they would need to get a hold of her to convince Hoffa to lend them the plane. "I'll tell her to talk to (Hoffa's pilot). She'll fly the fucking plane herself if she was told to."[43] While in one sense Giacalone's comments frame Pagano as a subordinate, as an underworld foot soldier who follows orders, their conversation assumes that it is Pagano, not Giacalone or Zerilli, who has the necessary leverage with Hoffa to execute the plan. Giacalone's metaphor is telling, as it imagines Pagano in the captain's seat, commanding the aircraft while Zerilli and Giacalone sit passively behind her in seats in the passenger cabin.

Sylvia Pagano's stature within her cohort of professional associates is striking, notably unusual for a woman during the mid-twentieth century. According to sociologist Chris M. Smith, women widely participated in the illicit economy before to 1920 because the underworld was decentralized.[44] This was true for both white women and women of color. As LaShawn Harris argues, "the burgeoning underground economy served as a catalyst in Black women's creation of employment opportunities, occupational identities, and survival strategies that provided financial stability and a sense of labor autonomy and mobility."[45] But as both Smith and Harris show, many of those opportunities vanished after the passage of Prohibition and during the Great Depression. Both because the lucrative nature of the illegal alcohol trade was attractive to wealthy actors, and because the underworld got more involved with labor organizing in the masculine-gendered domain of wage work (see chapter 1), organized crime became much more hierarchical, which elevated prominent white men's stature. That hierarchy also weakened the position of women who had participated in the underground economy through decentralized, small-time enterprises such as petty theft, brothel management, and low-level drug dealing and gambling.[46] The trend intensified after World War II, when Cold War anxieties elevated the ideology of domesticity,[47] and as eastern and southern European immigrant families' newly stable, suburban whiteness reinforced assumptions that Jewish and Italian women were wives, mothers, and caregivers, and not number runners, brothel madams, or labor operatives.

While Sylvia Pagano occupied a social location that was both atypical and illegible for a white woman in the mid-twentieth century, FBI surveillance confirms that she lived a highly mobile metropolitan lifestyle. While her domestic life took place in an early twentieth-century central city neighborhood with towering brownstones, a local butcher named Louie, and a steady stream of delivery boys, most of the Jewish and Sicilian underworld operatives who were her business partners had moved to Detroit's sprawling automobile suburbs and spent their time in ritzy homes with swimming pools, on country club sun decks, and on the golf course.

11:55 a.m., February 26, 1963: Pagano's steel gray Pontiac Grand Prix is in the driveway of Mike Rubino's 3,500-square-foot, five-bedroom house in Grosse Point Park. 12:15 p.m. A man comes out and drives the car over to Sicilian family higher-up Tony Cimini's four-bedroom, four-bathroom house, and then quickly returns. The Grand Prix then leaves Rubino's at 12:33, possibly with Pagano behind the wheel.[48] Daytime business frequently took Pagano to the Hillcrest Country Club in suburban Mount Clemens. With an expansive pool terrace and neatly manicured golf course that hosted Ladies Professional Golf Association events in the 1950s, law enforcement believed that underworld higher-up Giacomo Tocco owned a controlling stake in Hillcrest. Throughout the two years that the FBI had wiretapped her phones, Pagano is regularly heard calling the front desk, asking the receptionist to send a caddy out to the greens and fairways to carry a message to her associates.[49] It also seems that Pagano had attempted to buy the golf club with a group of investors affiliated with La Cosa Nostra in 1963, though that deal later fell through.[50]

Sylvia Pagano loved the cars she drove from the city to the suburbs. She bought the brand-new Grand Prix in on January 8, 1963, for the equivalent in today's money of $35,800 in cash.[51] With a 389-cubic-inch 4-barrel V8 under the hood, Pagano drove one of the era's classic muscle cars. While she may have enjoyed the Pontiac, it is also clear that Pagano liked to upgrade. When the FBI followed Pagano to meetings related to her insurance businesses with CSPF fund manager Allan Dorfman in the spring of 1964, Pagano was driving a cherry red Oldsmobile Cutlass that was even sportier than the Grand Prix and was a year newer.[52]

Pagano also traveled extensively for business. In an era when United Airlines still offered its "The Chicago Executive: A Club in the Sky for Men Only" business shuttle service between Chicago and New York, one on which women—except for the stewardesses—were not allowed,[53] Pagano was a road warrior. May 7, 1964: Pagano is sitting at the gate at Detroit's Willow Run airport, waiting for the departure of TWA Flight 177, a Convair 880 bound for Saint Louis. An undercover FBI agent hovers nearby. The gate agent pages Pagano with an urgent message: call Jimmy Hoffa at Teamster headquarters in Washington right away.[54]

It is clear that by the early 1960s Sylvia Pagano had become a successful businesswoman and an architect of the underground economy in Detroit and beyond. Her success would have been a source of envy for most businessmen, because of both the wealth she generated and the power she wielded. FBI surveillance confirms many of these facts beyond a reasonable doubt. The question that labor activists and historians must ask, then, is how Pagano became the boss that she was. How, we must ask, did Pagano achieve a degree of autonomy and mobility that was off-limits to most white women during the mid-twentieth century?

Queer Domesticity:
Business, Friendship, and Love inside Apartment 606C

Sylvia Pagano's access to the public world of men was the result of her relationship to the private sphere. By the early 1960s, apartment 606C had become a venue for what historian Nayan Shah calls "queer domesticity." Through his study of people who immigrated from East and South Asia to the US West Coast in the early twentieth century, Shah shows that marginal work placed people far outside the border of the nuclear family: living oceans away from parents, spouses, and children; cohabitating with other workers rather than with blood relatives; finding sex through homosexual and commercial encounters rather than in long-term, monogamous heterosexual relationships. While accounting for the pain of the broken bonds that comes with global migration, Shah's work is particularly compelling because it also theorizes the new lifeworlds that such people build in their unconventional homes, places where they pool financial resources, build political movements, and share friendship and intimacy in a way that makes an exploitive world more survivable and more joyful.[55]

Shaw writes about a particular context, about how anti-Asian racism, immigration policy, and labor law systematically denied nonwhite immigrants the privileges that had made Sylvia Pagano, Anthony Giacalone, and Jimmy Hoffa into middle-class American white people by the 1950s. But despite the vastly different historical milieu, Shah's insights help explain why Sylvia Pagano achieved the stature that she did. Pagano, Hoffa, and their friends came of age in the Depression-era US industrial city, one largely made up of migrant workers from Appalachia, from the US South, and from eastern and southern Europe. Out of necessity, and as Pagano's own coming-of-age demonstrates, most of those workers formed friendships, intimacies, and households that flouted the norms of the conventional nuclear family. By the time Pagano was providing investment consultations for the Teamsters in the 1960s, however, that Depression-era urban paradigm had given way to a middle-class suburban one. Shah compels us to consider that rather than uncritically adopting suburban cultural norms and abandoning the queer domesticity that was a defining feature of the immigrant industrial city of the 1930s, Sylvia Pagano and her friends adopted some of the unconventional family structures that had defined the world of their youth. In these porous, flexible kinship networks, Pagano found social mobility and gained access to money, power, autonomy, and pleasure typically reserved for men.

The queer domesticity of apartment 606C was particularly evident during the turbulent summer of 1963. These were probably the busiest months of Jimmy Hoffa's career as he was making the final push to compel trucking companies to sign the National Master Freight Agreement, a watershed deal that standardized wages for long-distance truckers across the entire industry. Since the middle of the 1950s, long-haul truckers had been paid even better than their peers in other heavily unionized industries, earning 11 percent more than miners, 8 percent more than manufacturing workers, and 1.5 percent more than meatpackers.[56] This deal would lock in that advantage and augment it with an additional pay bump plus a mandatory employer contribution of 10.3 percent of an employee's wage to the Teamsters pension and welfare funds.[57] This nationwide deal represented an apex of trade union power in the United States, and it delivered a solidly middle-class lifestyle to people who grew up in poverty and who were never able to access formal education. Hammering out that agreement took virtually all of Jimmy Hoffa's time and much of the time of Josephine Hoffa and Sylvia Pagano, who traveled to twenty-nine states promoting the deal in 1963.[58]

While that push was hopeful and invigorating, it also took a toll on Jimmy Hoffa's personal life, as he was virtually never home. Meanwhile, Robert F. Kennedy's dragnet was closing in on Hoffa, relentlessly surveilling, cataloguing, and appraising every aspect of his public and private life in an unceasing effort to purge him from the Teamsters union and send him to jail, which finally happened in 1967. Those two details—Jimmy Hoffa's absence during the freight agreement push and the constant threat of imprisonment—were debilitating to Josephine Hoffa. August 14, 1963: Pagano is on the phone with Josephine Hoffa. Hoffa is sobbing, and Pagano can be heard trying to comfort her to no avail on multiple phone calls throughout the day. Sometime in the previous few days, and during a period of extreme drinking, Josephine Hoffa had begun to suffer a mental health break. "Something just snapped inside her mind," Pagano can be heard telling her daughter in law Mary Ann O'Brien. Pagano went on to describe how Josephine Hoffa was strapped to a bed in the hospital, spending most of the day and night heavily sedated. Pagano seems to have been the primary point person for this family emergency and can be heard talking to Jimmy Hoffa—who was on the road working for the NMFA—to communicate what was happening and to strategize about the response.

Jimmy Hoffa was clearly shaken, and he ordered Pagano to keep either herself or Chuckie O'Brien next to Josephine Hoffa at all times and to hide this information from strangers and from the press. Pagano coordinated the news of the crisis to the inner circle of Teamster and underworld leaders. During that same phone call, for example, Pagano tells Mary Ann O'Brien that Bill Bufalino is already down at the hospital with Josephine Hoffa.[59]

During this intense period when she was trying to protect Josephine Hoffa's privacy and her health, Sylvia Pagano faced a second dilemma in the Hoffa family. August 15, 1963: the day after the painful phone calls to Josephine Hoffa's hospital room. Pagano has to break the news to Josephine Hoffa's mother, whom everyone refers to as "Ma," that the family intended for her to move into a nursing home. Jimmy Hoffa and Pagano knew that the stairs in the Hoffa's small home on Robson Street in Detroit where Ma had been living were no longer safe for her. The announcement was clearly upsetting to Ma. That afternoon, Pagano took Ma on a guided tour of what would become her new home. Pagano can be heard on the microphone raving about how luxurious the space was, enthusiastically describing the daily laundry service that Ma would receive, and reminding Ma that she would have her own private suite. Pagano's efflorescence clearly did nothing to sell Ma on the move to the home.[60] August 21, six days later: Pagano has to call Jimmy Hoffa to tell him that Ma "flew the coop," somehow temporarily disappearing from the Hoffas' house in an apparent protest against the move to the nursing home. On the telephone, Hoffa can be heard exasperated, angry, and distressed at what he sees as Ma's self-involved stunt in the middle of the wider struggle with Josephine Hoffa's mental health. Later that day, Pagano notifies Chuckie O'Brien that she is not telling Josephine Hoffa any of this given the fragility of her state, a decision that clearly placed even more burden on Pagano because it forced her to manage the crisis alone while Jimmy Hoffa was on the road.[61]

While she provided care for the Hoffas and their children, the queer domesticity of apartment 606C also involved romance and sex. While the nature of those connections varied over time, all of these intimacies took place far beyond the boundary of the traditional nuclear family. During the period the FBI microphone recorded, Pagano was having a romantic relationship with her primary business partner Anthony Giacalone, a man her son Chuckie called "Uncle Tony."[62] And for a period before her mental health crisis worsened in the summer and fall of 1963, Josephine Hoffa was also having an intimate relationship with Anthony Cimini, a member of the Detroit underworld who co-owned at least one business with Giacalone and Pagano. July 26, 1963: It is 1:30 p.m. on a Saturday afternoon. Sylvia

Pagano, Josephine Hoffa, Anthony Cimini, and Anthony Giacalone are all in Pagano's living room, listening to records and having afternoon cocktails. In passing, they note that Pagano has been "going with" Giacalone for six years and that Cimini and Josephine Hoffa had been together for a year. This afternoon gathering was a typical way for Pagano to entertain in her home. While she certainly hosted dinners and often invited guests for the typical 1950s five o'clock cocktail party, Pagano's favored social event was the long Sicilian lunch. On dozens of occasions, Pagano can be heard convening with Giacalone around 1 p.m., cooking as the two discussed the Teamsters and other business and as Ruby or Marie punctuated the conversation with the vacuum. Sometimes they would retire to the bedroom. On this particular Saturday, the two couples spent the whole afternoon together and could be heard exchanging sweetly romantic goodbyes as both the Tonys left Pagano's apartment around 5:30.[63]

While we cannot know exactly how Sylvia Pagano understood the linkage between business, friendship, and romantic love in her relationships, we do know that she sometimes spoke about them in candid terms. Words captured on the microphone in the living room of apartment 606C reveal, for example, that while she felt deeply connected to Anthony Giacalone, she did not imagine that their kinship should or would transition into a traditional, monogamous marriage. April 17, 1963: At 3:15 in the afternoon Pagano is on the phone with a friend whom FBI agents cannot identify. The friend asks Pagano if she is going to marry Giacalone. "Getting married?" Pagano interjects, seemingly exasperated. "Oh are you kidding? No." She then begins speaking to her friend in Giacalone's voice to explain where she stands in the relationship. "Sylvia, remember I've got a family. I have children and I would never leave them. I will never leave them and I know that you wouldn't want me to leave them. You must find someone who can take care of you, and I don't just mean anybody because you've gotta have somebody. This is the way he talks to me."[64] The tone of Pagano's words is simply frank. She does not seem irritated by what she portrays as Giacalone's conventionally patriarchal assumption that she needed a husband breadwinner, even though her daily life obviously proved otherwise. But nor does she seem to pine for him or to express a wish or a hope that Giacalone would eventually play that role. It seems that both Pagano and Giacalone probably assumed that she would, most likely, marry someone else someday.

Sylvia Pagano's matter-of-fact way of talking about her relationship with Giacalone is consistent with her tough, businesslike tone in most of the conversations that the FBI microphone captured in apartment

606C. In a few instances, however, Pagano showed great vulnerability as she described the unconventional life that she lived. August 15, 1963, 11:30 a.m.: Pagano is on the phone with Josephine Hoffa the day after she checked into the hospital. She speaks what are some of the most introspective, most painful words in the transcript. "Are you listening to me? Because I love you Josephine. I don't want anything to happen to you. You are all I've got. I haven't got anybody. Sure, I mean I got my mother, but I mean, same time, she can take care of herself and everything. That's all I got. I got nobody else."[65] At first glance, the loneliness in these words is baffling in the wider context of Pagano's dealings. Sylvia Pagano lived a strikingly full life, full of friends, dynamic businesses, social mobility, and money. But in this moment of self-doubt, a shrewd businesswoman writes off all her assets. She writes off Jimmy Hoffa, Anthony Giacalone, all her businesses, and her luxury apartment. She writes off the Teamsters and she writes off La Cosa Nostra. Her only love, the only one she can count on, is Josephine Hoffa.

After three decades of queer scholarship and activism that has transformed the way we think about the past, we must consider all possible meanings to the words, "Because I love you Josephine, you are all I have got," even though we have little concrete evidence to interpret what Pagano meant here. While romantic love could certainly be evident in these words, I argue that a different queer formation is coming into view. In a pained moment, Sylvia Pagano acknowledged that she lived far outside the box that society had made for her in the 1950s and early 1960s and that living outside the box was a lonely place to be. Yes, she spoke to Jimmy Hoffa constantly about interesting, substantive events. Yes, she could get Anthony Provenzano or any other underworld higher-up on the phone in minutes. Yes, she could buy a brand-new four-barrel V8 Pontiac in cash and drive it as fast as she wanted. Yes, many people told vivid stories about the many handsome men for whom Sylvia Pagano was an object of desire. But here, in a moment of doubt, Pagano knew that she owned none of these things. She knew full well that there was no place for a single woman in the mid-twentieth century to run a business, to lead the labor movement, or to challenge the culture of the American family on her own terms. At least in this moment, Pagano knew that as an atypical person, everything she had built could vanish. A friendship was all that Sylvia Pagano had, which during a moment of crisis was little solace in a society that values blood kinship, marriage, monogamy, and domesticity over the more ambiguous concept of friendship as the defining feature of a relationship you can count on.

Pressing though Pagano's dilemmas most certainly were, there is little historical evidence with which to process them. A year after this pained telephone conversation, and presumably because the trajectory of its case against La Cosa Nostra changed, the FBI removed the microphone from apartment 606C and stopped surveilling Pagano. Amid growing public awareness of and backlash against the FBI's counterintelligence campaign against the civil rights movement, the justice department strove to hide the illegal wiretaps it had authorized in the early 1960s, which delayed the dissemination of information about the Pagano surveillance. Meanwhile, Jimmy Hoffa went to prison in 1967 after being convicted of jury tampering. Losing her direct line to the general president of the International Brotherhood of Teamsters undoubtedly undermined Pagano's professional stature and weakened her financial position. Three years later, while Hoffa continued to serve his sentence in the Lewisburg Federal Penitentiary in Pennsylvania, Sylvia Pagano's story ended abruptly. During a business trip to New York on December 17, 1970, she suffered a heart attack. At fifty-six years old, Sylvia Pagano died. Her son Chuckie O'Brien spoke of his debilitating depression that followed her death and of the scores of Teamsters who lined up to attend her funeral.[66] Yet until the new wave of scrutiny that followed Jimmy Hoffa's disappearance in July of 1975, the woman who helped shape the Teamsters' financial and political strategy during the peak of the union's political and economic power remained absent in the widespread coverage of those victories.

Knowing Sylvia Pagano

The public finally met Sylvia Pagano two days after Jimmy Hoffa vanished on his way to meet Anthony Giacalone for lunch at the Machus Red Fox restaurant in the Detroit suburb of Bloomfield Hills. On August 1, 1975, as television, radio, and print sources provided uninterrupted coverage of Hoffa's spellbinding disappearance, the *Detroit News* ran a story on page 15A with the headline "Tony Jack had Mystery Woman Friend" above a black-and-white photograph of Sylvia Pagano.[67] The paper had widely covered Anthony Giacalone, so much so that reporters regularly used his nickname "Tony Jack." This was, however, the first time the *Detroit News* had described Pagano in any detail. The background narrative about Pagano—which came from writers' anonymous sources in law enforcement—was wildly inaccurate. But because the paper had also obtained the transcript from the microphone inside apartment 606C, it presented a detailed, factual account of Pagano's relationship to the Detroit, Chicago, and New

York underworlds and to the top leadership of the International Brotherhood of Teamsters.

Given the unprecedented detail in thousands of pages of documents about Pagano's life, and because of how compelling, relevant, and intimate many of the words on the transcript are, it is tempting to believe that these texts provide a neutral portrait of Sylvia Pagano's life. Such an assumption is, however, deeply flawed. White men in law enforcement produced all these documents: reports from FBI informants embedded within La Cosa Nostra, descriptions from plain-clothes officers who followed Pagano, summaries of interviews with neighbors, and the transcription of Pagano's own words, among many others. In these texts, we see Pagano not as she was, but as middle-class professional men saw a single woman who had come from working-class Sicilian immigrant roots, and who lived what they would have seen as an unconventional lifestyle.

The story they told was often explicit in its exoticism, one that described a swarthy woman shrouded in mystery. FBI agents interviewed Mr. and Mrs. Frank Wilson, for example, who lived two floors above Pagano in apartment 812C at the Alden Park Manor. Mr. Wilson was apparently uncomfortable with the invasion of Pagano's privacy when the FBI approached him, and he provided no useful information about her life. Mrs. Wilson, however, was candid, and FBI agents seemed to relish the details in her story. She spoke of a dark, mystical, ethnic woman who lived downstairs in apartment 606C. Pagano is "black haired and looks like a Gypsy, always wearing tight toreador pants. She usually speaks a foreign language," FBI agents scribbled as Mrs. Wilson spoke.[68] Similarly, the agents interviewed Howard Dwyer, a self-described bachelor who worked in the personnel department at Chrysler and whose home FBI agents described as "sharing a bedroom wall" with apartment 606C. The bachelor dwelled on the men who came into Pagano's apartment, describing them as "big and tough" and admitting that he got interested in Pagano's personal life after seeing Jimmy Hoffa on multiple occasions get out of the service elevator and walk into her apartment.[69]

While middle-class ideas about ethnicity, class, and sex influenced both the story that Dwyer and Wilson told about Pagano and the FBI agents' accounts of the interviews, such assumptions also shaped the way agents heard Pagano's words. The FBI officials who transcribed the microphone's recordings created not a verbatim reproduction of all words uttered inside apartment 606C, but rather a truncated account based on their theory of what they hoped would be a criminal case against La Cosa Nostra. Large sections of the recording were therefore not transcribed, labeled "impertinent" after officials decided that such events would not advance the prosecution. Perhaps even more importantly, agents only transcribed the conversations inside apartment 606C that took place in English. Pagano and most of her associates in the Sicilian syndicate were bilingual, however, and often jumped from fluent English to fluent Italian as they conducted businesses. When they did so, FBI agents wrote the all-capitals word "ITALIAN" into the record, and then resumed transcribing when dialogue returned to English. Because of this procedure, scores of hours of conversation inside apartment 606C remain unaccounted for.

The English words the agents did write down reflected their own cultural paradigm as much as it reflected Pagano's. Some of Pagano's personal traits, for example, rattled the FBI. Transcribers seemed disturbed by how often Pagano cursed, noting her frequent use of profanity in memos about her dealings, and they refused to transcribe the words "fuck," "fucker," "fucking," or "fucked." Other objectionable content did not bother them. When Anthony Giacalone used anti-Black and anti-Chinese racial slurs, they transcribed them fully and did not remark on their usage, rendering those words equivalent to any other neutral description of a person.[70]

These and other biases heavily abridged the narrative that the FBI produced about Sylvia Pagano's personal and professional affairs. Perhaps most importantly, FBI agents rarely identified Black people who appear in the transcript, instead attributing Black people's words to "a negro" without a name. In the thousands of pages of the Pagano transcript, for example, agents never identified any Black person with a last name. Bob the interior decorator, Sam the maintenance man, and Ruby and Marie the maids were in Pagano's apartment talking to her on many, many days. But even though Pagano probably spent more time with Ruby and Marie than she did with Anthony Giacalone or Jimmy Hoffa, we have no record of their full legal identities. One should wonder if Ruby and Marie—and Sylvia Pagano—took advantage of these omissions. Ruby and Marie vacuumed constantly, more than anyone would reasonably vacuum, and often while guests were over. They could have known that the noise of a vacuum cleaner would block a suspected microphone from recording conversations, which it indeed did in dozens of places on the transcript marked "conversation unclear—vacuuming." We must at least consider whether Ruby and Marie were doing this on purpose, covering up business that Pagano was doing with them or with others that they did not want outside listeners to hear. Why, for example, was the vacuum on for almost every conversation Pagano had with Bob, the interior decorator? Could the many conversations the vacuum blocked out have revealed a business relationship between Bob and Pagano that ran deeper than green fabric samples? Since we know that Sam the maintenance man carried a letter for a CSPF loan request from Mike Polizzi to Sylvia Pagano on June 13th, 1963,[71] could Sam have had a deeper, more sophisticated relationship to the Teamsters or to La Cosa Nostra that would teach us more about both organizations? Given the FBI agents' racist assumptions about Black people's place in the world, we do not know the answers to these questions.

While the federal government was compiling and transcribing its interpretation of the words of everyone who entered apartment 606C, it was also weaponizing those words to undermine the people being surveilled. The FBI communicated no details about Sylvia Pagano's business activity. But it seems that agents did spread graphic information about her sex life that they obtained through the microphone. December 4, 1963: Detroit family higher-ups Pete Licavoli and Mike Rubino call Anthony Giacalone into an emergency meeting. They tell him that a rumor is circulating that Giacalone, Anthony Cimini, Josephine Hoffa, and Sylvia Pagano are "playing house," having illicit domestic and sexual relationships. Giacalone blows up in anger, demanding to know how his associates obtained the information and admitting that underworld lawyer Larry Burns had also recently heard the gossip. Rubino tells Giacalone that he suspected the information was intentionally leaked by an FBI agent, perhaps an undercover infiltrator. FBI documents show that Rubino's hunch was indeed correct and that agents had purposely spread the account of Pagano, Josephine Hoffa, and the Tonys' long Sicilian lunch that Saturday afternoon in July 1963.[72] Records do not reveal why agents decided to leak the story. We might assume, however, that since Jimmy Hoffa was the prime target of the Justice Department's investigation, and because the story describes two of Jimmy Hoffa's closest associates—Anthony Giacalone and Sylvia Pagano—orchestrating his wife's extramarital affair, that federal operatives spread the information to provoke anger, paranoia, and embarrassment in Hoffa, emotions that would work in concert to weaken him.

Through the FBI's crass sexual storytelling, a far wider swath of the US public met Sylvia Pagano. By the end of the 1970s, a number of detailed journalistic accounts of Jimmy Hoffa's disappearance had been published, all of which relied on anonymous sources in law enforcement. Unlike the 1950s, when media accounts elided Pagano's role in the Teamsters and in La Cosa Nostra, the new, younger generation of journalists made Pagano quite visible, giving her a supporting role in a story about Hoffa. Her character, however, taught audiences much more about the culture of the 1970s than it did about the operations of the International Brotherhood of Teamsters when Pagano was alive. The United States was in the middle of the sexual revolution when these books began to tell Pagano's story. That upheaval had two countervailing consequences. On the one hand, the political activism of women's and gay liberationists, Black and Chicana feminists, and lesbian separatists allowed people to speak much more frankly about sex. In the wake of their movement, the mainstream media began to cover topics that had long been taboo: abortion, transgender expression, nonmonogamy, and sex work.[73] But on the other hand, because middle-class white men still held almost every job in the media, at corporations, in the government, and in higher education, most of the new sexual representation came from their perspective. Therefore, when journalists wrote about Pagano after reading the microphone transcript and interviewing men in law enforcement, the person they spoke about was a projection of the way middle-class white men thought about women during the sexual revolution.

Most prominent in the new genre was the work of Dan Moldea, a former Teamster truck driver turned Kent State University graduate student and journalist for NBC News. Moldea's work was rigorously researched and accessibly written, appearing first as a series of articles in *Playboy*, and then as the six-hundred-page book *The Hoffa Wars*. While erotic and pornographic images undoubtedly fueled *Playboy*'s sales, the magazine was also a venue for legitimate cultural analysis. As media studies scholar Bill Osgerby argues, *Playboy* had been selling a young, manly world of consumption, narcissism, and leisure since publication began in 1953. Articles aimed not to arouse readers sexually, but rather to stimulate young middle-class men's curiosity about other men's lives that diverged from their own, which in this case was the hardscrabble world of the working class: the picket line brawls, the torrid love affairs, the backroom deals, and the Mafia blackmail.[74] Moldea's research produced essays that fit comfortably within *Playboy*'s business model for men's lifestyle journalism. Much of the text drew on interviews with anonymous FBI agents and local police officers who levied scathing condemnations of Jimmy Hoffa as a thug and a crook and who told raunchy stories about women's relationships, motivations, and desires.

All six references to Sylvia Pagano in *The Hoffa Wars* are about sex. Moldea introduces Pagano as a "darkly attractive woman" who had a "clerical job with a union."[75] Drawing the reader to her arousingly ethnic appearance, Moldea presents no information about the union local or the industry in which she worked. And by describing her dealings as clerical work, Moldea exemplifies some men in the New Left's tendency to see typing, cleaning, and food preparation—rather than political strategy—as women's principal contribution to social movements.[76] The vulgar, sexually charged words of anonymous sources in law enforcement provided the structure for Moldea's telling of Pagano's backstory. He describes her, for example, as Jimmy Hoffa's "former mistress," an odd word choice given that Hoffa would have been unmarried and in his early twenties when such an affair would have taken place.[77] In another case, a nameless source Moldea calls "a Washington D.C. law enforcement official who is an expert on organized crime" claimed that underworld higher-up Frank Coppola "picked up where Hoffa left off, and began having an affair with Pagano."[78] The sources framed Jimmy Hoffa's personal life in similarly crude terms, claiming that he was having an affair with a woman they—once again—described as a "union secretary."[79] In this case, the source also described her as a "redhead," which exemplifies some middle-class men's tendency to refer to white women not with names, but rather with physical descriptions such as blonde or brunette. Perhaps most salaciously, Moldea and other journalists repeated the rumor that Pagano's son Chuckie O'Brien was not the biological son of the Kansas City underworld fixer Charles Lenton O'Brien, but rather Pagano and Hoffa's love child.[80] While there is no historical evidence to support this claim, it fits anonymous sources' wider narrative well, framing Pagano as an attractive yet empty vessel whom a long string of Teamsters and mobsters took turns having sex with as they built a man's world of business, labor, and politics.

Dan Moldea and other 1970s journalists taught us much about Jimmy Hoffa. But their sexually provocative writing proved just as incapable as the staid journalism of the 1950s of telling a complex, well-documented story about Sylvia Pagano. Like their 1950s counterparts, 1970s journalists could not locate Sylvia Pagano because they could not grapple with queer domesticity. By making sex hypervisible in Pagano's past, they crowded out the far more complex set of kinship practices and economic relationships that organized her life. Yes, Chuckie O'Brien saw Jimmy Hoffa as a father figure. But he most likely did so not because of his mother's illicit sexual past, but rather because he lost his own father as a seven-year-old and because he craved the fatherly attention that Hoffa, by all accounts, loved giving. Yes, Pagano left Chuckie O'Brien with the Hoffas on the weekends. But she did so not because romantic encounters with mobsters were her primary endeavor, but instead because she believed—like many working-class women who came before her—that being a good mother required, first and foremost, being a good provider. Yes, Pagano had a love affair with Anthony Giacalone while he was married to his wife Zina.

But the root of their intimate connections seems to have been the hustle they shared and the energy that both clearly gleaned from selling products and making deals. Without a set of historical tools to account for the unconventional and sometimes unruly intimate ties around which Pagano built her life, the journalists of the 1970s raised many more questions than they answered about Pagano. Absent a more critical account, labor scholars and activists left the twentieth century without getting to know Sylvia Pagano.

Conclusion: Toward a Queer Rereading of Labor's Past

By the time the FBI removed the microphone from apartment 606C in 1964, a new generation of activists and intellectuals was transforming the political landscape both in the United States and abroad. At first glance, the new social movements they were building resembled the grassroots, bottom-up, life-and-death physical struggles that defined Pagano and the Hoffas' world when they were young people during the Great Depression. Poor, rural African American sharecroppers were giving their lives as they battled the white mobs, the police fire hoses, and the Molotov cocktails of racial terror in Selma, Birmingham, and Meridian. Gay and transsexual sex workers and homeless youth would fight the police at Compton's Cafeteria and the Stonewall Inn. They, in tandem with struggles against colonization, imperialism, and militarism across the globe, were creating a new paradigm for the political, demanding a downward redistribution of money and power via the particularities of race, gender, sexuality, and culture.

Despite the tactical similarities, vast differences separated the turmoil of the US immigrant industrial city of the 1930s from the new social movements of the 1960s and 1970s. While activists on the margins, from Fanny Lou Hamer to Sylvia Rivera, resembled Hoffa's generation in that they lacked access to land, a fair wage, and a formal education, many of the new social movements' leaders were the middle-class, college-educated, native-born, monolingual in English children of people like Pagano and the Hoffas. They took aim at the institutions and values that they understood as having defined the previous generation, values they would have seen in the social world inside apartment 606C: consumerism, the nationalism of the "American standard of living," racial segregation, patriarchy, and compulsory heterosexuality, among others. Jimmy Hoffa was indeed hostile to some of the younger generation's critiques and often used pejoratives such as "longhairs" to define and dismiss the countercultural activism of the 1960s. Hoffa, for example, remarked to labor journalist Paul Jacobs as they walked down the "Boulevard of the Beats" on Grant Street in San Francisco in the early 1960s, "If I had a bunch of Detroit cops here, I would clean these joints out in no time. All these people need is a bath."[81] Hearing Hoffa's observations as dated and provincial, younger activists dismissed Hoffa and Pagano's generation—and big unions more generally—as a retrograde, reactionary force that, as historian Jefferson Cowie demonstrates in his foundational book *Stayin' Alive*, drove a wedge between the labor movement and the new social movements.

As younger activists helped hammer in that wedge, Sylvia Pagano disappeared. At first glance, this is surprising, as Pagano exemplified what many 1960s radicals—and especially women's liberationists—wanted to be: an independent woman who had supported herself since she was a teenager, who had been the sole breadwinner for a middle-class household for much of her life, and who had ample access to financial assets, political power, and sexual gratification. As she spent nights with the Giacalone brothers, Tony Cimini, the Hoffas, Chuckie O'Brien, and others in apartment 606C, Pagano rebuffed the status quo of mid-twentieth-century domesticity that the younger activists were also contesting. But in another sense, Pagano was anathema to women's liberation. She worked around powerful men on their terms rather than on her own. She lacked the formal education to understand analytical concepts like patriarchy and compulsory heterosexuality. She suffered indignities in her public life because of her gender. And perhaps most importantly, Pagano came from a cohort of Catholic and Jewish immigrants who, despite their parents' and grandparents' highly ambiguous relationship to whiteness, either lacked the tools to understand or did not want to engage the category of race that had become a motivating factor for the social movements of the 1960s. Pagano was thus an illegible subject during the 1960s zeitgeist, part of a cohort of labor women that many younger activists dismissed because of what was visible: a connection to union and underworld men who were crass in demeanor and who could not or would not understand the changing world around them. In an era when Ella Baker and Mario Savio and Cesar Chavez and Angela Davis were changing the world, Jimmy Hoffa had become a vestige of a past that many younger activists wanted to forget.

This chapter has challenged such a disavowal. I compel today's labor activists to revisit Sylvia Pagano and others who fall outside the conventional paradigms for historical representation, as the cultural complexity of their business enterprises, their political mobilization, their friendships, their intimacies, and their desires has much to teach us. The story we learned about them from Robert F. Kennedy, from the FBI, and from the middle-class press was, after all, not a neutral description of events, but rather part of an ideological apparatus that aimed to push people who had grown up in the unruly spaces of the industrial city into the box of mid-twentieth-century suburban domesticity. By revealing and confirming a different narrative of the Teamsters' past, one exposes the ideological work of Kennedy's tale. If we would have known about Sylvia Pagano, we would have seen the spaces she inhabited—her downtown apartment, the working-class bars her underworld friends owned, the suburban mansions of her associates, the sunny terrace of the Hillcrest Country Club— not as comfortable venues for midcentury culture, but rather as unsettled, contested places. In such locations, those where Jimmy Hoffa and Sylvia Pagano helped recruit hundreds of thousands of union members, turning the city into the Teamsters metropolis, activists struggled over the meaning of their race, gender, sexuality, and class even as they lacked the language to articulate those dilemmas. If we had known about Sylvia Pagano, we would have known much more about these debates, which suggest that the struggle for economic justice is always a cultural struggle. Sylvia Pagano reminds us of these tensions, pushing us toward a newer, queerer understanding of labor's past.

Queer Nightlife in the Teamsters Metropolis
Teamster Unionism as an Embodied Practice

The Everard Baths were a foundation of gay public life in New York City in the middle of the twentieth century. Located on West Twenty-Eighth Street in a neighborhood that was called the Tenderloin for a time, the bathhouse was marked by an ornate, elaborately painted Victorian façade when it opened in 1888. Guests escaped the relentless heat, choking dust, and nauseating odors of Manhattan's summer streets to enjoy refreshing fountains and sparkling, cool water in wide marble pools.[1] This was not a public bathing facility for tenement dwellers who lacked indoor plumbing. Rather, the Everard was an exclusive amenity for the health and comfort of the city's white Protestant elite. But within a few decades, as posh hotels moved northward along Park Avenue and as the federal government began to encourage the white middle class to move upward and outward to suburbs in the Hudson Valley, on Long Island, and in Connecticut and New Jersey, gay men—a group that had always used the Everard to make social, professional, and intimate connections—became its sole customers. By 1950, the bathhouse was a place for public sex. In the pool on the lower level, in the steam room, and in the small cubicles upstairs, men let their guard down in a violent world, engaging in frottage, performing fellatio, and having insertive and receptive anal sex with lovers, friends, and strangers. While the facility included spaces to relax, smoke, drink, and socialize, and while bathhouses would help launch a new wave of gay political activism in subsequent decades, the fact that people called the Everard the "Ever-Hard"[2] in the mid-twentieth century reflects the primarily sexual nature of the space.[3]

The proprietors of small service businesses like the Everard took an immense personal risk when their establishments provided a place for queer people to gather. According to historian George Chauncey, homosexuality and gender nonconformity were widely visible to middle-class people during the "pansy craze" of Prohibition-era New York.[4] But after repeal, when the "good government" reforms of liberal mayor Fiorello LaGuardia made it more difficult to pay protection bribes to public officials, and as heterosexual marriage, traditional gender roles, monogamy, and domesticity became ideological tools to stabilize a culture that had been shaken by the Great Depression and world wars, gay public life faced a daunting new wave of repression. Not only did police physically and sexually assault patrons during frequent raids on gay bars,[5] but state law made it illegal to serve "homosexuals, degenerates, and/or undesirables" in any New York City bar until 1967.[6] Even at venues without the Everard's transgressive sexual culture, barkeeps could lose their license and their livelihood by simply serving food or drink to a gay or transgender person.

Historical evidence suggests that by the 1950s, some small business owners were willing to take this risk because the institutions of the Teamsters metropolis had their backs. In 1949, a Jewish entrepreneur named Irving Fine bought the Everard Baths. He did so with financing from Irving Mishel, the owner of a "factoring" company that loaned money to eastern and southern European immigrants who lacked generational wealth and creditworthiness but who wanted to start small businesses in the service sector. To bring additional stability to these undercapitalized industries, Mishel and his associates began working with the International Brotherhood of Teamsters to organize the workers at some of the establishments they had financed. Doing so helped standardize wages, which would make it more difficult for newer firms with lower labor costs to undercut the small businesses that Mishel bankrolled. To convince his clients to acquiesce to these initiatives, Mishel leveraged the primary asset of immigrant entrepreneurs who lacked political connections and conventional financial resources: the muscle of the Jewish and Sicilian underworlds.[7]

Those unruly tactics were critical to the production of queer public space. By 1950, Jimmy Hoffa's associates in the Genovese family—one of the "five families" of La Cosa Nostra in New York and New Jersey—had made a widespread investment in a new service business: queer nightlife. As Phillip Crawford demonstrates in his meticulously researched book *The Mafia and the Gays*, Genovese operatives owned, controlled, or loaned money to scores of lesbian bars, drag cabarets, gay bathhouses, adult bookstores, and pornographic movie theaters between the 1940s and the 1980s. Many of the most famous institutions of the dissident sexual underground of the mid-twentieth century were, at least for a time, fronts for La Cosa Nostra: the Bon Soir, the Cherry Lane, the Hip-o-Drome, the Stonewall, and indeed the Everard Baths.[8] The Genovese family's soldiers and their Teamster allies were often imagined to be paragons of conventional masculinity and traditional family values, with bulging muscles, flying fists, roaring voices, and conservative ideas about husband breadwinners and dependent wives. But in at least some cases, La Cosa Nostra's physical fortitude provided a defensive shield for those on the margins of mid-twentieth-century culture: gay people, gender outlaws, homeless youth, sex radicals, hustlers, and call girls.

Pivotal though this alliance between the Teamsters, the underworld, and small-time entrepreneurs most certainly was for queer people in the 1950s, it faded from relevance in the later decades of the twentieth century. LGBTQ activists soon built a campaign that pushed through civil rights laws that helped protect queer-owned and queer-patronized bookstores, bars, theaters, and community centers, which rendered protection payments to La Cosa Nostra moot. As the gay bar–underworld alliance waned, the International Brotherhood of Teamsters' Hoffa-era zeitgeist also passed. By the late 1960s, amid the federal government's relentless surveillance and their own increasingly unscrupulous affairs, the set of personal relationships at the center of this book had ruptured. Jimmy Hoffa went to jail for four years beginning in 1967 and never returned to the Teamsters' presidency. Sylvia Pagano died unexpectedly in New York in 1970. Pagano's longtime friend, business partner, and lover Anthony Giacalone—along with Hoffa's primary Genovese-family ally Anthony Provenzano—was widely suspected to have participated in the sequence of events that led to Hoffa's disappearance on July 31, 1975. In the efflorescence of the social movements of the 1960s, one that would transform the Stonewall from a Genovese-family front into the namesake for militant queer activism, the Teamsters union began to seem like a vestigial remnant of an industrial metropolis that had disappeared into the past.

Despite those painful setbacks, the Hoffa-era Teamsters union has much to teach contemporary labor scholars and activists. This final chapter takes stock of those contributions, all of which lead back to a single point: Jimmy Hoffa's Teamsters union was a culturally revered, economically impactful social movement because it challenged the embodied experience of life according to the Protestant work ethic. Max Weber famously argued that US capitalism flourishes because of a religiously inflected secular system of values that governs our bodies, pushing us toward hard work and away from the delight of rich entrees and sweet desserts, away from the comfort of a long night's sleep, away from pleasure of sexual release, and away from the cool breezes of an afternoon on the beach.[9] That discipline created an immensely productive economic system during the nineteenth century. But it also left many people hungry, tired, isolated, and depressed. Perhaps because the Teamsters union was a loose coalition of eastern and southern European immigrants and Black and Brown migrants from the Caribbean, Asia, and Latin America who had suffered under the logic of the Protestant ethic, the Teamster movement fought for a different embodied experience, one demanding access to both the consumer comforts of suburbia and the unrestrained indulgence of the old neighborhoods of the central city. In the process, Teamster activists built a countercultural movement, and often took aim at the elite institutions that constituted the liberal, meritocratic values of the United States. That conflict was abundantly evident in the Teamsters' Genovese allies' investment in gay public sexual space in the 1950s. While Ivy League sociology, psychology, and public health professors, the managers of large corporations, and policymakers in the mid-twentieth-century bureaucracy all imagined the patrons of the Everard Baths to be degenerates who deserved no protections of citizenship,[10] the infrastructure of the Teamsters metropolis helped finance, supply, and operate a place where queer people could live their lives. It has been a central argument of this book that the willingness to take that risk—to make a countercultural intervention that thwarted American Protestant culture while opening a space for people whom society had cast aside—drove the International Brotherhood of Teamsters' remarkable success in the mid-twentieth century.

Deindustrializing the Teamsters Metropolis

Soon after Jimmy Hoffa was inaugurated as general president of the International Brotherhood of Teamsters in 1957, the US metropolis entered a watershed political economic transformation, one that economists Barry Bluestone and Bennett Harrison famously called "the deindustrialization of America."[11] Prior to 1960, the bulk of the goods that US households consumed were manufactured in the central cities of northern and eastern metropolitan areas. Jimmy Hoffa rose to prominence in the labor movement because he successfully organized many of the workers who made these products: pens and pillows, curtains and chemicals, electronics and plastics. In part to evade the high labor costs associated with the union wage, wholesalers and retailers began to use a global supply chain after 1960, sourcing their goods from new, far-lower-wage plants that first appeared in Mexico, then in the Caribbean and Central America, and later on in China, Vietnam, and Bangladesh. Manufacturing that remained on shore moved to newer, larger production facilities in the suburbs and to plants in the southern and western United States where unions were weaker and pay was lower. By the 1970s, the small factories and warehouses where Hoffa acolytes, immigrant entrepreneurs, and underworld operatives had used brute force to build the Teamsters union were closing for good.

Cultural change amplified the process of deindustrialization. Driving the shift were new ideas about the city and the suburbs, ideas that came from inside the Teamsters' house. As the metropolitan mobility depicted in this book has shown, a generation of workers who had suffered through the Great Depression and world wars celebrated new access to conspicuous consumption in the suburbs. Hundreds of thousands of workers joined the Teamsters to secure the wage increases that would pay for those material pleasures. But as the interwar crisis drifted into the past, children who had grown up in Teamster-funded suburban comfort began to scorn consumer society as crass, superficial, and vapid. Younger people yearned for a new world that they imagined would be more sophisticated, authentic, and meaningful than the homogeneous, segregated, depoliticized suburbs where they had grown up.[12]

A new generation found that world in the central city neighborhoods that their parents had left behind. In 1961, the famed urbanist Jane Jacobs published *The Death and Life of Great American Cities*. She argued that the design of certain urban districts that had flourished during the first decades of the twentieth century, including Chicago's Back of the Yards, Boston's North End, and New York's Greenwich Village, encouraged social heterogeneity. A mix of new and old buildings made space affordable to people of differing social classes. A combination of residential and commercial establishments kept streets busy at all hours of the day, which made it safer for people to walk alone. Short blocks reduced distances between destinations, making it easier for elders and parents with small children to move between their daily endeavors. Jacobs framed the city as a place where dense, eclectic urban geography helped people build more fulfilling lives than they could live in the suburbs.[13]

Jacobs's ideas, and the social movement she inspired that defended central city neighborhoods against urban renewal and freeway construction, changed the value of a place at the center of the story in this book: the industrial lofts where small-scale manufacturers assembled their products.

As stiff new overseas competition eroded their profits, urban manufacturers sought rent reductions to stay afloat. Sagging rents pushed landlords to find new, more profitable uses for their assets. According to sociologist Sharon Zukin's influential book *Loft Living*, landlords found that more profitable use in younger people's yearning for authentic and inspiring urban space. The owners began converting downtown factory buildings into artist lofts, live-work spaces that became the anchor for a flourishing new art scene in the 1960s. Unlike the previous generation of social realists who had used technical skill to depict the world as it appeared, younger artists turned to abstract styles. Rather than teaching their audience concrete lessons about history, politics, and power, Robert Rauschenberg, Elaine and Willem DeKooning, and other abstract expressionists asked their viewers questions about being and meaning. And instead of addressing those queries in sterile, white-wall galleries uptown, Rauschenberg's cohort began to show their work in the places they made it, convening with other artists and intellectuals in rustic, live-work spaces downtown to debate the pressing existential questions of the day.[14] As the 1960s gave way to the 1970s, more artists joined the trend and rented their own repurposed industrial lofts, which drove up rents and made it more difficult for the remaining manufacturers to continue to operate.

Sharon Zukin argues that, rather than a localized land use change, the conversion of small factories into artist lofts was an early example of a new form of urban political economy, one she termed the "artistic mode of production." The new regime of accumulation repurposed urban space from an old world of manufacturing into a new world of consumption, entertainment, and finance. As rents rose and old, eastern and southern European–owned factories closed, the urban labor market shifted from a goods base to a services base. Changing land uses and new employment opportunities ushered in a new set of ideas about the city, one that celebrated creative, fashionable, and fulfilling new downtown lifestyles and that confined urban problems from to traffic congestion to pollution to underworld corruption to labor unrest in an industrial era that the backers of the artistic mode of production claimed was over.[15]

While the rise of the artistic mode of production upended manufacturing unions' organizing agendas, the International Brotherhood of Teamsters was well-positioned to adapt to a changing political economy. As sociologist Arlie Russell Hochschield and journalist Barbara Ehrenreich have demonstrated, the transition to a postindustrial economy created millions of new jobs after 1970, most of which went to recent immigrants and women of color. For every position lost in a shuttered downtown lampshade, varnish, or ball-point-pen factory came new demand for services in gentrifying neighborhoods: for people to wash clothes, to clean apartments, to care for children, to prepare take-out food, to wait tables, and to staff nightclubs.[16] Because of Jimmy Hoffa and his predecessors' commitment to organizing marginal service workers, Teamster organizers were already versed in helping those categories of employees organize. Unlike the former CIO industrial unions that represented manufacturing workers at the largest corporations in the United States, Dan Tobin, Dave Beck, and Jimmy Hoffa had pushed the Teamsters into small family businesses in the service sector, signing up employees in hair salons, gas stations, car dealerships, bars, restaurants, and warehouses. These were the very type of businesses that boomed in US downtowns after 1970. Unlike most other unions that followed the strictures of labor law, rules that bore far less fruit for workers after employers began an aggressive countermobilization against unions in the 1970s, the Teamsters had designed their own organizing techniques around the conditions of marginal work, deploying the organizational picket, setting up defensive cartels, and, when they saw it as necessary, using physical coercion. Some of those tactics could have been useful in helping the new cohort of service workers to organize. And as Teamster associate Irving Mishel's financing of the Everard Baths shows, the union's associates were willing to engage with the most stigmatized sectors of the economy, sectors that expanded after 1970 as elite demand for temporary work, undocumented work, and sex work grew with gentrification. Activists could have built upon these historical strengths to push the Teamsters into the cafes, boutiques, and retail outlets that became the leading edge of the metropolitan economy in the 1970s.

Breaking the Teamsters' Strategic Commitment to Unruly Unionism

The membership rolls of the International Brotherhood of Teamsters show that the union's leadership failed to take advantage of those opportunities. During the bumper crop organizing decades of the 1940s and 1950s, the International Brotherhood of Teamsters recorded annual net population gains of more than a hundred thousand workers. The breakneck pace continued until 1968, when the union counted 2.2 million active workers in its ranks. Thereafter, organizing slowed, and the union's roster shrunk for the remainder of the twentieth century.[17] The population decline was in part the result of the changing political economy of transportation. After the 1980 deregulation of the trucking industry became a centerpiece of the neoliberal reforms of the Carter and Reagan administrations, nonunion, low-wage upstart firms undercut established companies, which destroyed their businesses.[18] Hundreds of thousands of truck drivers who had reaped the benefits of the National Master Freight Agreement lost their careers in the decades that followed. Regardless of the headwinds that deregulation exemplified, however, other unions—especially the needle trades union UNITE, the hotel and restaurant union HERE, and the building services and health care workers union SEIU—found ways to increase membership as the economy changed.[19] A primary reason that the Teamsters failed to meet this challenge is that both internal and external forces severed the union's long-standing commitment to the heterodox, militant, unruly tactics that had driven the union's membership gains during the administrations of Dan Tobin, Dave Beck, and Jimmy Hoffa.

Chief among the external impediments was the federal government's expansive surveillance campaign, which sapped the union of the boldness that had defined its previous organizing vision. Beginning in 1963, Jimmy Hoffa gave the labor economists Estelle and Ralph James unprecedented access to his personal affairs in an effort to repair the damage that the McClellan Committee hearings had inflicted upon the reputation of the Hoffa family, the Teamsters union, and the labor movement as a whole. Internal documents and interviews with Hoffa showed that while Teamster contracts either matched or outpaced the impressive wage gains in the manufacturing, steel, and meatpacking industries in the 1950s, the long-anticipated National Master Freight Agreement was less robust than union members had hoped when it was ratified in 1964. The Jameses argued that Hoffa's growing legal exposure made him afraid of antagonizing employers and regulators, which led him to settle for smaller pay increases and to acquiesce to the regional wage differentials that owners had sought and that Hoffa had long opposed.[20] During the same period, Hoffa abandoned his commitment to the Conference on Transportation Unity, his long-touted plan for a single, standardized contract for all air, sea, rail, and trucking workers.[21] And while he had backed ambitious local campaigns to organize public employees in the south and service workers in all regions, Hoffa never launched a single nationwide campaign for service-sector bargaining as he had in the transport sector. According to the Jameses' research and to prominent historians, while Jimmy Hoffa, Harold Gibbons, and other Teamster leaders continued to expand the union in fits and starts, they took fewer risks on comprehensive, strategic, militant strategies as the 1960s progressed because surveillance by Congress, the FBI, and the IRS multiplied the costs of those risks.[22] That trend intensified after the FBI placed an undercover informant inside Hoffa's legal defense team, who helped break his string of acquittals by delivering a conviction for jury tampering in 1967. As a result, the most vocal, most dedicated advocate for strategic organizing in the service sector was stripped of the Teamster presidency and reported to the penitentiary in Lewisburg, Pennsylvania.

Internal dynamics within the Teamster leadership also compromised the union's capacity to organize. These details are more challenging to expose, as the FBI surveillance of Hoffa's inner circle ended amid the growing political backlash against intrusive, illegal government surveillance programs in the late 1960s. The most persuasive evidence to date comes from Harvard Law School professor Jack Goldsmith, the stepson of Chuckie O'Brien, the only child of Hoffa's longtime associate Sylvia Pagano. Based on both Teamster documents and his interviews with O'Brien before he passed away, Goldsmith argues that Hoffa made a fundamental mistake in arranging for Frank Fitzsimmons to lead the Teamsters while he served his sentence. Fitzsimmons had been close to Hoffa's family for decades and had often helped the Hoffas care for Chuckie O'Brien while Sylvia Pagano worked on deals between the Teamsters and La Cosa Nostra in the 1940s. According to Goldsmith, Hoffa hoped that Fitzsimmons would be a docile steward who would maintain Hoffa's plan for the union until his release from prison and return to the presidency, which of course never happened. But unlike Hoffa, Fitzsimmons lacked the relentless drive and the cultural iconoclasm that had propelled Hoffa's commitment to militant, unceasing organizing.[23] While Hoffa refused to go on hunting trips with other Teamster higher-ups because he objected to cruelty to animals, and while he insulted the sport of golf as "a waste of time by nitwits walking around with a stick to hit a white ball," Fitzsimmons loved lavish travel junkets and all-day golf outings. Whereas Hoffa was a chronic workaholic who personally forged the union's nationwide commitment to centralized bargaining and service-sector organizing, Fitzsimmons was content to let midlevel operatives run the union, which worsened the parochialism that undermined its strategic goals. And while historical evidence shows that Sylvia Pagano and Jimmy Hoffa rigorously evaluated Teamster loans to La Cosa Nostra to guarantee that they would help push the union into new sectors of the economy, Fitzsimmons took a hands-off approach to underworld operatives, who squandered retired Teamsters' pension dollars on schemes that provided no benefit to workers.[24] Goldsmith's research suggests that Fitzsimmons was not capable of or interested in maintaining the organizing juggernaut that Hoffa had helped build in the 1950s.

Though the union's internal workings remain open to historical debate, there is concrete evidence that Fitzsimmons spent much of his time making deals that did nothing to further the union's organizing efforts. After Jimmy Hoffa was incarcerated, Frank Fitzsimmons became a regular guest of President Richard Nixon. We know this because Nixon recorded his many meetings with Fitzsimmons. The audio transcripts of their conversations soon became part of the "Nixon tapes," which helped destroy Nixon's presidency during Watergate. In part because Nixon shared Fitzsimmons's and Hoffa's contempt for Robert F. Kennedy, Nixon's most likely opponent prior to Kennedy's assassination in June 1968, and in part because he loved the pomp and the adulation extended to guests of the president, Fitzsimmons became a staunch supporter of Nixon's 1968 White House bid. Although there was no conservative political consensus among Teamster leaders, Nixon's pollsters were aware that a majority of the white members of some Teamster locals were supporting George Wallace's overtly racist presidential campaign, and his staff made note of Fitzsimmons's rambling, reactionary speeches about the counterculture, about "the longhairs," and about perils of marijuana.[25] Nixon used this information to repackage Frank Fitzsimmons into an icon for his southern strategy, one he hoped would align white working-class union members with southern racists into a "silent majority" who opposed desegregation, affirmative action, the ERA, and the women's and gay liberation movements. Through his alliance with Fitzsimmons, Richard Nixon cast the Teamsters union as a powerful opponent of the student, antiwar, antiracist, and feminist movements that a younger generation of workers often embraced in the late 1960s.[26]

Frank Fitzsimmons's hands-off, elite-focused managerial style led the union astray from its strategic commitment to mass organizing after 1970. Teamster activists had used unruly tactics to recruit workers in previous decades not just because flamboyant comportment, emotional outbursts, and physical aggression were cultural means to dissent from the discipline of Protestant middle-class culture, but also because those tactics worked. As the chapters of this book have shown, to take on hostile employers and abusive, corrupt police, organizers had to put their bodies on the line and use all tools at their disposal, including illegal tools. The Teamsters remained a heterodox union during the Fitzsimmons years, and many local activists continued to use unruly tactics. But with Hoffa in prison and Fitzsimmons on the golf course with Nixon, the Teamsters lacked a rudder that guided local tenacity toward a coherent, national strategy for mass organizing. Absent that guidance, and as the broader attack on the labor movement intensified in the 1970s, the Teamster organizing machine sputtered, producing far fewer members than it had in the past.

A Countercultural Social Movement against the Protestant Ethic

The opportunistic culture of the Teamsters union failed to meet the moment in an era of rapid social change. Jimmy Hoffa's cohort of leaders had built a plainspoken, pragmatic union that eschewed political ideology and refused to commit to other unions' vision for wider social change.[27] They did this on purpose, because focusing on what the Teamsters could *do* for its members rather than prescribing who workers should *be*, what they should *think*, and how they should *feel* helped the union appeal to a wide cohort of immigrant workers whose political outlooks were diverse and often conflicting. But by the mid-1960s, younger people had started a mass movement around the existential queries that the Teamsters tended to avoid, questioning the meaning of families' ethnic and racial identities, asking how gender shapes one's sense of self, and interrogating the value of monogamy, domesticity, heterosexuality, and other bedrock cultural norms. Absent a union culture that engaged in these debates, and as Frank Fitzsimmons publicly belittled the answers to these questions that many young workers professed, the union often seemed to be an alibi for an inequitable status quo rather than a tool to fight for workplace justice in a changing society.

Decades have passed since these painful years for the Teamsters. As the incessant corruption allegations, criminal convictions, and Hoffa's vanishing without explanation or closure fade into the past, historical distance opens a space to re-evaluate the Hoffa-era Teamsters' lasting contribution to labor history. Despite both Jimmy Hoffa's and Frank Fitzsimmons's deep opprobrium for the counterculture of the 1960s, and regardless of younger activists' searing critique of what they saw as the union's inept, authoritarian, reactionary bureaucracy, the Teamsters metropolis had been a countercultural place in the 1950s. To organize every worker in every business on every block of both the city and the suburbs, Teamster activists had to deliver both better pay and—in the words of the struggle for the eight-hour day—time for "what we will," for workers to live beyond the discipline of the Protestant ethic. When workers acted according to their own desires rather than to the rhythm of the clock and the demands of the free market, they often built cultural worlds that openly violated middle-class respectability. They opened bars where people transgressed the boundaries of gender, race, and class. They started theaters that showed sexually explicit, lowbrow content. And they opened bathhouses and pornographic book-stores where people could act upon forbidden desires. Therefore, Team-ster activist strategies that began in economic opportunism sometimes evolved into bold, explicit, principled transgressions of bourgeois culture. For a US workforce in which far more people have been subjected to the discipline of the Protestant ethic than have reaped its richest rewards, those countercultural practices were an important part of the Teamsters' appeal.

Irving Mishel was one such operative who helped build the counter-culture of the mid-twentieth-century metropolis. His dealings are well-documented, because Mishel was one of the few underworld-aligned entrepreneurs who flipped to become a cooperating witness during the McClellan Committee hearings. Mishel was born in Brooklyn in 1922 and was orphaned at five years old.[28] After dropping out of high school to sup-port himself, he began a career as a bookmaker, and was soon helping build entertainment businesses with ties to Meyer Lansky, Lepke Buchalter, and other leading figures in the Jewish syndicate.[29] By the early 1940s, Mishel had become a factor, lending money to small, immigrant-owned ventures that provided supplies for bars, nightclubs, and theaters: firms that distrib-uted food and liquor, that operated candy concessions in movie houses, and that supplied jukeboxes, cigarette machines, and coin games to all of these businesses.[30] As chapters 1 and 2 showed, many of these enterprises joined defensive cartels, signing their workers up for union membership in the Teamsters or other AFL-aligned unions to stabilize wages and using union staff and funds to publicly shame competitors who refused to pay protection money to the cartel. These economic strategies blurred the line between licit and illicit. Most of Mishel's ventures provided legitimate ser-vices to customers, and many of his associates—especially the real estate developer Charlie Bernoff—ran well-respected, above-board operations. But several of Mishel's partners had served jail time for extortion in the 1940s, and all were suspected of making predatory loans designed to cap-ture control of competitors' companies.[31] Mishel testified that by 1947, he had soured on these risky and sometimes coercive deals with companies that delivered goods to nightclubs, and that he had decided to begin mak-ing more profitable investments in the bars themselves.[32]

Through this new investing strategy, Irving Mishel began to fund queer nightlife in New York City. In 1949, Mishel loaned money to Irving Fein, who had previously been an entrepreneur in the New York's garment dis-trict.[33] Although he held a stake in a legitimate company called Miss Kay Fashions, one of his partners in that company was Anthony Salerno, who it appears had been tasked with collecting protection money for La Cosa Nostra's defensive cartels in clothing manufacturing.[34] Perhaps through those underworld connections, Fein had learned that the Everard Baths had fallen on hard times, as New York's middle class had abandoned the public bathhouses downtown in favor of exclusive country clubs and private beaches in the suburbs. He may have also known that gay and bisexual men of all social classes—including well-off professionals who could afford to spend lavishly at the businesses they patronized—were using the Everard to make public sexual connections. If Fein could find a way to circumvent the oversight of the State Liquor Authority that explicitly prohibited serving queer patrons, and to evade the New York Police Department's ruthless busts, gay men could provide Fein with a lucrative niche market. Mishel saw the value in Fein's proposal and made the loan, which appears to have been a success. By the late 1950s, Irving Fein had sold all his other businesses and worked full-time running the Everard,[35] a venture he continued to operate until public officials forcibly closed all gay bathhouses during the AIDS crisis in 1986.[36] Building on Fein's success. Irving Mishel followed up with another loan, this time to Vincent Mauro, who was also buying up gay bars in what he hoped would be a lucrative new slice of the nighttime entertainment business.[37]

Irving Mishel had confidence in these investments because Vito Genovese, the head of one of New York's five families of the underworld, had already injected significant capital into lesbian bars, topless clubs, gay cabarets, and other queer nighttime entertainment businesses. Genovese was not the only underworld leader to finance such businesses, as operatives from both the Colombo and Bonanno families made similar deals. But as Phillip Crawford thoroughly demonstrates, the Genovese family was much more systematic about these investments. Genovese appointed two different lieutenants to manage the family's queer establishments: Anthony Strollo before he was murdered in an underworld dust-up in 1962, and then Matthew Ianniello who oversaw these properties well into the gay liberation era. Crawford shows that the Genovese family controlled both established gay bars such as the Stonewall and "breakout clubs," venues that had originally served traditional middle-class audiences and that, after transition to Genovese ownership, would feature exotic dancing and drag performance, employ queer workers, and serve queer customers until the city shut them down. That the NYPD often used the blanket term "Genovese fag joints" as a broad catchall for all of New York's gay bars illustrates the clear association between La Cosa Nostra and queer nightlife in the minds of the wider public.[38]

In addition to funding the baths and the bars of queer New York, the Genovese family was also among the most important underworld allies of Jimmy Hoffa. Among Vito Genovese's most powerful lieutenants was Anthony Provenzano, a former Teamster truck driver from New York's Lower East Side who became president of Teamsters Local 560 in Union City, New Jersey, and would eventually become an international vice president of the Teamsters. Provenzano had thrown his support behind Hoffa's push for a single, standardized trucking contract in New York in the 1950s and had supported Hoffa's bid to become the union's general president in 1957. After Hoffa won the election, Provenzano celebrated with Hoffa's inner circle at the Fontainebleau Hotel on Miami Beach. Chuckie O'Brien, for example, photographed Sylvia Pagano sharing an after-dinner drink during the inauguration festivities with Anthony Provenzano and his wife Maria at a cocktail table surrounded by the Fontainebleau's famous tropical plants.[39] Although there is no evidence that Provenzano ever personally invested in queer nightlife, it does appear that Anthony Strollo—who managed gay bar operations for the Genoveses—was Provenzano's original mentor and connection to La Cosa Nostra.[40] By the late 1950s, Hoffa's close allies in the underworld were operating the most transgressive, most countercultural spaces in New York, Chicago,[41] and other large cities.

It is tempting to frame the Genoveses' stake in queer nightlife in purely transactional terms, as aggressive government repression left a small number of bars to serve a relatively large queer population, which drove up returns on investment for the underworld. But there is evidence of a deeper cultural affinity between Teamster-aligned groups like the Genovese family and the queer clubs they owned. Vito Genovese's generation had grown up in a world where Sicilian immigrants were stigmatized for their loud attire, emotional outbursts, unrestrained sexuality, and unscrupulous affairs. To protect themselves in a xenophobic society, they lived in accordance with Omertà, the Sicilian code of silence that shunned anyone who shared the secretes of the family. Gay bars and bathhouses operated with a similar logic, as internal honor and external secrecy were necessary to protect patron's physical safety and economic livelihood from the immense violence of state-sponsored homophobia and transphobia. And perhaps even more importantly, there is evidence that higher-ups in La Cosa Nostra patronized the establishments they financed despite the vast sigma against doing so. In her memoir, the comedian, actress, and singer Kay Ballard remembered regularly seeing Vito Genovese and his associates socializing with patrons while she performed for an all-gay audience at the Bon Soir, a Genovese-owned gay bar in the 1950s. She argued that these men "were always polite, well dressed, and quite generous" and that they "threw the greatest parties for us on closing nights, complete with dinner and guests for everyone in the show."[42] Genovese was among the most feared, most powerful leaders of La Cosa Nostra during this period,[43] the direct heir of the Lucky Luciano gang who had ordered an unsuccessful hit on predecessor Frank Costello and who had the Luciano syndicate renamed in his honor. Although we have no record of Vito Genovese's ideas about gay or transgender people, this paragon of underworld masculinity socialized in an affirmative manner with the "homosexuals, degenerates, and/or undesirables" that he would not have been able to serve had he complied with the laws that he never respected.

While the principle of Omertà kept most of the underworld's political commitments hidden, some people with ties to La Cosa Nostra openly politicized gender and sexuality. In 1959, the New York State Liquor Authority (SLA) pulled the license of the Big Dollar Bar on Thirty-Fourth Street in Manhattan's Murray Hill neighborhood. The authorities accused the Big Dollar of operating a "disorderly premise" because it "permitted homosexuals, degenerates, and/or undesirables" to patronize the establishment. Thomas Vasta, the proprietor of the Big Dollar who had ties to the Genovese family, sued the SLA, arguing that merely serving drinks to gay people does not make a business disorderly.[44] Vasta lost his case, but others soon followed his lead, with grassroots activists from the homophile group the Mattachine Society staging protests, and with both aboveboard and underworld-aligned proprietors of other queer bars filing their own antidiscrimination suits. Success finally came in 1967 after another entrepreneur with purported ties to La Cosa Nostra sued the SLA. In November 1965, a plain-clothes detective had entered the Julius Restaurant in Greenwich Village, which William Fugazy—who was suspected of being a member of the Lucchese underworld family—had purchased a year earlier. The officer reported seeing men with "tight clothes, limp wrists, shrill voices, and mincing gaits," who called each other "honey" and "deary." As a result of these findings, the SLA pulled the Julius' liquor license in April 1966. Fugazy sued, making among other claims that the SLA's policy violated gay men's civil rights enumerated in the constitutions of both New York and the United States. Although the court decided the case narrowly to avoid the constitutional question about civil rights, it nevertheless overturned the SLA's rule, which effectively legalized gay public social space in New York City.[45] Gay, lesbian, bisexual, and transgender people—and not La Cosa Nostra fronts or defensive labor cartels—conceptualized and operationalized the liberation movements of the late

1960s. But the historical record undoubtedly shows that associates of the Teamsters and of the underworld helped to fund and to defend the countercultural spaces that helped that movement germinate.

Conclusion: Toward an Embodied Reading of Teamster History

The overwhelming majority of rank-and-file Teamsters would never have known that some of Jimmy Hoffa's close associates were creating space in the metropolis for men to have anonymous same-sex intimacy. Given Hoffa's well-known contempt for sexually explicit entertainment, one might guess that Hoffa himself never knew about these deals and would have disparaged them if he had. Many union members who knew about drag cabarets, lesbian bars, and bathhouses would have condemned those places, as they were the aberrant antithesis of the middle-class suburban domesticity that brought rich rewards for so many Teamsters in the 1950s. Workers embraced suburban culture for legitimate reasons, as the fringe of the metropolis had finally delivered safety, stability, space, and comfort to people whose families had survived pogroms, dispossession, famine, and political repression. Conventional heterosexual domesticity was indeed a refuge for people whose kin networks had been torn apart by war, displacement, and economic crisis in the decades before they joined the Teamsters.

Dedicated though he certainly was to delivering the suburban comforts that union members demanded, the other, equally important foundation of Jimmy Hoffa's popularity, as *Teamsters Metropolis* has shown, was his personal and public ambivalence about the bourgeois values that suburbanization entrenched. Hoffa saw what Max Weber did, that the US economy flourished because it disciplined workers' bodies. Weber argued that as US society secularized in the nineteenth century, the muscle memory of the strict asceticism of seventeenth- and eighteenth-century Protestantism made people continue to discipline themselves, living by the values of self-restraint, deferred gratification, and personal responsibility.[46] Those values led people to repress the full spectrum of their physical desires, which reserved more of the body's capacity for producing goods that would be sold on the free market. During Hoffa's rise to power, suburban culture had become the catalyst for the bodily discipline that Weber theorized. Though this newer form of regulation came with far more luxuries than nineteenth-century working-class life, suburbanization nevertheless strictly contained the body's aims and desires. Suburban culture, for example, allowed for sexual pleasure but contained it within monogamy, domesticity, and the single-family home.[47] Suburban life allowed for the indulgence of conspicuous consumption but contained the joy of that indulgence by making it a reward for long hours of productive labor. That containment came with strict limitations on workers' horizons: state-sponsored racial segregation, compulsory heterosexuality, and a deep cultural derision of the unrestrained heterogeneity that had defined life in the immigrant industrial metropolis of the early twentieth century where Hoffa and his peers had come of age.

For some Teamster operatives, then, the purpose of trade unionism was to open a space for embodied pleasure and freedom. Hoffa and his peers recognized that for the overwhelming majority of workers, toil makes people's bodies feel pain, hunger, anxiety, fear, and boredom. Labor activism had to be about reversing those negative sensations, which would allow workers to experience pleasure, safety, satiation, and contentment in their lives. Thus, while queer public space was far, far removed from many rank-and-file workers' lives in the 1950s, both the International Brotherhood of Teamsters and the Everard Baths delivered fleeting pleasures in a painful world. Perhaps that is why Jimmy Hoffa's associates rebuffed the painful stigma of transphobia and homophobia to help queer people find what they looked for. That unruly endeavor, the commitment to providing gratification for marginal workers who found so little comfort in the mid-twentieth century, is the most enduring contribution of the International Brotherhood of Teamsters to the US labor movement.

Notes

Introduction

1. FBI, "RIF#124-10342-10285, Subject Anthony Giacalone ELSUR," April 5, 1963, Mary Ferrell Foundation, www.maryferrell.org, mff_pdf87761, 7, accessed June 22, 2022.
2. FBI, "RIF#124-10342-10056, Subject Anthony Giacalone ELSUR," October 8, 1963, Mary Ferrell Foundation, www.maryferrell.org, mff_pdf89224, 3, accessed June 22, 2022.
3. FBI, "RIF#124-10342-10285, 7.
4. In 1963, the FBI placed a microphone inside of Sylvia Pagano's apartment in downtown Detroit, and wiretapped her telephones. They had also previously placed a microphone inside the headquarters of the Home Juice Company, a small business owned by Pagano's friend and lover Anthony Giacalone, who was also a higher-up in Detroit's Sicilian underworld. For thorough documentation of Pagano's work as a financial adviser to Hoffa, see chapter 5 of this volume. See also Jack Goldsmith, *In Hoffa's Shadow: A Stepfather, a Disappearance in Detroit, and My Search for the Truth* (New York: Farrar, Straus and Giroux, 2019).
5. FBI, "Report of SA James L. Shanahan to the FBI, RIF#124-10342-10387, Subject Anthony Giacalone, ELSUR 92-228-1294," August 11, 1964, Mary Ferrell Foundation, www.maryferrell.org, mff_pdf142504, 2, accessed January 7, 2022, 2 (hereafter FBI, RIF#124-10342-10387).
6. Lauren Jae Gutterman, *Her Neighbor's Wife: A History of Lesbian Desire within Marriage* (Philadelphia: University of Pennsylvania Press, 2019), 22.
7. FBI, "RIF#124-10296-10099, Subject APR, Teamsters Union, Assoc, Buss, Crim, and Gambling; Act CR 92-2956-63, Report of SA Robert L. Moore," March 18, 1963, Mary Ferrell Foundation, www.maryferrell.org, mff_pdf73362, 9, accessed January 10, 2022.
8. FBI, "RIF#124-10342-10402, Subject Anthony Giacalone, ELSUR 92-228-1253, Memo from John Schelburne to the FBI," May 26, 1964, Mary Ferrell Foundation, www.maryferrell.org, mff_pdf88841, 1, accessed January 7, 2022.

9. Jack Goldsmith, personal interview, June 21, 2021.
10. US Congress, Senate, Select Committee on Improper Activities in the Labor or Management Field, *Investigation of Improper Activities in the Labor or Management Field, Part 48*, 86th Congress, 1st session, March 23, 24, 25, April 7, 8, 9, 10, 14, 15, 1959 (Washington, DC: Government Printing Office, 1959), 17,518 (hereafter MCH, *Part 48*), 17,476–17,480.
11. MCH, *Part 48*, 17,608.
12. "Bufalino: The Father of Rule 9," *Detroit Free Press*, February 7, 1963.
13. For a history of the relationship between heterosexual domesticity, the family wage, and the mid-twentieth-century labor movement, see Dorothy Sue Cobble, *The Other Women's Movement: Workplace Justice and Social Rights in Modern America* (Princeton, NJ: Princeton University Press, 2005).
14. See chapter 5 for a thorough analysis of these relationships and the historical documents to support that analysis.
15. Ralph C. and Estelle Dinerstein James, *Hoffa and the Teamsters: A Study of Union Power* (Princeton, NJ: D. Van Nostrand, 1965), 342–43, 350–51.
16. Nelson Lichtenstein, *State of the Union: A Century of American Labor* (Princeton, NJ: Princeton University Press, 2013), 98–141.
17. Andrew Wender Cohen, *The Racketeer's Progress: Chicago and the Struggle for the Modern American Economy* (Cambridge, UK: Cambridge University Press, 2004), 14.
18. Cohen, *The Racketeer's Progress*, 18.
19. Donald Garnel, *The Rise of Teamster Power in the West* (Berkeley: University of California Press, 1972), 171–76.
20. US Congress, Senate, Select Committee on Improper Activities in the Labor or Management Field, *Investigation of Improper Activities in the Labor or Management Field, Part 13*, 85th Congress, 1st session, August 20, 21, 22, and 23, 1957 (Washington, DC: Government Printing Office, 1957), 4,954 (hereafter MCH, *Part 13*).
21. James and James, *Hoffa and the Teamsters*, 132–43.
22. There is an extensive literature on the immigrant neighborhoods of the industrial city in the period between the end of the Civil War and the 1924 immigration restriction. For texts relevant to this book, see LaShawn Harris, *Sex Workers, Psychics, and Numbers Runners: Black Women in New York City's Underground Economy* (Urbana: University of Illinois Press, 2016); Saidiya Hartman, *Wayward Lives, Beautiful Experiments: Intimate Histories of Riotous Black Girls, Troublesome Women, and Queer Radicals* (New York: W. W. Norton, 2020); Annelise Orleck, *Common Sense and a Little Fire: Women and Working-Class Politics in the United States, 1900–1965* (Durham, NC: Duke University Press, 1995).
23. Dianne Harris, *Little White Houses: How the Postwar Home Constructed Race in America* (Minneapolis: University of Minnesota Press, 2013), 111–57.
24. For a particularly cogent discussion of the political economy of race as it intersected with suburban space, see Grace Kyungwon Hong, *The Ruptures of American Capital: Women of Culture Feminism and the Culture of Immigrant Labor* (Minneapolis: University of Minnesota Press, 2006), 67–106.
25. Lila Corwin Berman, *Metropolitan Jews: Politics, Race, and Religion in Postwar Detroit* (Chicago: University of Chicago Press, 2015).
26. Richard Rothstein, *The Color of Law: A Forgotten History of How Our Government Segregated America* (New York: W. W. Norton, 2017), 77–93.

27. Scores of newspaper advertisements for segregated car wash workers ran in the Detroit papers until at least the mid-1950s. See, for example, Tower Auto Wash, classified advertisement, *Detroit Free Press*, January 8, 1955, 15.

28. MCH, *Part 48*, 17,518.

29. MCH, *Part 48*, 17,608.

30. "Bufalino: The Father of Rule 9."

31. FBI, "RIF#124-10296-10099, Subjects APR, Teamsters Union, Assoc., Buss., Crim and Gambling; ACT," March 18, 1963, Mary Ferrell Foundation, mff_pdf73362, www.maryferrell.org, 7–8, accessed June 18, 2021.

32. "79 Webber Place," www.redfin.com, accessed August 11, 2021.

33. "12353 Wilshire Drive," www.zillow.com, accessed August 11, 2021.

34. Google street view, 2566 Pennsylvania St., Detroit, MI, https://www.google.com /maps/place/2566+Pennsylvania+St,+Detroit,+MI+48214/@42.3673549,-82.98 77646,3a,75y,151.34h,90t/data=!3m6!1e1!3m4!1shWfIfG6WKFgyjP2ZP5Z9Jw! 2e0!7i16384!8i8192!4m5!3m4!1s0x8824d484a1036f6f:0x8c1fffef3af5fdebf!8m2!3 d42.3674696!4d-82.9874139, accessed December 21, 2021.

35. John Bartlow Martin, "The Struggle to Get Hoffa Part II: The Making of a Labor Boss," *Saturday Evening Post*, July 4, 1959, 56.

36. For a thorough description of the kinship network of Jimmy Hoffa, Josephine Hoffa, Sylvia Pagano, and Chuckie O'Brien that revolved around Hoffa's Robson Street home in Detroit, see Jack Goldsmith, *In Hoffa's Shadow: A Stepfather, A Disappearance in Detroit, and My Search for the Truth* (New York: Farrar, Straus and Giroux, 2019), 11–95.

37. The FBI wiretap of the home of Sylvia Pagano in 1963 and 1964 provides incontrovertible evidence of these relationships. See, for example, FBI, "RIF#124-10342-10014, Subjects Anthony Giacalone ELSUR," July 25–27, 1963, Mary Ferrell Foundation, mff_pdf120178, www.maryferrell.org, accessed June 18, 2021.

38. Rachel Kranson, *Ambivalent Embrace: Jewish Upward Mobility in Postwar America* (Chapel Hill: University of North Carolina Press, 2017), 3.

39. For a summary of the Wagner Act bargaining process that remains the foundation of labor law in the United States, see Michael Gold, *An Introduction to Labor Law* (Ithaca, NY: Cornell University ILR Press, 2011).

40. John R. Commons, *Races and Immigrants in America* (1907; repr. New York: The Macmillan Company, 1920), 63–70.

41. David Witwer, *Corruption and Reform in the Teamsters Union* (Urbana: University of Illinois Press, 2008), 78–85.

42. "Court Helps Bartender Out on a Limb," *Detroit Free Press*, December 3, 1959, 3.

43. MCH, *Part 48*, 17,470–17,476.

44. Ken McKormick, "Tells Tale of Stolen Jukebox," *Detroit Free Press*, June 8, 1954, 3.

45. "Bufalino Accused in Beating," *Detroit Free Press*, December 23, 1954, 4.

46. MCH, *Part 48*, 17,572–17,576.

47. To understand how the Wagner Act changed the practice of collective bargaining, see Nelson Lichtenstein's description of Walter Reuther's transition from 1930s leftist to 1950s corporatist in Nelson Lichtenstein, *Walter Reuther: The Most Dangerous Man in Detroit* (Urbana: University of Illinois Press, 1997).

48. Labor economists Ralph and Estelle James followed Jimmy Hoffa on the road as he organized in the early 1960s. Their supportive account of Hoffa's work pro-

vides detailed description of the culture of the union, especially as it pertains to food, clothing, entertainment, and kinship. See James and James, *Hoffa and the Teamsters*.

49. Janet R. Jakobsen, "Sex + Freedom = Regulation: Why?" *Social Text* 23, no. 3–4 (Fall/Winter 2005): 286.

50. Jakobsen, "Sex + Freedom = Regulation," 289.

51. Jakobsen, "Sex + Freedom = Regulation," 293.

52. Hong, *The Ruptures of American Capital*, 67–106; see also Elaine Tyler May, *Homeward Bound: American Families in the Cold War Era* (New York: Basic Books, 2017 [1988]).

53. Emily Filler, personal interview, June 23, 2021.

54. FBI, "RIF#124-10342-10016, Subject Anthony Giacalone ELSUR," July 16, 1963, Mary Ferrell Foundation, www.maryferrell.org, mff_pdf120180, 10, accessed June 18, 2021.

55. Jack Goldsmith, personal interview, June 22, 2021.

56. FBI, "RIF#124-10342-10303, Subject Anthony Giacalone ELSUR," February 21, 1963, Mary Ferrell Foundation, www.maryferrell.org, mff_pdf87780, 4, accessed June 18, 2021.

57. Jimmy Hoffa's daughter Barbara described Pagano's multiple marriages in detail to federal agents in her FBI interview that took place on August 5, 1975, six days after her father vanished. There are no other documents to verify any of those claims, and no other FBI witness corroborated this information. See FBI, "RIF#124-10348-10066, Subject Anthony Provenzano," September 22, 1975, Mary Ferrell Foundation, www.maryferrell.org, mff_pdf84056, 47, accessed June 18, 2021.

58. Gutterman, *Her Neighbor's Wife*, 13.

59. Robert Bussel, *Fighting for Total Person Unionism: Harold Gibbons, Ernest Calloway, and Working-Class Citizenship* (Urbana: University of Illinois Press, 2015).

60. David Witwer, personal interview, June 25, 2021.

61. Goldsmith, *In Hoffa's Shadow*, 260.

62. Bill Osgerby, *Playboys in Paradise: Masculinity, Youth, Leisure-Style in Modern America* (Oxford, UK: Berg, 2001).

63. Eve Kasofsky Sedgwick, *Touching Feeling: Affect, Pedagogy, and Performativity* (Durham, NC: Duke University Press, 2003), 123–52.

64. Goldsmith, *In Hoffa's Shadow*, 95.

65. Goldsmith, *In Hoffa's Shadow*, 75.

66. Goldsmith, *In Hoffa's Shadow*, 124.

67. Goldsmith, *In Hoffa's Shadow*, 178–79.

68. Nayan Shah, *Contagious Divides: Epidemics and Race in San Francisco's Chinatown* (Berkeley: University of California Press, 2001), 120–57.

Chapter 1

1. Monimania, "Caruso's," accessed July 13, 2020, https://www.pinterest.com/pin/16184879893662490/.

2. "Caruso Matchbook MS Italian Restaurant Bar Lounge Pizza Levittown Long

Island NY," accessed July 13, 2020, https://www.pinterest.com/pin/559290847 465341805/.

3. US Congress, Senate, Select Committee on Improper Activities in the Labor or Management Field, *Investigation of Improper Activities in the Labor or Management Field, Part 46*, 86th Congress, 1st session, December 4 and 9, 1958; February 10, 11, 12, 13, 17, 18, 1959 (Washington, DC: Government Printing Office, 1959), 16,860–16,861 (hereafter MCH, *Part 46*).

4. Nelson Lichtenstein, *State of the Union: A Century of American Labor* (Princeton, NJ: Princeton University Press, 2013); Kim Phillips-Fein, *Invisible Hands: The Businessmen's Crusade Against the New Deal* (New York: W. W. Norton, 2010); Robert O. Self, *All in the Family: The Realignment of American Democracy since the 1960s* (New York: Hill and Wang, 2013).

5. John Kenneth Galbraith, *The Affluent Society* (New York: Houghton Mifflin, 1958); Lorraine Hansberry, *A Raisin in the Sun* (New York: Methuen Publishing, Ltd., 2001 [1959]); Herbert Marcuse, *One Dimensional Man* (Boston: Beacon Press, 1991 [1964]).

6. Lila Corwin Berman sharply challenges binary distinctions between the urban and suburban lifeworlds, arguing instead that postwar American Jews lived "metropolitan" lives, often living in the suburbs but politically and economically engaged in the city. I borrow her idea about metropolitanism to frame the way white Jews and Catholics moved through the immediate postwar city. See Lila Corwin Berman, *Metropolitan Jews: Politics, Race, and Religion in Postwar Detroit* (Chicago: University of Chicago Press, 2015).

7. See, for example: Dianne Harris, *Little White Houses: How the Postwar Home Constructed Race in America* (Minneapolis: University of Minnesota Press, 2012); Lynn Spigel, *Welcome to the Dreamhouse: Popular Media and Postwar Suburbs* (Durham, NC: Duke University Press, 2001); Richard Rothstein, *The Color of Law: A Forgotten History of How Our Government Segregated America* (New York: W. W. Norton, 2017).

8. I use the term "new immigrant" to mark the group of mostly Catholic and Jewish immigrants who arrived from eastern and southern Europe between the end of the US Civil War and the passage of the Johnson-Reed Act in 1924. To understand the history and racialization of this cohort, see Mae Ngai, *Impossible Subjects: Illegal Aliens and the Making of Modern America, Revised Edition* (Princeton, NJ: Princeton University Press, 2014), 21–55.

9. Ngai, *Impossible Subjects*, 21–55.

10. "Jukeboxes Unlimited," accessed July 13, 2020, https://jukeboxesunlimited.com /rockola1465.html.

11. MCH, *Part 46*, 16,974.

12. Karen Ho, *Liquidated: An Ethnography of Wall Street* (Durham, NC: Duke University Press, 2009); Ryan Patrick Murphy, *Deregulating Desire: Flight Attendant Activism, Family Politics, and Workplace Justice* (Philadelphia: Temple University Press, 2016), 95–102.

13. MCH, *Part 46*, 16,860.

14. Steve Fraser and Gary Gerstle, *The Rise and Fall of the New Deal Order, 1930–1980* (Princeton, NJ: Princeton University Press, 1990).

15. MCH, *Part 46*, 16,747–16,750.

16. US Congress, Senate, Select Committee on Improper Activities in the Labor or Management Field, *Investigation of Improper Activities in the Labor or Management Field, Part 48*, 85th Congress, 1st session, March 23, 24, 25, April 7, 8, 9, 10, 14, and 15, 1959 (Washington, DC: Government Printing Office, 1959), 17,352–356 (hereafter MCH, *Part 48*).

17. US Congress, Senate, Select Committee on Improper Activities in the Labor or Management Field, *Investigation of Improper Activities in the Labor or Management Field, Part 48*, 86th Congress, 1st session, February 26, 1958, February 19, 24, 25, and March 10, 1959 (Washington, DC: Government Printing Office, 1959), 17,125–131 (hereafter MCH, *Part 47*).

18. Nelson Lichtenstein, *Walter Reuther: The Most Dangerous Man in Detroit* (Urbana: University of Illinois Press, 1997).

19. John T. McGreevy, *Parish Boundaries: The Catholic Encounter with Race in the Twentieth-Century Urban North* (Chicago: University of Chicago Press, 1998), 24–27.

20. McGreevy, *Parish Boundaries*, 12–13.

21. McGreevy, *Parish Boundaries*, 27.

22. Michael Alexander, *Jazz Age Jews* (Princeton, NJ: Princeton University Press, 2001), 7.

23. Alexander, *Jazz Age Jews*, 2–5.

24. Alexander, *Jazz Age Jews*, 22.

25. Alexander, *Jazz Age Jews*, 18.

26. Rachel Kranson, *Ambivalent Embrace: Jewish Upward Mobility in Postwar America* (Chapel Hill, NC: University of North Carolina Press, 2017), 47.

27. Kranson, *Ambivalent Embrace*, 116.

28. McGreevy, *Parish Boundaries*, 80.

29. Kranson, *Ambivalent Embrace*, 3.

30. To understand the racialized sexual nature of bodily comportment and the connection between bodily comportment and sexuality studies, see Roderick A. Ferguson, *Aberrations in Black: Toward a Queer of Color Critique* (Minneapolis: University of Minnesota Press, 2003).

31. Some of the widest-read books of the 1950s commented on the relationship between restrained comportment and work at the large corporation. William H. Whyte's *The Organization Man* is a notable nonfiction text in this genre. Sloan Wilson's *The Man in the Gray Flannel Suit* addresses similar themes through fiction. Both books were published in 1956 during the height of the Teamsters' organizing growth in the service sector.

32. Kranson, *Ambivalent Embrace*, 74.

33. Kranson, *Ambivalent Embrace*, 77.

34. MCH, *Part 46*, 16,860.

35. David Montgomery, *Citizen Worker: The Experience of Workers in the United States with Democracy and the Free Market during the Nineteenth Century* (Cambridge, UK: Cambridge University Press, 1993), 115–62.

36. Andrew Wender Cohen, *The Racketeer's Progress: Chicago and the Struggle for the Modern American Economy* (Cambridge, UK: Cambridge University Press, 2004), 60–62.

37. Cohen, *The Racketeer's Progress*, 93.
38. Cohen, *The Racketeer's Progress*, 97.
39. "Indictment Lists 6 in Movie Kickback," *New York Times*, April 27, 1951, 19.
40. Display Ad 52—No Title, *New York Times*, October 7, 1947, 56.
41. Display Ad 16—No Title, *New York Times*, November 7, 1949, 10.
42. "Indictment Lists 6 in Movie Kickback."
43. "William Brandt of Movie Chain, Pioneer in the Film Industry, Is Dead," *New York Times*, July, 20, 1965, 33.
44. Irving Spiegel, "Flatbush and the Bronx: William Brandt Discovers Two Gold Mines on his Own Door Step," *New York Times*, October 11, 1942, X2.
45. "Glen or Glenda," IMDB.com, July 21, 2023, https://www.imdb.com/title/tt004 5826/.
46. MCH, *Part 46*, 16,890.
47. Norman Abrams and Neal Patterson, "Nip Movie Concession Kickbacks," *New York Daily News*, April 27, 1951, 141.
48. MCH, *Part 46*, 16,890.
49. "Indictment Lists 6 in Movie Kickback."
50. MCH, *Part 46*, 16,890. Note that in the McClellan Committee hearings, as was often the case when the senators and witnesses spoke of women, they do not name Beatrice Richer. They instead refer to her as "the woman." Based on Charles Bernoff's sworn testimony in front of the McClellan Committee in February 1959 and coverage in the *New York Times* and *New York Daily News* from the early 1950s, it is beyond a reasonable doubt that "the woman" is indeed Beatrice Richer.
51. "Nip Movie Concession Kickbacks."
52. "Indictment Lists 6 in Movie Kickback." See also Norman Abrams and Neal Patterson, "Smash Movie Concession Kickbacks," *New York Daily News*, April 27, 1951, 56.
53. MCH, *Part 46*, 16,783–16,786.
54. MCH, *Part 46*, 16,867–16,690.
55. MCH, *Part 46*, 16,800–16,802.
56. MCH, *Part 46*, 16,863.
57. US Congress, Senate, Select Committee on Improper Activities in the Labor or Management Field, *Investigation of Improper Activities in the Labor or Management Field, Part 41*, 85th Congress, 2nd session, November 13, 14, 17, 18, and 20, 1958 (Washington, DC: Government Printing Office, 1959), 15,410 (hereafter MCH, *Part 41*).
58. MCH, *Part 41*, 15,385–15,389.
59. Peter G. Vellon, *A Great Conspiracy Against Our Race: Italian Immigrant Newspapers and the Construction of Whiteness in the Early 20th Century* (New York: New York University Press, 2014), 15–36.
60. Kranson, *Ambivalent Embrace*, 60–71.
61. "Racket Witness Turns Mum," *Rochester Democrat and Chronicle*, February 14, 1959, 2.
62. MCH, *Part 46*, 16,800.
63. "Bandits Rob Café," *Brooklyn Daily Eagle*, June 26, 1953, 1.
64. MCH, *Part 46*, 16,801–16,802.
65. Kathi Peiss, *Cheap Amusements: Working Women and Leisure in Turn-of-the-Century New York* (Philadelphia: Temple University Press, 1986).

66. Jack Goldsmith, *In Hoffa's Shadow: A Disappearance in Detroit, and My Search for the Truth* (New York: Farrar, Straus and Giroux, 2019), 53.

67. Hoffa spoke extensively about his idea that activists needed to increase the size of the labor movement as a whole and increase the size of the bargaining unit from the scale of the firm to the scale of the region and nation. For a summary of ideas about the scale of the movement, see Ralph C. and Estelle Dinerstein James, *Hoffa and the Teamsters: A Study of Union Power* (Princeton, NJ: D. Van Nostrand, 1965), 125–40; see also David Witwer, *Corruption and Reform in the Teamsters Union* (Urbana: University of Illinois Press, 2008), 132–43.

68. Dan Austin, "Hotel Detroiter," HistoricDetroit.org, accessed July 15, 2020, https://www.historicdetroit.org/buildings/hotel-detroiter.

69. MCH, *Part 48*, 17,472–17,475.

70. MCH, *Part 48*, 17,480.

71. MCH, *Part 48*, 17,471.

72. MCH, *Part 48*, 17,482.

73. Goldsmith, *In Hoffa's Shadow*, 110–24. For a discussion of how the Italian underworld developed in New York City and how the Appalachian meeting fits into that arc, see C. Alexander Hortis, *The Mob and the City: The Hidden History of How the Mafia Captured New York* (New York City: Prometheus, 2014).

74. US Congress, Senate, Select Committee on Improper Activities in the Labor or Management Field, *Investigation of Improper Activities in the Labor or Management Field, Part 35*, 85th Congress, 2nd session, July 31 and August 1, 1958 (Washington, DC: Government Printing Office, 1958), 13,159.

75. Dan Moldea uses anonymous FBI sources to make the claim about Hoffa connections to Santo Perrone in the 1930s. See Dan Moldea, *The Hoffa Wars: Teamsters, Rebels, Politicians, and the Mob* (New York: Paddington Press, 1978), 25.

76. Jack Goldsmith's recent biography of Chucky O'Brien emphasizes the centrality of Sylvia Pagano in Hoffa's ties to La Cosa Nostra and claims that Hoffa's first ties to the Sicilian underworld came during the struggle with the CIO in the early 1940s. See Goldsmith, *In Hoffa's Shadow*, 57–59.

77. Thaddeus Russell explicitly refutes the earlier claims by Moldea and other journalists that had dated Hoffa's connection to La Cosa Nostra to the late 1930s and early 1940s. See Thaddeus Russell, *Out of the Jungle: Jimmy Hoffa and the Remaking of the American Working Class* (New York: Knopf, 2001), 88–89. See also Witwer, *Corruption and Reform in the Teamsters Union*, 78–85, for a discussion of historical theoretical approaches to understanding ties between Hoffa and the underworld.

78. US Congress, Senate, Select Committee on Improper Activities in the Labor or Management Field, *Investigation of Improper Activities in the Labor or Management Field, Part 12*, 85th Congress, 1st session, July 1, August 14, 15, 16, and 19, 1957 (Washington, DC: Government Printing Office, 1957), 4,748 (hereafter MCH, *Part 12*).

79. MCH, *Part 12*, 4,750.

80. US Congress, Senate, Select Committee on Improper Activities in the Labor or Management Field, *Investigation of Improper Activities in the Labor or Management Field, Part 11*, 85th Congress, 1st session, July 31, August 1, 2, 5, and 6, 1957 (Washington, DC: Government Printing Office, 1957), 3,720–3,723.

81. MCH, *Part 12*, 4,748–4,750.

82. MCH, *Part 12*, 4,756.
83. MCH, *Part 12*, 4,770–4,773.
84. MCH, *Part 46*, 16,757.
85. Melvyn Dubofsky and Foster Rhea Dulles, *Labor in America: A History, Fourth Edition* (New York: Wiley-Blackwell, 2001), 346.
86. James and James, *Hoffa and the Teamsters*, 14.
87. James and James, *Hoffa and the Teamsters*, 325–41.
88. James and James, *Hoffa and the Teamsters*, 353–60.
89. MCH, *Part 46*, 16,661–16,666.

Chapter 2

1. US Congress, Senate, Select Committee on Improper Activities in the Labor or Management Field, *Investigation of Improper Activities in the Labor or Management Field, Part 46*, 85th Congress, 1st session, December 4 and 9, 1958; September 24, 25, 26, 27, 28, and November 5, 1957 (Washington, DC: Government Printing Office, 1957), 5,378, 5,391–5,401 (hereafter MCH, *Part 14*).
2. Jennifer Delton, *Making Minnesota: Civil Rights and the Transformation of the Democratic Party* (Minneapolis: University of Minnesota Press, 2002).
3. MCH, *Part 14*, 5,401.
4. MCH, *Part 14*, 5,727–5,729.
5. The large trove of documents that the McClellan Committee assembled heavily influenced the journalistic coverage of the events both as they happened and in the flourish of book-form journalistic accounts of the 1950s that appeared soon after Hoffa disappeared. Dan Moldea and Steven Brill's books are the most widely read examples of this genre. See Dan Moldea, *The Hoffa Wars: Teamsters, Rebels, Politicians, and the Mob* (New York: Paddington Press, 1978), and Steven Brill, *The Teamsters* (New York: Simon & Schuster, 1979). More recent academic scholarship has processed the long-term significance of the McClellan Committee's work. Thaddeus Russell's PhD dissertation, which became the book *Out of the Jungle*, is an example of the more recently scholarly genre, as is David Witwer's *Corruption and Reform in the Teamsters Union*. See Thaddeus Russell, *Out of the Jungle: Jimmy Hoffa and the Remaking of the American Working Class* (New York: Knopf, 2001), and David Witwer, *Corruption and Reform in the Teamsters Union* (Urbana: University of Illinois Press, 2008). McClellan Committee documents have also shaped more recent journalistic accounts of the Teamsters in the 1950s. See James Neff, *Vendetta: Bobby Kennedy vs. Jimmy Hoffa* (New York: Little, Brown, and Company, 2012), and Jack Goldsmith, *In Hoffa's Shadow: A Stepfather, a Disappearance in Detroit, and My Search for the Truth* (New York: Farrar, Straus and Giroux, 2019).
6. Witwer, *Corruption and Reform in the Teamsters Union*, 184.
7. Lynn Spigel theorizes the connection between social sanitation and suburban space. See Lynn Spigel, *Welcome to the Dreamhouse: Popular Media and Postwar Suburbs* (Durham, NC: Duke University Press, 2001), 31–59.
8. While I disagree with James Neff's central theme that Hoffa had a vendetta against Robert F. Kennedy, he offers a well-documented and rigorous discussion of the McClellan Committee's original formation in 1956. See: Neff, *Vendetta*, 36–38.
9. Robert F. Kennedy, *The Enemy Within* (New York: Harper, 1960), 6–7.

10. Neff, *Vendetta*, 38.
11. The recording is indeed worth listening to. See Sam Ervin, "Bridge Over Troubled Water," CBS Records, 1973, accessed July 17, 2020. https://www.youtube.com/watch?v=hcMXi24QE7Y.
12. Kennedy, *The Enemy Within*, 4.
13. Kennedy, *The Enemy Within*, 4.
14. Neff, *Vendetta*, 23–27.
15. For an analysis of 1950s suburban masculinity, see Elaine Tyler May, *Homeward Bound: American Families in the Cold War Era* (New York: Basic Books, 2017 [1988]). To understand how race and sexuality shaped this paradigm of masculinity, see Grace Kyungwon Hong, *The Ruptures of American Capital: Women of Culture Feminism and the Culture of Immigrant Labor* (Minneapolis: University of Minnesota Press, 2006), 67–106.
16. US Congress, Senate, Select Committee on Improper Activities in the Labor or Management Field, *Investigation of Improper Activities in the Labor or Management Field, Part 46*, 86th Congress, 1st session, December 4 and 9, 1958; February 10, 11, 12, 13, 17, 18, 1959 (Washington, DC: Government Printing Office, 1959), 16,636 (hereafter MCH, *Part 46*).
17. Christopher Gray, "Crowning Achievements for Two Brother-Architects," *New York Times*, March 2, 2008, accessed July 21, 2020. https://www.nytimes.com/2008/03/02/realestate/02scap.html.
18. MCH, *Part 46*, 16,637.
19. James Barron, "An 86-Year-Old's Head-to-Toe Makeover Is Complete," *New York Times*, September 11, 2013, accessed July 22, 2020. https://cityroom.blogs.nytimes.com/2013/09/11/the-86-year-old-park-central-hotels-head-to-toe-makeover-is-complete/.
20. MCH, *Part 46*, 16,759–16,762.
21. Gray, "Crowning Achievements for Two Brother-Architects,"
22. See Miranda Joseph's discussion of "performative production" to understand the theoretical root of my argument here. Miranda Joseph, *Against the Romance of Community* (Minneapolis: University of Minnesota Press, 2002), 30–68.
23. "412 Pine Manor," Redfin.com, accessed July 24, 2020. https://www.redfin.com/IL/Wilmette/412-Pine-Manor-Dr-60091/home/13776040.
24. US Congress, Senate, Select Committee on Improper Activities in the Labor or Management Field, *Investigation of Improper Activities in the Labor or Management Field, Part 47*, 86th Congress, 1st session, February 26, 1958, February 19, 24, 25, and March 10, 1959 (Washington, DC: Government Printing Office, 1959), 16,964–965 (hereafter MCH, *Part 47*).
25. MCH, *Part 47*, 16,969–16,974.
26. MCH, *Part 47*, 16,973.
27. MCH, *Part 47*, 16,986.
28. Kennedy, *The Enemy Within*, 161, 38.
29. May, *Homeward Bound*, 14.
30. Julie Abraham, *Metropolitan Lovers: The Homosexuality of Cities* (Minneapolis: University of Minnesota Press, 2009), 170–72.
31. Clayton Howard, *The Closet and the Cul-de-Sac: The Politics of Sexual Privacy in Northern California* (Philadelphia: University of Pennsylvania Press, 2019), 55–

56, 106. See also Steven Vider, *The Queerness of Home: Gender, Sexuality, and the Politics of Domesticity after World War II* (Chicago: University of Chicago Press, 2021), 13.

32. Hong, *The Ruptures of American Capital*, 67–106.

33. US Congress, Senate, Select Committee on Improper Activities in the Labor or Management Field, *Investigation of Improper Activities in the Labor or Management Field, Part 5*, 85th Congress, 1st session, March 26 and 27, 1957 (Washington, DC: Government Printing Office, 1957), 1,578 (hereafter MCH, *Part 5*).

34. Witwer, *Corruption and Reform in the Teamsters Union*, 161.

35. MCH, *Part 5*, 1,595–1,599.

36. MCH, *Part 5*, 1,596.

37. MCH, *Part 5*, 1,597.

38. MCH, *Part 5*, 1,598.

39. MCH, *Part 5*, 1,598.

40. The fall 2020 Nieman-Marcus collection, for example, features a Tom Ford Cashmere Chesterfield Coat for $5,890. There are many others like it. Niemanmarcus. com, accessed August 26, 2020. https://www.neimanmarcus.com/p/tom-ford-ca shmere-chesterfield-coat-prod200160273?utm_source=google_shopping&adpo s=&scid=scplpsku171401708&sc_intid=sku171401708&ecid=NMCS__GooglePL A&gclid=EAIaIQobChMI84rF0eW56wIVUfDACh28UQoHEAQYASABEgKCa fD_BwE&gclsrc=aw.ds.

41. MCH, *Part 5*, 1,597.

42. MCH, *Part 5*, 1,592.

43. Federal Deposit Insurance Corporation, *History of the Eighties—Lessons for the Future* (Washington, DC: Federal Deposit Insurance Corporation, 2000), 187.

44. Emily S. Rosenberg, *Financial Missionaries to the World: The Politics and Culture of Dollar Diplomacy, 1900–1930* (Durham, NC: Duke University Press, 2004), 7.

45. Rosenberg, *Financial Missionaries to the World*, 8.

46. US Congress, Senate, Select Committee on Improper Activities in the Labor or Management Field, *Investigation of Improper Activities in the Labor or Management Field, Part 48*, 86th Congress, 1st session, March 23, 24, 25, April 7, 8, 9, 10, 14, 15, 1959 (Washington, DC: Government Printing Office, 1959), 17,378 (hereafter MCH, *Part 48*).

47. MCH, *Part 48*, 17,378.

48. MCH, *Part 46*, 16,896.

49. MCH, *Part 48*, 17,378.

50. MCH, *Part 46*, 16,758.

51. US Congress, Senate, Select Committee on Improper Activities in the Labor or Management Field, *Investigation of Improper Activities in the Labor or Management Field, Part 11*, 85th Congress, 1st session, July 31, August 1, 2, 5, and 6, 1957 (Washington, DC: Government Printing Office, 1957), 3,804 (hereafter MCH, *Part 11*).

52. MCH, *Part 11*, 3,653.

53. MCH, *Part 47*, 16,969.

54. MCH, *Part 11*, 3,720.

55. MCH, *Part 14*, 5,391.

56. US Congress, Senate, Select Committee on Improper Activities in the Labor or Management Field, *Investigation of Improper Activities in the Labor or Management*

Field, Part 11, 85th Congress, 2nd session, September 2, 3, 4, 9, and 10, 1958 (Washington, DC: Government Printing Office, 1958), 14,574 (hereafter MCH, *Part 39*).

57. US Congress, Senate, Select Committee on Improper Activities in the Labor or Management Field, *Investigation of Improper Activities in the Labor or Management Field, Part 38*, 85th Congress, 2nd session, August 21, 26, 27, 28, and 29, 1958 (Washington, DC: Government Printing Office, 1958), 14,360 (hereafter MCH, *Part 38*).

58. MCH, *Part 39*, 14,574.

59. Kennedy, *The Enemy Within*, 72.

60. Mae Ngai, *Impossible Subjects: Illegal Aliens and the Making of Modern America* (Princeton, NJ: Princeton University Press, 2014), 21–55.

61. MCH, *Part 48*, 17,339.

62. MCH, *Part 48*, 17,340.

63. MCH, *Part 48*, 17,349.

64. Aaron Sternfield, "Jukebox Commercials May Bring in Extra Operator Loot," *Billboard Music Week*, April 17, 1961, 1.

65. "Coin Staffer Starts Jobbing Firm," *Billboard*, June 7, 1952, 95.

66. "Trades and Professions Due to Roll," *Jewish Floridian*, January 29, 1960, 2.

67. MCH, *Part 48*, 17,339.

68. "Baitler in Trinidad," *Billboard*, March 2, 1963, 62.

69. "Coinmen You Know," *Billboard*, February 2, 1952, 94.

70. "GE Group Solves Sitter Problem," *The Key West Citizen*, March 26, 1954, 3.

71. MCH, *Part 48*, 17,339, 17,349.

72. 1361 NW 133rd St., trulia.com, accessed August 26, 2020, https://www.trulia.com /p/fl/miami/1361-nw-133rd-st-miami-fl-33167--2093983712.

73. "Donald and Josephine Helow," *Fitchburg Sentinel*, December 27, 1941, 4.

74. "Passenger List, Carrier: LIB. SS. Florida No. 653, Voyage 2829," Miami, Florida, October 5, 1959.

75. "PA-503, HAV-CUBA-MIAMI, FL, Admitted," May 15, 1960.

76. "New Exporters in Field," *Cash Box*, November 17, 1962, 58.

77. "Homes for Sale," *The Voice*, June 12, 1964, 35, "The Catholic News Archive," accessed August 26, 2020. https://thecatholicnewsarchive.org/?a=d&d=fcatl9 640612-01.1.35.

78. "Death Files, 1936–2007," *National Archives*, accessed August 26, 2020. https:// aad.archives.gov/aad/record-detail.jsp?dt=2999&mtch=1&cat=all&tf=F&sc=29 343,29348,29350,29353,29354,29355,29362,29370,29371,29372&bc=sl,fd&txt_29 348=Leonard&op_29348=0&nfo_29348=V,16,1900&txt_29350=Baitler&op_29 350=0&nfo_29350=V,21,1900&rpp=10&pg=1&rid=1738720.

79. "Donald J. Helow," *Fort Lauderdale Sun-Sentinel*, July 24, 2007, "Legacy.com," accessed August 26, 2020. https://www.legacy.com/obituaries/sunsentinel/ob ituary.aspx?n=donald-j-helow&pid=91323282.

80. Julio Capó Jr., *Welcome to Fairyland: Queer Miami before 1940* (Chapel Hill: University of North Carolina Press, 2017).

81. Phil Tiemeyer, *Plane Queer: Labor, Sexuality, and AIDS in the History of Male Flight Attendants* (Berkeley: University of California Press, 2013).

82. US Congress, Senate, Select Committee on Improper Activities in the Labor or Management Field, *Investigation of Improper Activities in the Labor or Management*

Field, Part 56, 86th Congress, 1st session, July 10, 13, and 14, 1959 (Washington, DC: Government Printing Office, 1959), 19,488–491 (hereafter MCH, *Part 56*).

83. MCH, *Part 56*, 19,510.
84. MCH, *Part 56*, 19,514.
85. MCH, *Part 56*, 19,516.
86. MCH, *Part 56*, 19,523–19,524.
87. MCH, *Part 56*, 19,832–19,833.
88. MCH, *Part 56*, 19,832.
89. MCH, *Part 56*, 19,516.
90. MCH, *Part 56*, 19,834.
91. Witwer, *Corruption and Reform in the Teamsters Union*, 184–87.
92. Witwer, *Corruption and Reform in the Teamsters Union*, 157.
93. Witwer, *Corruption and Reform in the Teamsters Union*, 204–11.
94. Speech Before the University of Georgia Law School, Athens, May 6, 1961, cited in Witwer, *Corruption and Reform in the Teamsters Union*, 204.
95. Witwer, *Corruption and Reform in the Teamsters Union*, 207.
96. Witwer, *Corruption and Reform in the Teamsters Union*, 206.
97. A particularly explicit example of the notion that unions turned itinerant workers into family breadwinners exists in the National Maritime Union's 1967 coffee table book about its own history. See National Maritime Union, *On a True Course*, 1967, 88–91.
98. Vider, *The Queerness of Home*, 7–8.
99. Lauren Jae Gutterman, *Her Neighbor's Wife: A History of Lesbian Desire within Marriage* (Philadelphia: University of Pennsylvania Press, 2020), 49–76.
100. Daniel Hurewitz, *Bohemian Los Angeles and the Making of Modern Politics* (Berkeley: University of California Press, 2007).

Chapter 3

1. Charles O'Brien, "A Celebratory Evening in Miami Beach on October 5, 1957," photograph, Jack Goldsmith, *In Hoffa's Shadow: A Stepfather, a Disappearance in Detroit, and My Search for the Truth* (New York: Farrar, Straus and Giroux, 2019).
2. Kevin Plotner and Rebecca Plotner, *The Fontainebleau Miami* (New York: Schiffer Publishing, 2008), 22–27; Morris Lapidus, *Too Much Is Never Enough* (New York: Rizzoli International Publications, 1996), 183.
3. Lapidus, *Too Much Is Never Enough*, 166.
4. Lapidus, *Too Much Is Never Enough*, 167.
5. Ann Armbruster, *The Life and Times of Miami Beach* (New York: Knopf, 1995), 147.
6. Victor Riesel, "He 'Gives Away' Hoffa's Millions," *Miami News*, February 1, 1961, 8.
7. Plotner and Plotner, *The Fontainebleau Miami*, 47.
8. Kathi Weeks, *The Problem with Work: Feminism, Marxism, Antiwork Politics, and Postwork Imaginaries* (Durham, NC: Duke University Press, 2011), 11–12.
9. Julio Capó Jr., *Welcome to Fairyland: Queer Miami before 1940* (Chapel Hill: University of North Carolina Press, 2017), 27–45
10. Plotner and Plotner, *The Fontainebleau Miami*, 7–9.

11. Charles Abrams, "Only the Very Best Christian Clientele: Discrimination in Hotels and Resorts, USA, 1955," *Commentary*, January 1, 1955, 10.
12. Lapidus, *Too Much Is Never Enough*, 142–44.
13. Lapidus, *Too Much Is Never Enough*, 135.
14. Lapidus, *Too Much Is Never Enough*, 35.
15. Lapidus, *Too Much Is Never Enough*, 33.
16. Gail Bederman, *Manliness and Civilization: A Cultural History of Gender and Race in the United States, 1880–1917* (Chicago: University of Chicago Press, 1996), 175–79.
17. Bederman, *Manliness and Civilization*, 203.
18. Christine Stansell, *American Moderns: Bohemian New York and the Creation of a New Century* (Princeton, NJ: Princeton University Press, 2009).
19. Lapidus, *Too Much Is Never Enough*, 53.
20. Lapidus, *Too Much Is Never Enough*, 85.
21. Lapidus, *Too Much Is Never Enough*, 149.
22. Lapidus, *Too Much Is Never Enough*, 144.
23. Plotner and Plotner, *The Fontainebleau Miami*, 23.
24. Deborah Desilets, *Morris Lapidus: An Architecture of Joy* (New York: Rizzoli International Publications, 2010), 112; Lapidus, *Too Much Is Never Enough*, 179.
25. Desilets, *Morris Lapidus*, 15.
26. Armbruster, *The Life and Times of Miami Beach*, 149.
27. Plotner and Plotner, *The Fontainebleau Miami*, 22.
28. Lapidus, *Too Much Is Never Enough*, 165.
29. Lapidus, *Too Much Is Never Enough*, 178.
30. Norman Giller and Sarah Giller Nelson, *Designing the Good Life: Norman M. Giller and the Development of Miami Modernism* (Gainesville: University Press of Florida, 2007), 113.
31. Giller and Nelson, *Designing the Good Life*, 121.
32. Lapidus, *Too Much Is Never Enough*, 163; Giller and Nelson, *Designing the Good Life*, 113.
33. Steven Gaines, *Fool's Paradise: Players, Poseurs, and the Culture of Excess on South Beach* (New York: Broadway Books, 2009), 73.
34. Lapidus, *Too Much Is Never Enough*, 188–89.
35. Capó, *Welcome to Fairyland*, 98–104.
36. Capó, *Welcome to Fairyland*, 107–24.
37. Capó, *Welcome to Fairyland*, 46.
38. Capó, *Welcome to Fairyland*, 47.
39. Chad Heap, *Slumming: Sexual and Racial Encounters in American Nightlife, 1885–1940* (Chicago: University of Chicago Press, 2010).
40. Armbruster, *The Life and Times of Miami Beach*, 163.
41. Ralph C. and Estelle Dinerstein James, *Hoffa and the Teamsters: A Study of Union Power* (Princeton, NJ: D. Van Nostrand, 1965), 216.
42. US Congress, Senate, Select Committee on Improper Activities in the Labor or Management Field, *Investigation of Improper Activities in the Labor or Management Field, Part 12*, 85th Congress, 1st session, July 1, August 14, 15, 16, 19, 1957 (Washington, DC: Government Printing Office, 1957), 4,750–4,754.

43. Donald Garnel, *The Rise of Teamster Power in the West* (Berkeley: University of California Press, 1972), 3.

44. Garnel, *The Rise of Teamster Power in the West*, 171.

45. James R. Hoffa and Donald I. Rogers, *The Trials of Jimmy Hoffa: An Autobiography* (Chicago: Henry Regnery Company, 1970), 105–14.

46. Hoffa and Rogers, *The Trials of Jimmy Hoffa*, 92.

47. Hoffa and Rogers, *The Trials of Jimmy Hoffa*, 107.

48. Jeremy Rifkin and Randy Barber, *The North Will Rise Again: Pensions, Power, and Politics in the 1980s* (Boston: Beacon Press, 1978), 97–101; James and James, *Hoffa and the Teamsters*, 214–16.

49. Alexander S. Lipsett, *Labor's Partnership in Industrial Enterprise: A New Approach to Investment of Union and Pension Funds* (New York: Floyd L. Carlisle, 1950), 9.

50. David Witwer, *Corruption and Reform in the Teamsters Union* (Urbana: University of Illinois Press, 2003), 177–78.

51. Harry Robert Bartell Jr. "Unions and Pension Funds" (PhD. diss., Cornell University, 1963), 193–97.

52. James and James, *Hoffa and the Teamsters*, 230–33.

53. The name of this fund would change over the year as the scope of the members whose pensions it funded grew. By 1960, the fund was known as the Central States, Southeast, and Southwest Areas Pension Fund. Note also that there were many other pension funds for Teamster members, the overwhelming majority of which Hoffa had no sway. See Witwer, *Corruption and Reform in the Teamsters Union*, 180–82.

54. James and James, *Hoffa and the Teamsters*, 238–44.

55. Giller and Nelson, *Designing the Good Life*, 54, 65–67.

56. "State's Women Lawyers Organize to Meet," *Miami News*, June 24, 1951, 27; *France v. Hart*, 170 So. 2d 52 (1964), 64–455, District Court of Appeal of Florida, Third District, December 22, 1964.

57. James and James, *Hoffa and the Teamsters*, 381–87.

58. "The Castaways," Critiki.com, accessed October 27, 2020. https://www.critiki .com/location/the-castaways-miami-beach-709/.

59. "Charles Foster McKirahan," gini.com, accessed October 27, 2020. https://www .geni.com/people/Charles-Mckirahan/6000000017697422337.

60. "The Castaways," The Cardboard America Motel Archive, accessed October 27, 2020. http://motelpostcards.blogspot.com/2010/03/castaways-miami-beach-fl orida.html.

61. Paul Jacobs, *The State of Unions* (New York: Athenaeum, 1963), 23.

62. Jacobs, *The State of Unions*, 10.

63. James and James, *Hoffa and the Teamsters*, 45.

64. John Bartlow Martin, "The Struggle to Get Hoffa Part II: The Making of a Labor Boss," *Saturday Evening Post*, July 4, 1959, 54.

65. Martin, "The Struggle to Get Hoffa Part II," 54.

66. Hoffa and Rogers, *The Trials of Jimmy Hoffa*, 12.

67. Hoffa and Rogers, *The Trials of Jimmy Hoffa*, 18.

68. Hoffa and Rogers, *The Trials of Jimmy Hoffa*, 17.

69. Goldsmith, *In Hoffa's Shadow*, 66.

70. Dorothy Sue Cobble, *The Other Women's Movement: Workplace Justice and Social Rights in Modern America* (Princeton, NJ: Princeton University Press, 2005).
71. See chapter 5 for a sourcing and analysis of this relationship.
72. Weeks, *The Problem with Work*, 18–19.
73. Nelson Lichtenstein, *State of the Union: A Century of American Labor* (Princeton, NJ: Princeton University Press, 2013), 145–75.
74. James and James, *Hoffa and the Teamsters*, 341–44.
75. Tom Lownes, "Teamsters Hit Citrus Juice Firm," *Miami Herald*, February 12, 1958, 41.
76. Robert Shogan, "And Jim Digs In," *Miami News*, July 12, 1959, 1+.
77. Jane Berger, *A New Working Class: The Legacies of Public-Sector Employment in the Civil Rights Movement* (Philadelphia: University of Pennsylvania Press, 2021).
78. Dom Bonafede, "Hoffa Sets Sights on New Fields," *Miami Herald*, February 22, 1959, 29.
79. Lownes, "Teamsters Hit Citrus Juice Firm."
80. Bonafede, "Hoffa Sets Sights on New Fields."
81. Dom Bonafede, "Teamsters Eye Dade Politics," *Miami Herald*, June 19, 1960, 52.
82. "Add Miami Hospital to Hoffa's Mortgages," *Miami News*, February 6, 1961, 15.
83. Agnes Ash, "Hoffa and Friends at Miami Beach," *Miami News*, July 3, 1961, 1A+.
84. Agnes Ash, "Hoffa Buying Way In," *Miami News*, December 26, 1960, 20.
85. "Teamster Fund Buys Miami Luxury Hotel," *Reading Eagle*, September 28, 1960, 54.
86. "The New Everglades Hotel," postcard, Pan American Printers, Miami, date unknown circa 1960, cardcow.com, accessed October 28, 2020. https://www.cardcow.com/412512/new-everglades-hotel-miami-florida/?campaign=10952965803&param1=value1&param2=value2&shopping=rocks&level=account&&product_id=412512&aa=bb&placement=&target=pla-293946777986&campaign=10952965803&adgroup=111212683567&creative=459531732388&network=g&keyword=&storecode=&gclid=Cj0KCQjwreT8BRDTARIsAJLI0KI6b7VWhyg97KE4zwfUSSmrzjwksduAEJQ2U7y06lrRBoIaVKuyGSwaAggcEALw_wcB.
87. Donald M. Rothberg and Dick Barnes, "Teamster $$: Where Some Went," *Ocala Star-Banner*, September 1, 1975, 6A.
88. "Montmartre Hotel in Miami Beach," retroplanet.com, accessed October 28, 2020. https://blog.retroplanet.com/montmartre-hotel-in-miami-beach/.
89. "Melvin Grossman Architects," UNLV Special Collections and Archives, business listing, accessed October 28, 2020. https://www.library.unlv.edu/speccol/archdb2/index.php/firms/view/527.
90. Lapidus, *Too Much Is Never Enough*, 220.
91. James and James, *Hoffa and the Teamsters*, 381–87.
92. "Union Fund has Millions in Florida," *Miami Herald*, August 2, 1962, 41.
93. Victor Riesel, "Four Freedoms Hotels, Idea of Labor Chiefs," *Sheboygan Press*, March 29, 1960, 14.
94. "President Madison Hotel Miami Beach," postcard, 1960, ebay.com, accessed October 28, 2020. https://www.ebay.com/itm/Miami-Beach-FL-President-Madison-Hotel-1960-/323153123323.
95. Burt Garnett, "Union Tries an Experiment," *Miami News*, February 28, 1961, 11.
96. Jack Oswald, "They Set Up 'Shop' at Retirement Hotel," *Miami News*, December 15, 1960, 44.

97. *Miami News*, June 24, 1962, 71.

98. Bob Swift and Dom Bonafede, "Teamsters' Pension Cash Invested in Plush Motel," *Miami Herald*, August 31, 1958, 1.

99. "Neat Mixture," *Miami Herald*, October 28, 1963, 17.

100. "B'nai B'rith Chapters Sign New Charters," *Miami News*, November 9, 1958, 45.

101. Witwer, *Corruption and Reform in the Teamsters Union*, 157–83.

102. Agnes Ash, "Hoffa's Cash Piles Up Too Fast to Spend," *Miami News*, December 23, 1960, 8.

103. Charles Hesser, "Hoffa Moving in on Miami," *Miami News*, January 16, 1959, 1+.; Shogan.

104. Hesser.

105. Bonafede, "Hoffa Sets Sights on New Fields."

106. Shogan, "And Jim Digs In."

107. Swift and Bonafede, "Teamsters' Pension Cash Invested in Plush Motel."

108. "Gold Coast Deal Bared by Hoffa," *Miami Herald*, September 19, 1958, 9.

109. Dom Bonafede, "Teamsters Tough Money Lenders," *Miami Herald*, January 17, 1959, 19.

110. Shogan, "And Jim Digs In."

111. Bonafede, "Teamsters Eye Dade Politics."

112. Gene Miller, "Bail Jumping Pal of Hoffa Hunted Here," *Miami Herald*, November 8, 1962, 67.

113. US Congress, Senate, Select Committee on Improper Activities in the Labor or Management Field, *Investigation of Improper Activities in the Labor or Management Field, Part 15*, 85th Congress, 1st session, September 24–28, November 5, 1957 (Washington, DC: Government Printing Office, 1957), 5,364–5,401.

114. "Teamster Loan to Fix Up Hotel in Miami Bared," *Miami Herald*, May 16, 1964, 114.

115. Miller, "Bail Jumping Pal of Hoffa Hunted Here."

116. Witwer, *Corruption and Reform in the Teamsters Union*, 146–48.

117. To understand the racialization of the mind and the body in the context of European colonial expansion, see Edward Said, *Orientalism* (New York: Pantheon Books, 1978); to understand the intersection between the racialization of the mind and the body and its connection to dissident sexuality, see Siobhan Somerville, *Queering the Color Line: Race and the Invention of Homosexuality in American Culture* (Durham, NC: Duke University Press, 2000).

118. "Pool Bar," postcard, circa 1960, motelpostcards.blogspot.com, accessed October 28, 2020, http://motelpostcards.blogspot.com/2010/03/castaways-miami-beach-florida.html.

119. Armbruster, *The Life and Times of Miami Beach*, 157.

120. Lapidus, *Too Much Is Never Enough*, 195.

121. Lapidus, *Too Much Is Never Enough*, 183.

122. Ada Louise Huxtable, "Show Offers 'Joy' of Hotel Architecture," *New York Times*, October 15, 1970, 60.

123. "Miami on the Beach?" *The Economist*, March 18, 1961.

124. Armbruster, *The Life and Times of Miami Beach*, 154.

125. "Creeping Bankruptcy (650), Advance for AMs of Sunday," *Associated Press Newsfeatures*, July 10, 1960.

126. James and James, *Hoffa and the Teamsters*, 381–87.
127. Gaines, *Fool's Paradise*, 91–97.
128. Herald Wire Services, "Hoffa Gets Five Years for Union Fund Fraud," *Miami Herald*, August 18, 1964, 23.
129. "Open Hotel for Union Members," *The Chicago Defender (National Edition)*, March 18, 1961, 21.
130. Lapidus, *Too Much Is Never Enough*, 183.

Chapter 4

1. Bob Merrill, "Doggie in the Window," recorded by Patti Page (New York: Mercury Records, 1953).
2. Ken Shipley, "The Shiptown Label," *Eccentric Soul Records No. 81—The Shiptown Label* (Chicago: Eccentric Soul Records, 2021).
3. Daphne Duval Harrison, *Black Pearls: Blues Queens of the 1920s* (New Brunswick, NJ: Rutgers University Press, 1988), 111.
4. Kristina Wilson, *Mid-Century Modernism and the American Body* (Princeton, NJ: Princeton University Press, 2021), 70, 87.
5. Leonard Buder, "Boycott Cripples City Schools; Absences 360,000 Above Normal; Negroes and Puerto Ricans Unite," *New York Times*, February 4, 1964, 1.
6. Edward C. Burks, "Four Hour Sit-In Staged at NLRB," *New York Times*, May 4, 1965, 26.
7. US Congress, Senate, Select Committee on Improper Activities in the Labor or Management Field, *Investigation of Improper Activities in the Labor or Management Field, Part 12*, 85th Congress, 1st session, July 1, August 14, 15, 16, and 19, 1957 (Washington, DC: Government Printing Office, 1957), 4,561–4,564 (hereafter MCH, *Part 12*).
8. "9 Anvil Lane, Levittown, NY 11756, redfin.com, accessed August 1, 2020, https://www.redfin.com/NY/Levittown/9-Anvil-Ln-11756/home/20313854.
9. David Kushner, *Levittown: Two Families, One Tycoon, and the Fight for Civil Rights in America's Legendary Suburb* (New York: Walker and Company, 2009), 10.
10. Kushner, *Levittown*, 18.
11. Kushner, *Levittown*, 90–189.
12. US Congress, Senate, Select Committee on Improper Activities in the Labor or Management Field, *Investigation of Improper Activities in the Labor or Management Field, Part 10*, 85th Congress, 1st session, July 31, August 1, 2, 5, and 6, 1957 (Washington, DC: Government Printing Office, 1957), 3,636–3,640 (hereafter MCH, *Part 10*).
13. MCH, *Part 10*, 3,666–3,668.
14. MCH, *Part 12*, 4,564.
15. MCH, *Part 10*, 3,643–3,647.
16. MCH, *Part 10*, 3,758.
17. MCH, *Part 10*, 3,752.
18. "Two Officers of Union Held as Extorters," *New York Times*, March 26, 1953, 35.
19. "Two Officers of Union Held as Extorters."

20. MCH, *Part 10*, 3,920–3,926.
21. Nelson Lichtenstein, *Walter Reuther: The Most Dangerous Man in Detroit* (Urbana: University of Illinois Press, 1997), 248–98.
22. Andrew Wender Cohen, *The Racketeer's Progress: Chicago and the Struggle for the Modern American Economy* (Cambridge, UK: Cambridge University Press, 2004), 103.
23. Cohen, *The Racketeer's Progress*, 219.
24. David Witwer, *Corruption and Reform in the Teamsters Union* (Urbana: University of Illinois Press, 2008), 10.
25. Witwer, *Corruption and Reform in the Teamsters Union*, 16.
26. Joe Willian Trotter Jr. *The Great Migration in Historical Perspective: New Dimensions of Race, Class, and Gender* (Bloomington: Indiana University Press, 1991).
27. Thomas Sugrue, *The Origins of the Urban Crisis: Race and Inequality in Postwar Detroit*, updated ed. (Princeton, NJ: Princeton University Press, 2014), 15–89.
28. Clayton Knowles, "60% Rise in Puerto Ricans and Negroes Is Seen Here," *New York Times*, November 30, 1959, 1.
29. Carmen Teresa Whalen, "Colonialism, Citizenship, and the Making of the Puerto Rican Diaspora: An Introduction," in *The Puerto Rican Diaspora: Historical Perspectives*, ed. Carmen Teresa Whalen and Victor Vázquez-Hernández (Philadelphia: Temple University Press, 2005), 1–42.
30. MCH, *Part 10*, 3,781–3,784.
31. MCH, *Part 10*, 3,792–3,795.
32. MCH, *Part 12*, 4,605.
33. MCH, *Part 10*, 3,692–3,697.
34. MCH, *Part 10*, 3,831.
35. For an insightful analysis of the political economy of industrial lofts in New York City, see Sharon Zukin, *Loft Living: Culture and Capital in Urban Change* (New Brunswick, NJ: Rutgers University Press, 1982).
36. Joshua M. Zeitz, *White Ethnic New York: Jews, Catholics, and the Shaping of Postwar Politics* (Chapel Hill: University of North Carolina Press, 2007), 19.
37. "Building: 315 W. 36th St.," streeteasy.com, accessed December 10, 2020, https://streeteasy.com/building/315-west-36-street-new_york.
38. "Business Spaces Leased," *New York Times*, January 8, 1938, 28.
39. MCH, *Part 10*, 3,778–3,881.
40. Scores of newspaper advertisements for segregated car wash workers ran in the Detroit papers until at least the mid-1950s. See, for example: Tower Auto Wash, classified advertisement, *Detroit Free Press*, January 8, 1955, 15.
41. The ties between Bill Bufalino and Vincent and Angelo Meli are well-established in popular and scholarly sources, as is Bufalino's control of Teamsters Local 985. For more information about the context under which Gus Richardson encountered Local 985, see Morris Goldman, Arthur Kaplan, and Bill Bufalino's testimony in US Congress, Senate, Select Committee on Improper Activities in the Labor or Management Field, *Investigation of Improper Activities in the Labor or Management Field, Part 48*, 86th Congress, 1st session, March 23, 24, 25, April 7, 8, 9, 10, 14, 15, 1959 (Washington, DC: Government Printing Office, 1959) (hereafter MCH, *Part 48*).
42. MCH, *Part 48*, 17,528–17,530.

43. Whalen, "Colonialism, Citizenship, and the Making of the Puerto Rican Diaspora," 5.
44. MCH, *Part 10*, 3,801.
45. Laura Briggs, *Reproducing Empire: Race, Sex, Science, and U.S. Imperialism in Puerto Rico* (Berkeley: University of California Press, 2002), 162–92.
46. Eithne Luibhéid, *Entry Denied: Controlling Sexuality at the Border* (Minneapolis: University of Minnesota Press, 2002), 1–30.
47. MCH, *Part 12*, 4,765.
48. MCH, *Part 12*, 4,754.
49. A. H. Raskin, "24,000 Teamsters Strike; Mayor's Plea Is Rejected; Tie-Up Imperils Commerce," *New York Times*, October 16, 1954, 1.
50. Raskin, "24,000 Teamsters Strike."
51. Stanley Levey, "3 Big Food Chains Sign Truck Pacts; 8,000 Men to Work," *New York Times*, October 17, 1954, 1.
52. A. H. Raskin, "Union Leaders Eye Split Truck Pacts," *New York Times*, October 22, 1954, 36.
53. Levey, "3 Big Food Chains Sign Truck Pacts," 1.
54. MCH, *Part 12*, 4,748.
55. MCH, *Part 12*, 4,765.
56. Levey, "3 Big Food Chains Sign Truck Pacts," 1.
57. MCH, *Part 12*, 4,750.
58. MCH, *Part 12*, 4,754.
59. MCH, *Part 12*, 4,756.
60. MCH, *Part 12*, 4,690–4,694.
61. MCH, *Part 12*, 4,688.
62. MCH, *Part 12*, 4,724–4,730.
63. The most comprehensive study of race in the Teamsters was conducted as part of a wider study of the position of Black workers in many industries. While the volume on the trucking industry is deeply revealing of Teamster practices related to race, it explicitly focuses on Black workers and makes only cursory mention of other workers of color. Thus, historians have a far less granular understanding of how Teamster racial policy applied to workers who were neither Black nor white. See Richard D. Leone, *The Negro in the Trucking Industry* (Philadelphia: Industrial Research Unit, Department of Industry, the Wharton School of Finance and Commerce, 1970).
64. Leone, *The Negro in the Trucking Industry*, 50–59.
65. Leone, *The Negro in the Trucking Industry*, 73.
66. Leone, *The Negro in the Trucking Industry*, 40–45.
67. David Witwer, *Corruption and Reform in the Teamsters Union* (Urbana: University of Illinois Press, 2003), 146.
68. Leone, *The Negro in the Trucking Industry*, 64.
69. Leone, *The Negro in the Trucking Industry*, 82.
70. MCH, *Part 10*, 3,828–3,829.
71. "Low Paid Group Here Found Hit by Union Racket," *New York Times*, August 3, 1957, 1; MCH, *Part 10*, 3,763.
72. MCH, *Part 10*, 3,828.

73. Adam Green, *Selling the Race: Culture, Community, and Black Chicago, 1940–1955* (Chicago: University of Chicago Press, 2008), 182.

74. Green, *Selling the Race*, 154. For further discussion of the way mass consumption and suburban living shaped the aspirations of Black and Brown people, see Kasey R. Keeler, *American Indians and the American Dream: Policies, Place, and Property in Minnesota* (Minneapolis: University of Minnesota Press, 2023); Jody Vallejo, *Barrios to Burbs: The Making of the Mexican American Middle Class* (Stanford, CA: Stanford University Press, 2012); Andrew Wiese, *Places of their Own: African American Suburbanization in the Twentieth Century* (Chicago: University of Chicago Press, 2005).

75. Wilson, *Mid-Century Modernism*, 17.

76. Green, *Selling the Race*, 11.

77. US Congress, Senate, Select Committee on Improper Activities in the Labor or Management Field, *Investigation of Improper Activities in the Labor or Management Field, Part 48*, 86th Congress, 1st session, March 23, 24, 25, April 7, 8, 9, 10, 14, 15, 1959 (Washington, DC: Government Printing Office, 1959), 17,518 (hereafter MCH, *Part 48*).

78. MCH, *Part 48*, 17,515.

79. Green, *Selling the Race*, 10.

80. MCH, *Part 48*, 17,515–17,528.

81. MCH, *Part 48*, 17,519.

82. MCH, *Part 48*, 17,523.

83. Delgado, 74.

84. Dan Wakefield, "Politics and the Puerto Ricans: Getting Out the Vote in Spanish Harlem," *Commentary*, March, 1958, commentarymagazine.com, accessed November 10, 2020, https://www.commentarymagazine.com/articles/dan-wakefield/politics-and-the-puerto-ricansgetting-out-the-vote-in-spanish-harlem/.

85. Delgado, 68–81.

86. Wakefield, "Politics and the Puerto Ricans."

87. MCH, *Part 12*, 4,603.

88. MCH, *Part 10*, 3,756.

89. MCH, *Part 12*, 4,605.

90. MCH, *Part 10*, 3,756–3,757.

91. MCH, *Part 10*, 3,784–3,787.

92. Ralph Katz, "2 Unions Accused in Bronx Dispute," *New York Times*, September 4, 1957, 28.

93. MCH, *Part 10*, 3,789.

94. MCH, *Part 10*, 3,793–3,799.

95. Katz, "2 Unions Accused in Bronx Dispute."

96. There were cases where illicit employers and paper locals did sue to try to protect their collusive contracts. At the Radley Metzger Company, management sued to defend its contract with Anthony Corallo's United Textile Workers Local 229, arguing that Charles Fay, the president of IUE Local 485 was a communist and that the Puerto Rican activists were under the sway of the Communist Party. Such examples are very rare in the historical record, however, and most paper locals were disbanded because of grassroots activism or because of the passage of the Landrum Griffin Act. See: Katz, "2 Unions Accused in Bronx Dispute."

97. MCH, *Part 10*, 3,790.
98. MCH, *Part 10*, 3,799.
99. Although Black and Brown workers in the New York paper locals were harassed, threatened, and intimidated at work, I found no historical evidence of workers being physically attacked in their homes or in their neighborhoods. This is a vastly different scenario than the situation facing Jewish and Italian operatives, who were subjected to physical violence at their homes from other Jewish and Italian operatives with connections to the underworld and to the Teamsters. See chapter two for citations documenting the way that physical violence was an organizing tool within the Teamsters metropolis.
100. See chapter 2 for a thorough discussion and documentation of Kennedy's relationship to the media. See also Witwer, , *Corruption and Reform in the Teamsters Union*, 155–90.
101. "Low Paid Group Here Found Hit by Union Racket."
102. Stanley Levey, "Labor Maps Fight on Racket Unions Operating in the City," *New York Times*, August 4, 1957, 1.
103. "Pact Raising Wages Ends Lamp Strike," *New York Times*, January 23, 1958, 8.
104. Carmen Teresa Whalen, "The Day the Dresses Stopped," in *Memories and Migrations: Mapping Boriqua and Chicana Histories*, ed. Vicki L. Ruiz and John R. Chávez (Urbana: University of Illinois Press, 2008), 121–50.
105. "5 Rights Leaders Ask Governor to Intervene in Hospital Strike," *New York Times*, February 8, 1965, 18.
106. "Lower East Side Plans Rent Rally," *New York Times*, January 12, 1964, 81; Buder, "Boycott Cripples City Schools," 20.
107. A. H. Raskin, "Teamsters Set Up Big Union Drives," *New York Times*, February 11, 1956, 13.
108. Kushner, *Levittown*, 147–75.
109. For recent work on the connections between the new social movements and unions, see Jane Berger, *A New Working Class: The Legacies of Public-Sector Employment in the Civil Rights Movement* (Philadelphia: University of Pennsylvania Press, 2021); Luis L. M. Aguiar and Joseph A. McCartin, eds., *Purple Power: The History and Global Impact of SEIU* (Urbana: University of Illinois Press, 2023); Roberta Rehner Iverson, *What Workers Say: Decades of Struggle and How to Make Real Opportunity Now* (Philadelphia: Temple University Press, 2022).

Chapter 5

1. "If These Walls Could Talk, Alden Towers," accessed June 12, 2021, https://www.aldentowers.com/.
2. FBI, "RIF#124-10342-10001, Subject Anthony Giacalone, ELSUR 92-228-1-1," March 9, 1963, Mary Ferrell Foundation, www.maryferrell.org, mff_pdf85188, 1–5, accessed January 7, 2022.
3. US Congress, Senate, Select Committee on Improper Activities in the Labor or Management Field, *Investigation of Improper Activities in the Labor or Management Field, Part 36*, 85th Congress, 2nd session, August 5, 6, 7, 8, and 12, 1958 (Washington, DC: Government Printing Office, 1958), 13,287 (hereafter McClellan Committee, *Hearings*).

4. John Bartlow Martin, "The Struggle to Get Hoffa Part II: The Making of a Labor Boss," *Saturday Evening Post*, July 4, 1959, 56.

5. Ralph C. and Estelle Dinerstein James, *Hoffa and the Teamsters: A Study of Union Power* (Princeton, NJ: D. Van Nostrand, 1965).

6. FBI, "RIF#124-10342-10014, Subject Anthony Giacalone, ELSUR 92-228-SUB 1-138, 140, 141," July 25, 1963, Mary Ferrell Foundation, www.maryferrell.org, mff_pdf120178, 5, accessed July 12, 2021 (hereafter FBI, RIF#124-10342-10014).

7. Multiple literatures describe the Teamsters' conservative business unionism. For a labor historical approach, see Nelson Lichtenstein, *State of the Union: A Century of American Labor* (Princeton, NJ: Princeton University Press, 2002), 142–46; for a rank-and-file dissident perspective, see Dan LaBotz, *Rank-and-File Rebellion: Teamsters for a Democratic Union* (London: Verso, 1991). For a cultural and labor historical approach to trade union conservatism in the 1960s and 1970s, see Jefferson Cowie, *Stayin' Alive: The 1970s and the Last Days of the Working Class* (New York: The New Press, 2010); for a feminist critique of business unionism, see Dorothy Sue Cobble, *The Other Women's Movement: Workplace Justice and Social Rights in Modern America* (Princeton, NJ: Princeton University Press, 2005).

8. FBI, "Report of SA James L. Shanahan to the FBI, RIF#124-10342-10387, Subject Anthony Giacalone, ELSUR 92-228-1294," August 11, 1964, Mary Ferrell Foundation, www.maryferrell.org, mff_pdf142504, 2, accessed January 7, 2022, 2 (hereafter FBI, RIF#124-10342-10387).

9. This biographical information comes from Harvard Law School professor Jack Goldsmith's extensive interviews with Chuckie O'Brien, who was a father figure to Goldsmith for a part of his life. As Goldsmith notes in his footnotes, FBI surveillance documents produced from the electronic surveillance of the Home Juice Company confirm many of these details. See Jack Goldsmith, *In Hoffa's Shadow: A Stepfather, a Disappearance in Detroit, and My Search for the Truth* (New York: Farrar, Straus and Giroux, 2019), 45–47.

10. Jack Goldsmith, personal interview, June 21, 2021.

11. Goldsmith, *In Hoffa's Shadow*, 48.

12. Goldsmith, *In Hoffa's Shadow*, 48.

13. FBI, RIF#124-10342-10387, 2.

14. Goldsmith, *In Hoffa's Shadow*, 48.

15. Goldsmith, personal interview, June 21, 2021.

16. "Whittier Hotel," historicdetroit.org, accessed May 25, 2021, https://historicdetroit.org/buildings/whittier-hotel.

17. Goldsmith, *In Hoffa's Shadow*, 60.

18. US Congress, Senate, Select Committee on Improper Activities in the Labor or Management Field, *Investigation of Improper Activities in the Labor or Management Field, Part 35*, 85th Congress, 2nd session, July 31 and August 1, 1958 (Washington, DC: Government Printing Office, 1958), 13,159.

19. Goldsmith, *In Hoffa's Shadow*, 58. Only Chuckie O'Brien's extensive interviews with Jack Goldsmith identify Anthony Giacalone as the person who organized the antiunion gang whose brick killed Arthur Queasebarth. It is undeniable, however, that Queasebarth was killed by an antiunion thug's brick, and most legitimate sources argue that this strike formed a turning point in the relationship between Hoffa, the Teamsters, and La Cosa Nostra.

20. The elision of Sylvia Pagano from the historical record significantly impacts how

we understand the Hoffa-Meli-Perrone meeting of 1941. Anonymous sources in law enforcement for Dan Moldea's *The Hoffa Wars* argue that this Hoffa-Meli-Perrone meetup indeed took place in 1941, and David Witwer also relies on those sources in his authoritative 2003 account of these events, in part because law enforcement relied on the reliable testimony of Teamster officials. Thaddeus Russell disputes the Moldea account in his 2001 book *Out of the Jungle*, taking a more orthodox approach by using the McClellan Committee documents to argue that the origin of the Hoffa-underworld connection occurred not until the late 1940s. Pagano's story (as revealed in Moldea, Witwer, and Goldsmith, among others), however, reveals that Hoffa, Brennan, Giacalone, and Pagano were in contact in the early 1940s, a time when Pagano had close ties to Frank Coppola and other high-ranking officials in the Detroit family. Chuckie O'Brien's testimony also corroborates this story. Therefore, although more research is still needed, I am confident enough of its validity that I wrote it as such. See Thaddeus Russell, *Out of the Jungle: Jimmy Hoffa and the Remaking of the American Working Class* (New York: Knopf, 2001), 88–89; Dan Moldea, *The Hoffa Wars: Teamsters, Rebels, Politicians, and the Mob* (New York: Paddington Press, 1978), 25; Goldsmith, *In Hoffa's Shadow*, 57–59.

21. Goldsmith, *In Hoffa's Shadow*, 66.
22. Goldsmith, *In Hoffa's Shadow*, 64–68; David Witwer, *Corruption and Reform in the Teamsters Union* (Urbana: University of Illinois Press, 2003), 169; Moldea, *The Hoffa Wars*, 63.
23. Goldsmith, *In Hoffa's Shadow*, 147.
24. Witwer, *Corruption and Reform in the Teamsters Union*, 184–87.
25. Robert F. Kennedy, *The Enemy Within* (New York: Harper, 1960).
26. Goldsmith, personal interview.
27. The transcripts of the microphone recordings make constant reference to the sound of the vacuum cleaner. Ruby and Marie operate the vacuum in all cases, and often when Anthony Giacalone was in the house with Pagano. Vacuuming often occurred frequently in short periods of time. On April 12, 1963, for example the vacuum runs for at least eight minutes starting at 4:32 p.m. and during a conversation between Pagano and Giacalone. The next day, April 13, the vacuum is back on, in this case while Pagano talks on the phone. See FBI, "RIF#124-10342-10050, Subject Anthony Giacalone, ELSUR 92-228-SUB 1-11, 20, 34–38," April 12–13, 1963, Mary Ferrell Foundation, www.maryferrell.org, mff_pdf120215, 4, 6, accessed January 7, 2022.
28. FBI, "RIF#124-10342-10016, Subject Anthony Giacalone, ELSUR 92-228-SUB 1-130-137," July 16, 1963, Mary Ferrell Foundation, www.maryferrell.org, mff_pdf120180, 10, accessed July 10, 2021.
29. FBI, "RIF#124-10342-10054, Subject Anthony Giacalone, ELSUR 92-228-SUB 1-216-222," October 10, 1963, Mary Ferrell Foundation, www.maryferrell.org, mff_pdf89222, 8, accessed January 7, 2022 (hereafter FBI, RIF#124-10342-10054).
30. FBI, "RIF#124-10342-10029, Subject Anthony Giacalone, ELSUR 92-228-SUB 1-100-105," June 17, 1963, Mary Ferrell Foundation, www.maryferrell.org, mff_pdf120193, 10, accessed June 15, 2022.
31. FBI, "RIF#124-10342-10054, 7.
32. FBI, "RIF#124-10342-10038, Subject Anthony Giacalone, ELSUR 92-228-SUB 1-79-81," May 27, 1963, Mary Ferrell Foundation, www.maryferrell.org, mff_pdf120202, 4, accessed June 15, 2022.

33. FBI, "RIF#124-10334-10116, Subject Anthony Provenzano, ELSUR 92-228-1-96," June 13, 1963, Mary Ferrell Foundation, www.maryferrell.org, mff_pdf115149, 12, accessed January 7, 2022 (hereafter FBI, "RIF#124-10334-10116).

34. FBI, "RIF#124-10336-10082, Subject James R. Hoffa Jr., ELSUR 92-228-1-182 183, 185, 209," September 9, 1963, Mary Ferrell Foundation, www.maryferrell.org, mff_pdf85912, 10, accessed January 7, 2022.

35. FBI, "RIF#124-10342-10058, Subject Anthony Giacalone, ELSUR 92–228-SUB 1-205-208," September 30, 1963, Mary Ferrell Foundation, www.maryferrell.org, mff_pdf89226, 5, accessed January 7, 2022.

36. FBI, "RIF#124-10336-10303, Subject James Riddle Hoffa, ELSUR 92-470-1484, Memo from John Schelburne to the FBI," January 31, 1964, Mary Ferrell Foundation, www.maryferrell.org, mff_pdf85215, 1, accessed January 7, 2022.

37. FBI, "RIF#124-10342-10427, Subject Anthony Giacalone, ELSUR 92-228-1202, Memo from John Schelburne to the FBI," April 20, 1964, Mary Ferrell Foundation, www.maryferrell.org, mff_pdf88865, 1, accessed January 7, 2022.

38. Witwer, *Corruption and Reform in the Teamsters Union*, 176–79.

39. FBI, "RIF#124-10334-10116, 11,21.

40. FBI, "RIF#124-10336-10107, Subject James R. Hoffa, ELSUR 92-228-1-360-549, Mary Ferrell Foundation, www.maryferrell.org, mff_pdf86287, 163, accessed January 7, 2022 (hereafter FBI, "RIF#124-10336-10107).

41. FBI, "RIF#124-10342-10402, Subject Anthony Giacalone, ELSUR 92-228-1253, Memo from John Schelburne to the FBI," May 26, 1964, Mary Ferrell Foundation, www.maryferrell.org, mff_pdf88841, 1, accessed January 7, 2022.

42. FBI, "RIF#124-10336-10098, Subject James R. Hoffa, ELSUR 92-438-1-71, 72, 85, 100, 113, 114, 116, 134, 228, 288," June 3, 1963, Mary Ferrell Foundation, www.maryferrell.org, mff_pdf85509, 116, accessed January 11, 2022.

43. FBI, "RIF#124-10336-10107, 111.

44. Chris M. Smith, *Syndicate Women: Gender and Networks in Chicago Organized Crime* (Berkeley: University of California Press, 2019), 1–17.

45. LaShawn Harris, *Sex Workers, Psychics, and Numbers Runners: Black Women in New York's Underground Economy* (Urbana: University of Illinois Press, 2016), 2.

46. Smith, *Syndicate Women*, 8–11; Harris, *Sex Workers, Psychics, and Numbers Runners*, 54–93.

47. Elaine Tyler May, *Homeward Bound: American Families in the Cold War Era* (New York: Basic Books, 2017 [1988]).

48. FBI, "RIF#124-10342-10285, Subject Anthony Giacalone, ELSUR 92-228-802, Memo from Harry R. Lunt to the FBI," April 5, 1963, Mary Ferrell Foundation, www.maryferrell.org, mff_pdf87761, 14, accessed January 7, 2022 (hereafter FBI, "RIF#124-10342-10285).

49. Pagano is heard calling the Hillcrest Country Club and having phone conversations with many of her associates from La Cosa Nostra who were playing golf at the Hillcrest throughout the FBI surveillance. See, for example: FBI, "RIF#124-10342-10358, Subject Anthony Giacalone, ELSUR 92-228-1044, Memo from Harry R. Lunt to the FBI," January 14, 1964, Mary Ferrell Foundation, www.maryferrell.org, mff_pdf121957, 12, accessed January 10, 2022.

50. FBI, "RIF#124-10342-10182, Subject Anthony Giacalone, ELSUR 92-228-908, Memo from Harry R. Lunt to the FBI," July 11, 1963, Mary Ferrell Foundation, www.maryferrell.org, mff_pdf87660, 3, accessed July 15, 2021.

51. FBI, "RIF#124-10342-10285, 7.

52. FBI, "RIF#124-10342-10459, Subject Anthony Giacalone, ELSUR 92-228-1148, Memo from Harry R. Lunt to the FBI," March 18, 1964, Mary Ferrell Foundation, www.maryferrell.org, mff_pdf88897, 6, accessed January 10, 2022.

53. Gary Leff, "United Had Men-Only Flights Until 1970: Here's the Manly Services They Offered," www.viewfromthewing.com, accessed February 4, 2022, https://viewfromthewing.com/united-airlines-men-only-executive-service/.

54. FBI, "RIF#124-10342-10387, Subject Anthony Giacalone, ELSUR 92-228-1294, Report of SA James L. Shanahan," August 11, 1964, Mary Ferrell Foundation, www.maryferrell.org, mff_pdf88825, 17, accessed January 7, 2022.

55. Nayan Shah, *Contagious Divides: Epidemics and Race in San Francisco's Chinatown* (Berkeley: University of California Press, 2001), 120–57; Shah also develops related concepts of "border intimacy" and "stranger intimacy," which also theorize how migration and labor exploitation produce dissident sexuality. See especially Nayan Shah, *Stranger Intimacy: Contesting Race, Sexuality, and the Law in the North American West* (Berkeley: University of California Press, 2012), 77–104.

56. Ralph C. and Estelle Dinerstein James, *Hoffa and the Teamsters: A Study of Union Power* (Princeton, NJ: D. Van Nostrand, 1965), 342–43, 350–51.

57. James and James, *Hoffa and the Teamsters*, 345–46.

58. FBI, "RIF#124-10342-10029, 10.

59. FBI, "RIF#124-10336-10095, Subject James R. Hoffa Jr., ELSUR 92-228-1-106-175," September 9, 1963, Mary Ferrell Foundation, www.maryferrell.org, mff_pdf85506, 25–26, accessed June 10, 2021 (hereafter FBI, RIF#124-10336-10095.

60. FBI, RIF#124-10336-10095, 28.

61. FBI, RIF#124-10336-10095, 33.

62. Goldsmith, *In Hoffa's Shadow*.

63. FBI, "RIF#124-10342-10014, 3–5.

64. FBI, "RIF#124-10336-10093, Subject James R. Hoffa Jr., ELSUR 92-228-1-39-94," April 17, 1963, Mary Ferrell Foundation, www.maryferrell.org, mff_pdf85504, 4–5, accessed June 10, 2021.

65. FBI, RIF#124-10336-10095, 15.

66. Jack Goldsmith, *In Hoffa's Shadow*, 170–80.

67. Seth Kantor, Robert Pavich, and Michael Wendland, "Tony Jack Had Mystery Woman Friend," *Detroit News*, August 1, 1976, 15A.

68. FBI, "RIF#124-10342-10303, Subject Anthony Giacalone, ELSUR 92-228-784, Memo from Harry R. Lunt to the FBI," February 21, 1963, Mary Ferrell Foundation, www.maryferrell.org, mff_pdf87780, 9, accessed January 10, 2022 (hereafter FBI, RIF#124-10342-10303).

69. FBI, RIF#124-10342-10303, 10–11.

70. The FBI edits out all forms of the word "fuck" all the way through the transcript, using only the abbreviation F---. They fully transcribe racial slurs on many instances. See, for example, FBI, "RIF#124-10342-10023, Subject Anthony Giacalone, ELSUR 92–228-SUB 1–115, 166," July 2, 1963, Mary Ferrell Foundation, www.maryferrell.org, mff_pdf120187, 3, accessed January 10, 2022.

71. FBI, "RIF#124-10334-10116, 11.

72. FBI, "RIF#124-10336-10301, Subject James R. Hoffa, ELSUR 92-470-1487, Memorandum to SAC Detroit from SA John L. Shelburne," February 7, 1964, Mary

Ferrell Foundation, www.maryferrell.org, mff_pdf85213, 3–7, accessed January 10, 2022.

73. For examples of the expanding representation of sexuality in the 1970s, see Ronald Michael Mazur, *The New Intimacy: Open-Ended Marriage and Alternative Lifestyles* (Boston: Beacon Press, 1973); George and Nena O'Neill, *Open Marriage: A New Life Style for Couples* (New York: M. Evans and Company, 1972); for a scholarly analysis of this process, see Ryan Patrick Murphy, "Lifestyle: Contesting a Category of Dissident Sexuality in U.S. Urban History," *GLQ* 26, no. 2 (April 2020): 273–301.

74. Bill Osgerby, *Playboys in Paradise: Masculinity, Youth, and Leisure-Style in Modern America* (Oxford, UK: Berg, 2001), 4.

75. Moldea, *The Hoffa Wars*, 25.

76. Alice Echols, *Daring to Be Bad: Radical Feminism in America, 1967–1975* (Minneapolis: University of Minnesota Press, 1989).

77. Moldea, *The Hoffa Wars*, 49.

78. Moldea, *The Hoffa Wars*, 25.

79. Moldea, *The Hoffa Wars*, 177.

80. Moldea, *The Hoffa Wars*, 25, 391.

81. Paul Jacobs, *The State of Unions* (New York: Athenaeum, 1963), 56.

Epilogue

1. Tom Miller, "The Long History of the Everard Baths," *Daytonian in Manhattan*, July 19, 2023, http://daytoninmanhattan.blogspot.com/2020/06/the-long-histo ry-of-everards-baths-26.html.

2. Paul Sorene, "A Night at New York's Banging Continental Baths," *Flashback: Everything Old is New Again*, April 29, 2018, https://flashbak.com/a-night-at-new-yor ks-banging-continental-baths-399561/.

3. "Everard Baths," *NYC LGBT Historic Sites Project*, July 19, 2023, https://www.ny clgbtsites.org/site/everard-baths/.

4. George Chauncey, *Gay New York: Gender, Urban Culture, and the Making of a Gay Male World, 1890–1940* (New York: Basic Books, 1994), 301–54.

5. Anna Lvosky, *Vice Patrol: Cops, Courts, and the Struggle Over Urban Gay Life Before Stonewall* (Chicago: University of Chicago Press, 2021); for a first-person account of police violence in gay bars in the 1950s and 1960s, see Leslie Feinberg, *Stone Butch Blues* (Ithaca, NY: Firebrand Books, 1993).

6. Phillip Crawford Jr., *The Mafia and the Gays, Second Edition* (self-published, 2022), 67–76.

7. US Congress, Senate, Select Committee on Improper Activities in the Labor or Management Field, *Investigation of Improper Activities in the Labor or Management Field, Part 46*, 86th Congress, 1st session, December 4 and 9, 1958; February 10, 11, 12, 13, 17, 18, 1959 (Washington, DC: Government Printing Office, 1959), 16,907–16,913 (hereafter MCH, *Part 46*).

8. Crawford, *The Mafia and the Gays*, 31–66, 111–16.

9. Max Weber, *The Protestant Ethic and the Spirit of Capitalism* (New York: Routledge, 2001 [1904]), 102–25.

10. Margot Canaday, *The Straight State: Sexuality and Citizenship in Twentieth-Century America* (Princeton, NJ: Princeton University Press, 2011).

11. Barry Bluestone and Bennett Harrison, eds., *The Deindustrialization of America: Plant Closings, Community Abandonment, and the Dismantling of Basic Industry* (New York: Basic Books, 1982).

12. Stuart Hall and Tony Jefferson, eds., *Resistance through Ritual: Youth Subcultures in Postwar Britain* (London: Taylor and Francis, 1976); Cullen Murphy, "The Search for a Whole Life: Turning Away from Status Syndrome," *Change* 6, no. 8 (1974): 14–18; Mary Rizzo, *Class Acts: Young Men and the Rise of Lifestyle* (Reno: University of Nevada Press, 2015); Ryan Patrick Murphy, "Lifestyle: Contesting a Category of Dissident Sexuality in U.S. Urban History," *GLQ* 26, no. 2 (April 2020): 273–301.

13. Jane Jacobs, *The Death and Life of Great American Cities* (New York: Vintage Books, 1961), 143–240.

14. Sharon Zukin, *Loft Living: Culture and Capital in Urban Change* (New Brunswick, NJ: Rutgers University Press, 1982), 89–93.

15. Zukin, *Loft Living*, 175–80.

16. Cameron Lynne Macdonald and Carmen Sirianni, eds., *Working in the Service Society* (Philadelphia: Temple University Press, 1996).

17. "Teamsters History and Timeline," *GW Libraries and Academic Innovation*, July 19, 2023, https://library.gwu.edu/teamsters-history-and-timeline.

18. Michael H. Belzer, *Sweatshops on Wheels: Winners and Losers in Trucking Deregulation* (Oxford, UK: Oxford University Press, 2000); for a cultural analysis of the changes in the truck-driving workplace after deregulation, see Anne Balay, *Semi Queer: Inside the World of Gay, Trans, and Black Truck Drivers* (Chapel Hill: University of North Carolina Press, 2018).

19. Luís M. Aguiar and Joseph A. McCartin, eds., *Purple Power: The History and Global Impact of SEIU* (Urbana: University of Illinois Press, 2023); Fran Quigley, *If We Can Win Here: The New Front Lines of the Labor Movement* (Ithaca, NY: Cornell University ILR Press, 2015).

20. Ralph C. and Estelle Dinerstein James, *Hoffa and the Teamsters: A Study of Union Power* (Princeton, NJ: D. Van Nostrand, 1965), 340–45.

21. James and James, *Hoffa and the Teamsters*, 137.

22. Robert Bussel, *Fighting for Total Person Unionism: Harold Gibbons, Ernest Calloway, and Working-Class Citizenship* (Urbana: University of Illinois Press, 2015), 118.

23. Jack Goldsmith, *In Hoffa's Shadow: A Stepfather, a Disappearance in Detroit, and My Search for the Truth* (New York: Farrar, Straus and Giroux, 2019), 154–59.

24. Goldsmith, *In Hoffa's Shadow*, 158.

25. Goldsmith, *In Hoffa's Shadow*, 160.

26. Goldsmith, *In Hoffa's Shadow*, 159–72.

27. David Witwer, *Corruption and Reform in the Teamsters Union* (Urbana: University of Illinois Press, 2008), 131–56.

28. MCH, *Part 46*, 16,196.

29. Norman Abrams and Neal Patterson, "Nip Movie Concession Kickbacks," *New York Daily News*, April 27, 1951, 141.

30. MCH, *Part 46*, 16,898–16,906.

31. MCH, *Part 46*, 16,888–16,893.

32. MCH, *Part 46*, 16,906.

33. MCH, *Part 46*, 16,907.

34. Crawford, *The Mafia and the Gays*, 114.

35. Crawford, *The Mafia and the Gays*, 115.
36. Crawford, *The Mafia and the Gays*, 114; Sorene, "A Night at New York's Banging Continental Baths."
37. MCH, *Part 46*, 16,912; Crawford, *The Mafia and the Gays*, 26.
38. Crawford, *The Mafia and the Gays*, 31–66.
39. Charles Lenton O'Brien, photograph, October, 1957, cited in Goldsmith, *In Hoffa's Shadow*, photo gallery.
40. Goldsmith, *In Hoffa's Shadow*, 86–88.
41. Crawford, *The Mafia and the Gays*, 188–206.
42. Kay Ballard and Jim Hesselman, *How I Lost 10 Pounds in 53 Years: A Memoir* (New York: Back Stage Books, 2006), cited in Crawford, *The Mafia and the Gays*, 11.
43. Goldsmith, *In Hoffa's Shadow*, 87.
44. Crawford, *The Mafia and the Gays*, 74.
45. Crawford, *The Mafia and the Gays*, 67–73.
46. Weber, *The Protestant Ethic and the Spirit of Capitalism*, 102–25.
47. Elaine Tyler May, *Homeward Bound: American Families in the Cold War Era* (New York: Basic Books, 2017 [1988]).

Bibliography

Abraham, Julie. *Metropolitan Lovers: The Homosexuality of Cities*. Minneapolis: University of Minnesota Press, 2009.

Aguiar, Luis L. M., and Joseph A. McCartin, eds. *Purple Power: The History and Global Impact of SEIU*. Urbana: University of Illinois Press, 2023.

Alexander, Michael. *Jazz Age Jews*. Princeton, NJ: Princeton University Press, 2001.

Armbruster, Ann. *The Life and Times of Miami Beach*. New York: Knopf, 1995.

Balay, Anne. *Semi Queer: Inside the World of Gay, Trans, and Black Truck Drivers*. Chapel Hill: University of North Carolina Press, 2018.

Bartell, H. Robert, Jr. *Unions and Pension Funds*. PhD dissertation, Cornell University, 1963.

Bederman, Gail. *Manliness and Civilization: A Cultural History of Gender and Race in the United States, 1880–1917*. Chicago: University of Chicago Press, 1996.

Belzer, Michael H. *Sweatshops on Wheels: Winners and Losers in Trucking Deregulation*. Oxford, UK: Oxford University Press, 2000.

Berger, Jane. *A New Working Class: The Legacies of Public-Sector Employment in the Civil Rights Movement*. Philadelphia: University of Pennsylvania Press, 2021.

Berman, Lila Corwin. *Metropolitan Jews: Politics, Race, and Religion in Postwar Detroit*. Chicago: University of Chicago Press, 2015.

Bluestone, Barry, and Bennett Harrison, eds., *The Deindustrialization of America: Plant Closings, Community Abandonment, and the Dismantling of Basic Industry*. New York: Basic Books, 1982.

Braden, Susan R. *The Architecture of Leisure: The Florida Resort Hotels of Henry Flagler and Henry Plant*. Gainesville: University Press of Florida, 2002.

Briggs, Laura. *Reproducing Empire: Race, Sex, Science, and U.S. Imperialism in Puerto Rico*. Berkeley: University of California Press, 2002.

Brill, Steven. *The Teamsters*. New York: Simon & Schuster, 1979.

Bussel, Robert. *Fighting for Total Person Unionism: Harold Gibbons, Ernest Calloway, and Working-Class Citizenship*. Urbana: University of Illinois Press, 2015.

Canaday, Margot. *The Straight State: Sexuality and Citizenship in Twentieth-Century America*. Princeton, NJ: Princeton University Press, 2011.

Capó, Julio, Jr. *Welcome to Fairyland: Queer Miami before 1940*. Chapel Hill: University of North Carolina Press, 2017.

Chauncey, George. *Gay New York: Gender, Urban Culture, and the Making of a Gay Male World, 1890–1940*. New York: Basic Books, 1994.

Cobble, Dorothy Sue. *The Other Women's Movement: Workplace Justice and Social Rights in Modern America*. Princeton, NJ: Princeton University Press, 2005.

Cohen, Andrew Wender. *The Racketeer's Progress: Chicago and the Struggle for the Modern American Economy*. Cambridge, UK: Cambridge University Press, 2004.

Commons, John R. *Races and Immigrants in America*. New York: The Macmillan Company, 1920 [1907].

Cowie, Jefferson. *Stayin' Alive: The 1970s and the Last Days of the Working Class*. New York: The New Press, 2010.

Crawford, Phillip, Jr. *The Mafia and the Gays*, 2nd ed. Self-published, 2022.

Culot, Maurice, and Jean-Francois LeJeune. *Miami: Architecture of the Tropics*. Princeton, NJ: Princeton Architectural Press, 1993.

Delgado, Linda C. "Jesús Colón and the Making of a New York Community, 1917 to 1974." In *Puerto Rican Diaspora: Historical Perspectives*. Theresa Carmen Whalen and Victor Vasquez, 68–87. Philadelphia: Temple University Press, 2005.

Delton, Jennifer. *Making Minnesota: Civil Rights and the Transformation of the Democratic Party*. Minneapolis: University of Minnesota Press, 2002.

Desilets, Deborah. *Morris Lapidus: An Architecture of Joy*. New York: Rizzoli International Publications, 2010.

Dubofsky, Melvyn, and Foster Rhea Dulles. *Labor in America: A History*, 4th ed. New York: Wiley-Blackwell, 2001.

Dudziak, Mary L. *Cold War Civil Rights: Race and the Image of American Democracy*. Princeton, NJ: Princeton University Press, 2000.

Echols, Alice. *Daring to Be Bad: Radical Feminism in America, 1967–1975*. Minneapolis: University of Minnesota Press, 1989.

Feinberg, Leslie. *Stone Butch Blues*. Ithaca, NY: Firebrand Books, 1993.

Ferguson, Roderick A. *Aberrations in Black: Toward a Queer of Color Critique*. Minneapolis: University of Minnesota Press, 2003.

Fraser, Steve, and Gary Gerstle, *The Rise and Fall of the New Deal Order, 1930–1980*. Princeton, NJ: Princeton University Press, 1990.

Fung, Archon, Tessa Hebb, and Joel Rogers, *Working Capital: The Power of Labor's Pensions*. Ithaca, NY: Cornell University ILR Press, 2001.

Gaines, Steven. *Fool's Paradise: Players, Poseurs, and the Culture of Excess on South Beach*. New York: Broadway Books, 2009.

Galbraith, John Kenneth. *The Affluent Society*. New York: Houghton Mifflin, 1958.

Garnel, Donald. *The Rise of Teamster Power in the West*. Berkeley: University of California Press, 1972.

Giller, Norman, and Sarah Giller Nelson, *Designing the Good Life: Norman M. Giller and the Development of Miami Modernism*. Gainesville: University Press of Florida, 2007.

Gold, Michael. *An Introduction to Labor Law*. Ithaca, NY: Cornell University ILR Press, 2011.

Goldsmith, Jack. *In Hoffa's Shadow: A Stepfather, a Disappearance in Detroit, and My Search for the Truth.* New York: Farrar, Straus and Giroux, 2019.

Green, Adam. *Selling the Race: Culture, Community, and Black Chicago, 1940–1955.* Chicago: University of Chicago Press, 2008.

Gutterman, Lauren Jae. *Her Neighbor's Wife: A History of Lesbian Desire within Marriage.* Philadelphia: University of Pennsylvania Press, 2019.

Hall, Stuart, and Tony Jefferson, eds., *Resistance through Ritual: Youth Subcultures in Postwar Britain.* London: Taylor and Francis, 1976.

Hansberry, Lorraine. *A Raisin in the Sun.* New York: Methuen Publishing, Ltd., 2001 [1959].

Harris, Dianne. *Little White Houses: How the Postwar Home Constructed Race in America.* Minneapolis: University of Minnesota Press, 2013.

Harris, LaShawn. *Sex Workers, Psychics, and Numbers Runners: Black Women in New York City's Underground Economy.* Urbana: University of Illinois Press, 2016.

Harrison, Daphne Duval. *Black Pearls: Blues Queens of the 1920s.* New Brunswick, NJ: Rutgers University Press, 1988.

Hartman, Saidiya. *Wayward Lives, Beautiful Experiments: Intimate Histories of Riotous Black Girls, Troublesome Women, and Queer Radicals.* New York: W. W. Norton, 2020.

Heap, Chad. *Slumming: Sexual and Racial Encounters in American Nightlife, 1885–1940.* Chicago: University of Chicago Press, 2010.

Ho, Karen. *Liquidated: An Ethnography of Wall Street.* Durham, NC: Duke University Press, 2009.

Hoffa, James R., and Donald I. Rogers. *The Trials of Jimmy Hoffa: An Autobiography.* Chicago: Henry Regnery Company, 1970.

Hong, Grace Kyungwon. *The Ruptures of American Capital: Women of Culture Feminism and the Culture of Immigrant Labor.* Minneapolis: University of Minnesota Press, 2006.

Hortis, C. Aldexander. *The Mob and the City: The Hidden History of How the Mafia Captured New York.* New York City: Prometheus, 2014.

Howard, Clayton. *The Closet and the Cul-de-Sac: The Politics of Sexual Privacy in Northern California.* Philadelphia: University of Pennsylvania Press, 2019.

Hurewitz, Daniel. *Bohemian Los Angeles and the Making of Modern Politics.* Berkeley: University of California Press, 2007.

Iverson, Roberta Rehner. *What Workers Say: Decades of Struggle and How to Make Real Opportunity Now.* Philadelphia: Temple University Press, 2022.

Jacobs, Jane. *The Death and Life of Great American Cities.* New York: Vintage Books, 1961.

Jacobs, Paul. *The State of Unions.* New York: Athenaeum, 1963.

Jakobsen, Janet R. "Sex + Freedom = Regulation: Why?" *Social Text* 23, no. 3–4 (Fall/Winter 2005): 285–308.

James, Ralph C., and Estelle Dinerstein James. *Hoffa and the Teamsters: A Study of Union Power.* Princeton, NJ: D. Van Nostrand, 1965.

Joseph, Miranda. *Against the Romance of Community.* Minneapolis: University of Minnesota Press, 2002.

Keeler, Kasey R. *American Indians and the American Dream: Policies, Place, and Property in Minnesota.* Minneapolis: University of Minnesota Press, 2023.

Kennedy, Robert F. *The Enemy Within*. New York: Harper, 1960.

Kofoed, Jack. *Moon Over Miami*. New York: Random House, 1955.

Kranson, Rachel. *Ambivalent Embrace: Jewish Upward Mobility in Postwar America*. Chapel Hill, NC: University of North Carolina Press, 2017.

Kuntz, Tom, and Phil Kuntz. *The Sinatra Files: The Secret FBI Dossier*. New York: Three Rivers Press, 2000.

Kushner, David. *Levittown: Two Families, One Tycoon, and the Fight for Civil Rights in America's Legendary Suburb*. New York: Walker and Company, 2009.

LaBotz, Dan. *Rank-and-File Rebellion: Teamsters for a Democratic Union*. London: Verso, 1991.

Lapidus, Morris. *Too Much Is Never Enough*. New York: Rizzoli International Publications, 1996.

Leone, Richard D. *The Negro in the Trucking Industry*. Philadelphia: Industrial Research Unit, Department of Industry, the Wharton School of Finance and Commerce, 1970.

Lichtenstein, Nelson. *State of the Union: A Century of American Labor*. Princeton, NJ: Princeton University Press, 2013.

Lichtenstein, Nelson. *Walter Reuther: The Most Dangerous Man in Detroit*. Urbana: University of Illinois Press, 1997.

Lipsett, Alexander S. *Labor's Partnership in Industrial Enterprise: A New Approach to Investment of Union and Pension Funds*. New York: Floyd L. Carlisle, 1950.

Littauer, Amanda. *Bad Girls: Young Women, Sex, and Rebellion before the Sixties*. Chapel Hill: University of North Carolina Press, 2015.

Luibhéid, Eithne. *Entry Denied: Controlling Sexuality at the Border*. Minneapolis: University of Minnesota Press, 2002.

Lvosky, Anna. *Vice Patrol: Cops, Courts, and the Struggle Over Urban Gay Life Before Stonewall*. Chicago: University of Chicago Press, 2021.

MacDonald, Cameron Lynne, and Carmen Sirianni, eds. *Working in the Service Society*. Philadelphia: Temple University Press, 1996.

Mailer, Norman. *Miami and the Siege of Chicago: An Informal History of the Republican and Democratic Conventions of 1968*. New York: World Publishing, 1968.

Marcuse, Herbert. *One Dimensional Man*. Boston: Beacon Press, 1991 [1964].

May, Elaine Tyler. *Homeward Bound: American Families in the Cold War Era*. New York: Basic Books, 2017 [1988].

Mazur, Ronald Michael. *The New Intimacy: Open-Ended Marriage and Alternative Lifestyles*. Boston: Beacon Press, 1973.

McGreevy, John T. *Parish Boundaries: The Catholic Encounter with Race in the Twentieth-Century Urban North*. Chicago: University of Chicago Press, 1998.

Moldea, Dan. *The Hoffa Wars: Teamsters, Rebels, Politicians, and the Mob*. New York: Paddington Press, 1978.

Montgomery, David. *Citizen Worker: The Experience of Workers in the United States with Democracy and the Free Market during the Nineteenth Century*. Cambridge, UK: Cambridge University Press, 1993.

Murphy, Cullen. "The Search for a Whole Life: Turning Away from Status Syndrome." *Change* 6, no. 8 (1974): 14–18.

Murphy, Ryan Patrick. *Deregulating Desire: Flight Attendant Activism, Family Politics, and Workplace Justice*. Philadelphia: Temple University Press, 2016.

Murphy, Ryan Patrick. "Lifestyle: Contesting a Category of Dissident Sexuality in U.S. Urban History," *GLQ* 26, no. 2 (April 2020): 273–301.

Neff, James. *Vendetta: Bobby Kennedy vs. Jimmy Hoffa*. New York: Little, Brown, and Company, 2012.

Ngai, Mae. *Impossible Subjects: Illegal Aliens and the Making of Modern America*, rev. ed. Princeton, NJ: Princeton University Press, 2014.

Nijman, Jan. *Miami: Mistress of the Americas*. Philadelphia: University of Pennsylvania Press, 2010.

O'Neill, George, and Nena O'Neill. *Open Marriage: A New Life Style for Couples*. New York: M. Evans and Company, 1972.

Orleck, Annelise. *Common Sense and a Little Fire: Women and Working-Class Politics in the United States, 1900–1965*. Durham, NC: Duke University Press, 1995.

Osgerby, Bill. *Playboys in Paradise: Masculinity, Youth, and Leisure-Style in Modern America*. Oxford, UK: Berg, 2001.

Peiss, Kathi. *Cheap Amusements: Working Women and Leisure in Turn-of-the-Century New York*. Philadelphia: Temple University Press, 1986.

Petkov, Steven, and Leonard Mustazza. *The Frank Sinatra Reader*. Oxford, UK: Oxford University Press, 1997.

Phillips-Fein, Kim. *Invisible Hands: The Businessmen's Crusade against the New Deal*. New York: W. W. Norton, 2010.

Plotner, Kevin, and Rebecca Plotner. *The Fontainebleau Miami*. New York: Schiffer Publishing, 2008.

Quigley, Fran. *If We Can Win Here: The New Front Lines of the Labor Movement*. Ithaca, NY: Cornell University ILR Press, 2015.

Rifkin, Jeremy, and Randy Barber. *The North Will Rise Again: Pensions, Power, and Politics in the 1980s*. Boston: Beacon Press, 1978.

Rizzo, Mary. *Class Acts: Young Men and the Rise of Lifestyle*. Reno: University of Nevada Press, 2015.

Rosenberg, Emily S. *Financial Missionaries to the World: The Politics and Culture of Dollar Diplomacy, 1900–1930*. Durham, NC: Duke University Press, 2004.

Rothstein, Richard. *The Color of Law: A Forgotten History of How Our Government Segregated America*. New York: W. W. Norton, 2017.

Ruiz, Vicki L., and John R. Chávez, eds. *Memories and Migrations: Mapping Boriqua and Chicana Histories*. Urbana: University of Illinois Press, 2008.

Russell, Thaddeus. *Out of the Jungle: Jimmy Hoffa and the Remaking of the American Working Class*. New York: Knopf, 2001.

Said, Edward. *Orientalism*. New York: Pantheon Books, 1978.

Sedgwick, Eve Kasofsky. *Touching Feeling: Affect, Pedagogy, and Performativity*. Durham, NC: Duke University Press, 2003.

Self, Robert O. *All in the Family: The Realignment of American Democracy since the 1960s*. New York: Hill and Wang, 2013.

Shah, Nayan. *Contagious Divides: Epidemics and Race in San Francisco's Chinatown*. Berkeley: University of California Press, 2001.

Shah, Nayan. *Stranger Intimacy: Contesting Race, Sexuality, and the Law in the North American West*. Berkeley: University of California Press, 2012.

Smith, Chris M. *Syndicate Women: Gender and Networks in Chicago Organized Crime*. Berkeley: University of California Press, 2019.

Somerville, Siobhan. *Queering the Color Line: Race and the Invention of Homosexuality in American Culture*. Durham, NC: Duke University Press, 2000.

Spigel, Lynn. *Welcome to the Dreamhouse: Popular Media and Postwar Suburbs*. Durham, NC: Duke University Press, 2001.

Stansell, Christine. *American Moderns: Bohemian New York and the Creation of a New Century*. Princeton, NJ: Princeton University Press, 2009.

Sugrue, Thomas. *The Origins of the Urban Crisis: Race and Inequality in Postwar Detroit*, updated ed. Princeton, NJ: Princeton University Press, 2014.

Tiemeyer, Phil. *Plane Queer: Labor, Sexuality, and AIDS in the History of Male Flight Attendants*. Berkeley: University of California Press, 2013.

Trotter, Joe William, Jr. *The Great Migration in Historical Perspective: New Dimensions of Race, Class, and Gender*. Bloomington: Indiana University Press, 1991.

Vallejo, Jody. *Barrios to Burbs: The Making of the Mexican American Middle Class*. Stanford, CA: Stanford University Press, 2012.

Vellon, Peter G. *A Great Conspiracy Against Our Race: Italian Immigrant Newspapers and the Construction of Whiteness in the Early 20th Century*. New York: New York University Press, 2014.

Vider, Steven. *The Queerness of Home: Gender, Sexuality, and the Politics of Domesticity after World War II*. Chicago: University of Chicago Press, 2021.

Weber, Max. *The Protestant Ethic and the Spirit of Capitalism*. New York: Routledge, 2001 [1904].

Weeks, Kathi. *The Problem with Work: Feminism, Marxism, Antiwork Politics, and Postwork Imaginaries*. Durham, NC: Duke University Press, 2011.

Whalen, Carmen Teresa, and Victor Vázquez-Hernández. *The Puerto Rican Diaspora: Historical Perspectives*. Philadelphia: Temple University Press, 2005.

Wilson, Kristina. *Mid-Century Modernism and the American Body*. Princeton, NJ: Princeton University Press, 2021.

Wiese, Andrew. *Places of their Own: African American Suburbanization in the Twentieth Century*. Chicago: University of Chicago Press, 2005.

Witwer, David. *Corruption and Reform in the Teamsters Union*. Urbana: University of Illinois Press, 2008.

Witwer, David, and Catherine Rios. *Murder in the Garment District: The Grip of Organized Crime and the Decline of Labor in the United States*. New York: The New Press, 2020.

Zeitz, Joshua M. *White Ethnic New York: Jews, Catholics, and the Shaping of Postwar Politics*. Chapel Hill: University of North Carolina Press, 2007.

Zukin, Sharon. *Loft Living: Culture and Capital in Urban Change*. New Brunswick, NJ: Rutgers University Press, 1982.

Index